Writing: Texts, Processes and Practices

APPLIED LINGUISTICS AND
LANGUAGE STUDY

GENERAL EDITOR

CHRISTOPHER N. CANDLIN

Chair Professor of Applied Linguistics
Centre for English Language Education & Communication Research
Department of English
City University of Hong Kong
Hong Kong

For a complete list of books in this series, see pp. v–vi

Writing: Texts, Processes and Practices

Edited by

Christopher N. Candlin
and
Ken Hyland

Longman

London and New York

P
211
.W7197
1999

Addison Wesley Longman Limited,
Edinburgh Gate,
Harlow,
Essex CM20 2JE,
United Kingdom
and Associated Companies throughout the world.

*Published in the United States of America
by Addison Wesley Longman Inc. New York*

First published 1999

ISBN 0–582–31750–9 PPR

Visit Addison Wesley Longman on the world wide web at
http://www.awl-he.com

British Library Cataloguing-in-Publication Data

A catalogue record for this book is available from the British Library

Library of Congress Cataloging-in-Publication Data

Writing : texts, processes, and practices / edited by Christopher N.
   Candlin and Ken Hyland.
      p.   cm. — (Applied linguistics and language study)
   Includes bibliographical references and index.
   ISBN 0–582–31750–9 (pbk.)
      1. Written communication.   I. Candlin, Christopher.   II. Hyland,
   Ken.   III. Series. ·
   P211.W7197   1999
   302.2′244—dc21   98–46959
                                                                            CIP

Set by 35 in 10/12pt New Baskerville
Printed in Malaysia, PP

APPLIED LINGUISTICS AND LANGUAGE STUDY

GENERAL EDITOR

CHRISTOPHER N. CANDLIN

Chair Professor of Applied Linguistics
Centre for English Language Education & Communication Research
Department of English
City University of Hong Kong
Hong Kong

Contents

List of contributors

ROBERT J. BARRETT is Professor of Psychiatry at the University of Adelaide and Clinical Director of Psychiatric Services at the Royal Adelaide Hospital. Both an anthropologist and a psychiatrist by training, he has an interest in the field of schizophrenia, which he has pursued both in Australia and Borneo.

VIJAY K. BHATIA is a Professor at the City University of Hong Kong. His research interests include discourse and genre analysis, English for specific purposes, professional communication, especially in the field of law, business, newspapers, advertising and philanthropic fundraising. His book *Analysing Genre-Language Use in Professional Settings*, published by Longman, is widely used by scholars interested in the analysis of discourse.

CHRISTOPHER N. CANDLIN is Chair Professor of Applied Linguistics at the City University of Hong Kong, and was until recently Professor of Linguistics and Executive Director of the Australian National Centre for English Language Teaching and Research (NCELTR) at Macquarie University, Sydney. His research and publishing interests are in professional–client discourse, language and literacy education and critical linguistics. He is currently President of the International Association of Applied Linguistics.

YU-YING CHANG is a linguistics PhD candidate at the University of Michigan. Her research interests include language for academic purposes, contrastive rhetoric, computer-mediated communication, sociolinguistics, and language in contact (multilingualism). She has published in *Applied Linguistics* and the *RELC Journal*.

SANDRA GOLLIN is currently Head of the Learning Centre, University of Western Sydney, Nepean. Her research and teaching experience in language and literacy development in academic and professional communication spans twenty-five years. She has worked in teacher professional development in The National Centre for English Language Teaching and Research, Macquarie University, Sydney.

KEN HYLAND is an Associate Professor at The City University of Hong Kong. He has taught in Britain, Sudan, Saudi Arabia, Malaysia, Papua New Guinea and New Zealand and has published widely on language teaching issues and academic discourse. His book on scientific hedging was published in 1998 by Benjamins.

ROZ IVANIČ is a Senior Lecturer in the Department of Linguistics and Modern English Language at Lancaster University. Her interests as a researcher and as an active participant in the academic community include academic writing as a social practice, issues of access to higher education, and alternative forms of knowledge and learning. Her publications include *Writing and Identity* and, with Romy Clark, *The Politics of Writing.*

MARY R. LEA is a research fellow in the Institute of Educational Technology at the Open University, UK. She has worked as both a researcher and practitioner in the area of student writing and learning in new, traditional and distance education universities. Her present research is concerned with understanding more about computer conferencing and student learning and is looking at the relationship between conferencing and students' assessed written work.

IAN G. MALCOLM is Professor of Applied Linguistics at Edith Cowan University in Perth, Western Australia. He has experience in language teaching and teacher education in Australia and China and has carried out research on many aspects of language education, especially in relation to English-speaking Indigenous Australians.

JOHN MILTON has taught EFL in Canada, the Middle East and China. He currently researches the writing of EFL students with the aid of computational techniques and develops computational tools and tutorials for learners of English, such as WordPilot, as described in Chapter 10. More information about this tool can be obtained at http://www.compulang. com/

GREG MYERS is a Senior Lecturer in the Department of Linguistics and Modern English Language at Lancaster University, where he teaches on the Culture, Media, and Communication Programme. He is author of *Writing Biology* (1990), *Words in Ads* (1994) and *Ad Worlds* (1998), and is now working on the dynamics of discussions in focus groups.

GUENTER A. PLUM has been fascinated by text for over twenty years, having taught systemic-functional linguistics at Sydney University and Macquarie University, researched L2 learning, genre and register variation, academic literacy, doctor-patient communication in HIV/AIDS, subtitled for TV, and managed a computational-linguistic development project in an IT company.

BRIAN STREET is Professor of Language in Education at King's College, London and Visiting Professor of Education in the Graduate School of Education, University of Pennsylvania. He has lectured extensively on literacy practices and published six books and over 60 scholarly articles. His recent collection of essays *Social Literacies* was awarded the David H. Russell Award for Teaching English by NCTE.

JOHN M. SWALES has been Professor of Linguistics and Director of the English Language Institute at the University of Michigan since 1987. Recent book-length publications include *Genre Analysis* (1990), *Academic Writing for Graduate Students* (with Chris Freak) (1994), and *Other Floors, Other Voices; A Textography of a Small University Building.*

SUE WELDON is an honorary research fellow in the Centre for Science Studies at Lancaster University, UK. Her research interests include the issue of public participation in environmental decision-making. She is also the publishing editor for Innovation in Higher Education publications in the Higher Education Development Centre at Lancaster.

PATRICIA WRIGHT is Distinguished Senior Research Fellow at Cardiff University, UK, where she leads a team exploring printed and interactive forms of health information. While previously based in Cambridge, she published over one hundred papers and chapters detailing how readers are influenced by the linguistic and visual design of the documents they use.

Editors' acknowledgements

Chris Candlin would like to recall with thanks the discussions with Mike Breen in the late 70s at the University of Lancaster where, as members of a group John Swales once referred to as 'The Lancaster Radicals', they called for an integration of work on texts, processes and practices in the context of research into English for Specific Purposes. More recently, something of the shape of the present book stems from a series of seminars given by him at the Beijing Foreign Studies University in November of 1996. His thanks, as ever, go to Sally.

Ken Hyland thanks colleagues and friends in Australia, Hong Kong and Britain for their conversations and texts in contributing to the view of writing presented in this book. To Lynn Wales and Malcolm Coulthard for getting him interested in these issues to begin with, and to Andrew Taylor for space to work on them. He owes a more personal debt to his wife, Fiona, for her encouragement and to his parents for moral support from afar.

The editors would like to thank in particular Jada Wong of the Department of English at the City University of Hong Kong for her assistance in preparing the composite bibliography for the volume.

Publisher's acknowledgements

We are grateful to the following for permission to reproduce copyright material:

Cambridge University Press for extracts from *The Psychiatric Team and the Social Definition of Schizophrenia* by R. J. Barrett and Friends of the Earth for an extract from the leaflet *Look Forward To a Better Future*, February 1998, © Friends of the Earth.

Introduction: Integrating approaches to the study of writing

CHRISTOPHER N. CANDLIN AND KEN HYLAND

A framework for exploring academic, workplace and professional writing

Our aim in this book is to approach the study of academic and professional writing from an integrated and multidisciplinary perspective. Through a collection of commissioned chapters, the book is designed to bring together the three dimensions underlying writing research announced in our title: the description and analysis of texts, the interpretation of the processes involved in writing, and the exploration of the connections between writing and the institutional practices which in large measure are constituted and sustained through writing.

We have also sought to make explicit the valuable links that can be made between research into writing as text, as process and as social practice, with some of the practical applications that such an integrated research paradigm suggests, in the contexts of the classroom, the workplace and the professions. At the same time, the chapters in this volume show how different approaches to the analysis of texts, different perspectives on the writing process, and different methodologies for research into writing, can be integrated and made to inform distinctive approaches to the practice of writing and writing instruction. In this way, theory and practice in writing inform each other in a reflective praxis.

This attempt to integrate the multiple elements comprising academic and professional writing may initially seem to be a rather daunting task. For one reason, written discourse serves a multitude of significant roles and purposes within educational, workplace

1

and professional settings, and it is therefore natural that the study of written discourse in these settings has been subjected to an equally various range of approaches and methodologies. What this research quite clearly tells us is that texts are multidimensional constructs requiring multiple perspectives for their understanding. Writing is much more than the generation of text-linguistic products. As such, writing research needs to move beyond a focus on the page or the screen to explore the uses to which writing is put, and to offer candidate explanations of how these uses may engender particular conditions of production and interpretation of texts in context. Writing as text is thus not usefully separated from writing as process and interpretation, and neither can easily be divorced from the specific local circumstances in which writing takes place nor from the broader institutional and socio-historical contexts which inform those particular occasions of writing.

Every act of writing is thus linked in complex ways to a set of communicative purposes which occur in a context of social, interpersonal and occupational practices. Equally, of course, each act of writing also constructs the reality that it describes, reproducing a particular mode of communication and maintaining the social relationships which that implies. Writing is also a personal and socio-cultural act of identity whereby writers both signal their membership in what may be a range of communities of practice, as well as express their own creative individuality.

This view of writing as a social act influenced by a variety of linguistic, physical, cognitive, cultural, interpersonal and political factors has achieved a certain orthodoxy. Indeed, research into the nature of academic, workplace and professional writing and its underpinning processes has, over the last twenty years, become something of a cottage industry, fuelled by a plethora of published work to guide our understanding. Linguists, educationalists, psychologists, teachers, composition researchers and sociologists have all had a hand in the exploration of writing, mapping it in very different ways according to their distinctive projections and purposes. The drawback of this extensive and variously purposed literature is that its very diversity works against its cohesiveness, and thus blunts its explanatory potential. Work in different fields of writing research often shows little overlap, or even mutual recognition, and little engagement takes place between writers of different disciplinary or theoretical affiliations. Amid excellent but singular treatments of the topic, even the most receptive reader may thus confront a confusing range of research frameworks whose distinct rhetorical framing of the construct of writing produces diverse discussions of what may be quite variegated data.

One problem is the sheer complexity and pervasiveness of the topic itself. As a recent study of local literacies (Barton and Hamilton, 1998) exemplifies, writing intrudes into every cranny of our personal as well as our workplace and professional worlds, and everything that is part of these worlds can in turn intrude into writing. Many of us live in highly literate environments in which writing forms a major part of the landscape, playing an important role in how we interact with others, interpret our realities, and define the persons we are. It serves as a means of measuring cognitive abilities, a way of facilitating the design, delivery and assessment of instruction and training, as a gateway allowing or restricting access to goods and services, a route for the accomplishing of personal goals and the negotiating of disciplinary knowledge, as well as serving to oil the wheels of the corporate/industrial enterprise. Within the academy, the workplace and the professions, writing is perhaps the central means by which our individual life chances are enabled or restricted, our daily realities explored and explained, and our professional communities and activities structured, instantiated and defined. In sum, the more we come to understand these academic, workplace and professional worlds, and the behaviour of those who work within them, the more we see how writing works to create the intersubjective, communal and personal understandings that make them possible.

It is in these senses, then, that we cannot regard writing as simply words on a page or screen, any more than we can regard it as the creation of isolated minds. A variety of sources has now generated a considerable body of research to underscore the essential situatedness of texts and of the processes which contribute to their creation and interpretation.

Systemic functional linguists, for example, have illustrated some of the ways that lexico-grammatical choices resonate with particular aspects of topic and writer–reader relationships (Halliday, 1978; Halliday and Martin, 1993). Rhetoricians have demonstrated how texts represent a coherent pattern of motivated writer choices implying interactional processes of construction reflecting wider social systems (Bazerman, 1988; Freedman and Medway, 1994; Thralls and Byler, 1993). Research in applied linguistics has emphasised how the analysis of generic structure contributes to an understanding of how the communicative purposes of writers respond to particular community practices (Bhatia, 1993; Swales, 1990) and how these may promote differential opportunities for participants (Bhatia, 1997). From a more critical discourse analytical perspective, research has also revealed how texts engage with key social issues surrounding the distribution of power and knowledge, and the ways that discourse conventions imbricate ideologies. It has also revealed how explicating these conventions can assist our understanding of institutional meanings and values (Fairclough, 1995; Kress, 1988).

In sum, we now know a great deal about the ways that texts work within a number of particular socio-cultural contexts and how they help instantiate, and are instantiated by, particular occupational practices. This is particularly true of academic domains, where a large number of studies are available, some emphasising a text-linguistic focus (e.g. Gosden, 1993; Hyland, 1998a; Ventola and Mauranen, 1996), and others a more sociological/ethnographic approach (e.g. Bazerman and Paradis, 1991; Berkenkotter and Huckin, 1995; MacDonald, 1994; Myers, 1990), or an abstract, more theoretical perspective (e.g. Dillon, 1991; Prelli, 1989). Studies of business and occupational writing are less common, but some valuable accounts exist (Bhatia, 1993; Coleman, 1989; Odell and Goswami, 1985; Thralls and Byler, 1993). A recent collection of papers (Bargiela-Chiappini and Nickerson, in press) focuses exclusively on business writing, exploring its nature from a genre and discourse analysis perspective and in relation to a variety of media. But just as this research has increasingly revealed the ever-growing complexity of the multiple roles and purposes which writing serves, so the need remains to unpack this complexity and to make the attempt to assert the overarching nature of writing, despite this variation and fragmentation.

There was a need for a volume, in our view, which drew on the insights offered by this research, but which at the same time offered such an overarching perspective on texts seen as situated in cognitive, social and cultural contexts, and made accessible through various methodological approaches. One motivation for creating this collection of original contributions therefore arises from a desire to take stock of this diversity, and to try to gather together and integrate these different perspectives and dimensions of texts. But we are also impelled by a second issue of writing research – the notion of praxis. While there is clearly a reciprocal relationship between theory and practice in writing research, in which evidence from the former enhances the latter and then feeds back to produce more informed research, or where issues initially arising in the practice of writing call for research-based study, this link has not always been evident, either in the published literature or in many classrooms. Theoretical models of writing, whether social, cognitive, structural or cultural, need to be contextualised within a wider research framework which acknowledges the other elements, and, in addition, the issues such models raise should feed into, and be tested by, work in instructional settings so as to facilitate reflective practice and to appraise the theoretical robustness of the models themselves.

The book is so organised as to represent and to engage with this integrated approach to the topic of writing. Each part links the three central dimensions of writing in the title of the volume, and the role each plays as a dimension of social practice. Parts I–III emphasise the description of writing as text, the interpretation of writing processes and the design of different methodologies for writing research. Part IV features a series of case studies which focus on the practical application of these orientations to writing and writing research and demonstrate their relevance in distinct academic, workplace and professional contexts. Within each part, three chapters highlight and explore a central dimension of the orientation in question, while demonstrating how that particular dimension relates to the others in the part and reaches out to other sections of the book.

Similarly, while the case studies in Part IV privilege lexicogrammatical, interpersonal or ethnographic means of exploiting writing research in practice, they are also closely interlinked to the research-based accounts in the other parts. Finally, the chapters themselves offer a picture of the rich contextual variety within writing to which we referred earlier. Such contexts range from the academy, to the practice of medicine and healthcare, and to organisational communication. They emphasise writing-focused interactions involving different social and discursive roles and relationships – tutors to students, professionals to professionals, experts to the lay community, researchers to researchers – and invoke a variety of distinctive attitudinal stances among writers and readers.

In short, the book is an argument for an integration of research and practice, in particular by insisting that linking the three dimensions of expression, interpretation and explanation is crucial for the appropriate realisation of writing programmes and practices in the range of contexts illustrated in the chapters, and more generally. In what follows, we set out the elements of the approach we have taken in more detail.

Perspectives on writing

1   *Expression: focus on texts*

Part I focuses on written texts as products of writing and examines three interconnected approaches to their analysis. It begins, appropriately, with a view of text as an artefact of form and structure. The linguistic features of written texts have been variously examined, but one of the more fruitful approaches has been to see textual variation and similarity in terms of lexico-grammatical and discursive patterning, as particular genres. Such generic products have a recognisable structural identity, what Bhatia (1993 and in this volume) refers to as generic integrity, but are also clearly related to particular forms of social action (Miller, 1984) and to shared social purposes (Swales, 1990). The importance of this research area is that it displays not only the dependence of texts on social context, on their conditions of production and interpretation, but also the constraints and choices that operate on writers in these contexts (e.g. Freedman and Medway, 1994; Halliday and Hasan, 1985). Studying texts in this way inevitably draws the analyst into a wider paradigm which locates the text as an element within both communication and social practice. Bhatia's chapter in this volume explicitly signals the need for this broadening of analysis with his call for the integration of an awareness of discipline-specific discursive processes, the appraisal of participant and organisational communicative purposes, and the study of textual form.

The approach to the analysis of written texts as interactive communication is taken up in Chapter 2. This perspective represents textual products as outcomes of writer discursive processes in interaction with the discursive processes of readers – attempts by writers to communicate with readers, if you like, by conveying certain intentions, purposes and actions concomitant with the ideational content of a message. Researchers in this perspective clearly also accept that writing is a social accomplishment, but, more than this, have assumed that discursive conventions in writing rest on large-scale organising principles, similar to those drawn on in face-to-face interaction. Such a focus emphasises the local context or co-text of interaction within the text, rather than its broader societal or institutional framing, and draws on pragmatic and ethnomethodological views of how texts are created and understood and how contexts of writing and reading are mutually negotiated and made relevant by co-participants in a process.

Key to this perspective are issues of face (Brown and Levinson, 1987; Myers, 1989), implicature and the maxims of interpretation and politeness such as those suggested by Grice (1975), Sperber and Wilson (1986), and Leech (1983), mechanisms for conveying newness of information and appealing to shared knowledge (Prince, 1992; Vande Kopple, 1986), and predictive models of discourse coherence based on schemata and scripts (Schank and Abelson, 1977; van Dijk and Kintsch, 1983). Writers and readers are seen to share, or at least orientate to, certain principles of interaction which employ a matrix of meanings, beliefs and values which extend beyond the text to the assumptions of those who use them. The chapter by Myers addresses how the analysis of written communication between students and teachers, between academic colleagues, and between government agencies and citizens, can be informed by such concepts, and how their application is valuable for teaching. At the same time, he emphasises the distinctive assumptions that writing and oral communication make about the conditions of production and reception of their messages.

A third perspective towards the analysis of written texts takes the view that they are prototypical instances of social and institutional practices. Chapter 3 thus necessarily encompasses wider issues than the interactionist, arguing that while writing draws on and helps constitute a local context, this is to be understood as encompassing a larger social and cultural reality. Here, then, particular discursive conventions are seen as 'authorised' and valued by social groups, institutional sites, or discourse communities. This means that the typical ways meanings are made and social relations expressed actually embody particular sets of power relationships, political interests and ideological positions, constitutive of those communities and sites.

On this perspective, any analysis of text needs to consider the overall framework of social meanings and socially based ideological schemata inscribed in its creation and interpretation. What this approach tells us, then, is that when writers engage in a particular genre or draw on particular interactional conventions, they are simultaneously adopting and reproducing particular social roles and relationships and ratifying literacy practices. It also suggests that to adopt different conventions in academic and professional contexts is often to redefine these roles and relationships and to explicitly contest the institutional dynamics that lie behind them. The site of Lea and Street's chapter is, appropriately enough, the academy. Their chapter focuses particularly on the varying perceptions of tutors and students concerning the nature of these ratified literacy practices, how they are formulated in the practices and texts of the academy, and how ethnographic research linked to textual study can illuminate the struggles among the participants in the delineation and significance of these practices. What emerges is more than an analysis of writing; such an approach explains how deeply embedded such preferred and dispreferred literacy practices are within alternative epistemologies of the disciplines in question.

2   Interpretation: focus on process

Part II moves away from issues of expression and text organisation to focus on three interlinked perspectives on the process of academic and professional writing: the cognitive, the social and the cultural. Each of these approaches seeks to link the activity of writing to the wider circumstances of its production.

Understanding the rich diversity of cognitive processes involved in professional writing critically depends on appreciating the purposes for which readers will use the text. Decisions about appropriate wording, structure, layout, graphics, materials, the representation of self and other, and how the reader is likely to interpret and act on the text, all play a critical role in writing in professional, workplace and academic contexts. Attempts to understand writers' mental processes during the act of composition go back to research in cognitive psychology in the early 1970s, and have become increasingly, if not always fully convincingly, refined through the work of Flower and Hayes (1981, 1984), de Beaugrande (1984) and Bereiter and Scardamalia (1987). Much of this work has been descriptive rather than explanatory (see Grabe and Kaplan, 1996), and, in its focus on writing seen as an individual act of information processing, has paid less attention than it might to the social conditions of the writing process. Nonetheless, it has provided examples of the rich diversity of cognitive processes engaged in the act of writing, and has offered a carefully constructed set of research protocols for the exploration of writers' composing practices and, in particular, the influence of planning, memory and writer objectives.

Of particular interest, therefore, to any study of the cognitive processes of professional writing is the degree of reciprocity holding between writer and reader, how writers come to construct their audience, and the effect this has on the text (Park, 1982, 1986). Unfortunately, much of the extensive research into writing from the perspective of cognitive psychology fails to situate it adequately socially, and often links writing to writer purposes in only very general ways. To understand the extent to which writers may be seen as independent creative beings, it is not sufficient to ground such an understanding simply on a mentalist analysis of writers' inner feelings and beliefs. Any comprehensive explanation of such creativity must incorporate all elements of the rhetorical situation, of which audience is a significant part. In our view, any cognitive perspective on writing must locate the writer within a given social context of writing practices, rather than isolated in the confines of psychological processes, if we wish to account for the interpersonal and social decisions that the writer makes.

It is the challenge of this perspective that is taken up in Wright's chapter. As a cognitive psychologist, she argues that research into the nexus between writers' composing and reader reception requires what she regards as a sophisticated orchestration of a wide range of cognitive resources. In particular, such research requires just the social perspective we have argued for above, emphasising the varied and parallel purposes of readers when interpreting non-fiction texts (as here in healthcare), and the implications such multiple reader goals have on the decisions writers make when realising their similarly plural goals in text. In short, we may say that interest in a cognitive perspective on writing processes lies as much in what it can say about the social representations which contribute to a writer's production of a text, and the extent these are socially shared or individual, as it does about the cognitive skills and strategies writers must employ. Fundamental to this perspective, then, is an understanding of the social relationship between writer and reader in the given case.

A second perspective on the writing process addresses this issue explicitly, focusing on the writer's awareness of the social context which defines the purpose and meaning of any piece of writing. A variety of different methodologies have contributed to our understanding here, drawing on ethnography (Myers, 1990b), sociolinguistics (B. Bernstein, 1990), social constructionism (Rorty, 1979; Bizzell, 1992), social semiotics (Halliday, 1978) and critical discourse analysis (Fairclough, 1992a; Kress, 1988). All point to writing processes occurring within a complex of understandings, meanings and knowledge as part of wider social and cultural structures. On this perspective, individuals write as community members and the specific properties of writing are seen as reflecting, and in part constituting, the interactions between members of social groups. Texts, and the writing processes which create them, are the ways we participate in institutions, construct our professional identities, and carry out our social and occupational roles.

The social perspective clearly complements the cognitive perspective and, as we shall see, the cultural perspective, in helping us understand the processes of writing. In addition, it illuminates our awareness of the ways that discursive forms and genres are institutionally valued, evaluated and validated. As Berkenkotter and Huckin point out, genres are not only the media of professional communication, but are:

> intimately linked to a discipline's methodology and they package information in ways that conform to a discipline's norms, values, and ideology. Understanding the genres of written communication in one's field is, therefore, essential to professional success.
>
> (Berkenkotter and Huckin, 1995: 1)

All discourse, and particularly the discourses of the professions, workplaces and the academy, are constructed, interpreted and acted upon in social sites of engagement and according to social norms. It is important to recall, however, that such discourses are not only contextually specific, they serve as well to regulate access to the roles, statuses and authority structures they realise in those contexts and those sites.

A central assumption is, then, that meanings are socially mediated, or are specific to social groups, and discourse is essentially field-dependent. Members of professional communities simultaneously reproduce their communities as they communicate through approved and familiar genres and conventional patterns of discourse. Thus, while the need to incorporate one's audience appropriately into one's writing is regarded as a crucial dimension of securing both professional and personal goals, it is also the way that acts of writing serve to reinforce existing structures of authority and professional practice. This perspective is directly exemplified in Hyland's chapter. His context is again the academy, but the focus has shifted to the evaluation of the interpersonal stance of the writer in the institutionally (and personally) crucial site of the research article. The intent is to demonstrate how writers adopt distinctive social and personal positions in the construction of academic papers, reflecting different positions vis-à-vis their propositions and their audiences, in line with the discursive conventions of their particular disciplines. Such a comparative approach highlights the importance of the social, but it also resonates with Wright's discussion of complex cognitive decision-making, and, as we shall see, with the cultural practices of disciplinary communities.

Finally in Part II, we emphasise a cultural perspective on the analysis of writing processes. In doing so, we are aware of the considerable interpretative baggage that any reference to 'culture' invokes. We take here an almost certainly simplistic position that culture as it relates to language choice and language use involves an understanding of values and of practices. Composing involves selecting and grouping experience in consistent and to a degree conventionalised ways, and thus implies the incorporation of a range of cultural knowledge and experience in any individual response to a writing task. Among many elements, gender, ethnicity and language play an important role.

From the point of view of ethnolinguistic cultures, writing has been seen as inherent in self-perception and cultural maintenance, as well as the site of struggle and change where diverse cultures meet. Given the broad sweep of such a view, it is perhaps regrettable that much applied linguistic research into the cultural influences on writing has focused chiefly on textual study of rhetorical and discursive variation of writers from presumed different linguistic and cultural backgrounds (e.g. Connor, 1996; Hinds, 1987; Kaplan, 1987; Purves, 1988). While this research has offered explanations for particular patterns and discourse organisational preferences of writers in terms of their cultural embeddedness, it has been far less successful in accounting for features of second language writing in terms of cognitive and cultural transfer from one language to another.

From the perspective of academic, workplace and professional writing, culture has been seen as a critical influence on the practices of writers through their institutional allegiances. Here texts are seen to instantiate the norms, beliefs, value systems and epistemological understandings of particular disciplines or professional communities. Myers expresses this succinctly:

> Disciplines are like cultures in that their members have shared, taken for granted beliefs; these beliefs can be mutually incomprehensible between cultures; these beliefs are encoded in a language; they are embodied in practices; new members are brought into culture through rituals.   (Myers, 1995: 5)

Culture provides an intellectual and communicative scaffold for the writer to construct community-based meanings and knowledge, a framework of conventions and understandings within which individuals can communicate concisely and effectively with their peers.

One way of approaching how this framework may be constructed is to follow the Brechtian principle of estrangement and attempt to disengage and stand outside our immediate contexts of familiarity. Such an opportunity may be provided for some readers at least in Malcolm's chapter, focusing as it does on indigenous cultures, as here in Australia. The potential for estrangement is considerable. The chapter addresses issues which have much more general relevance, one of which is his construct of a 'linguistic ecology' where writing may or may not have a place, or certainly where writing is variously valued by different members and in different contexts of interaction and sites. Where the introduction or privileging of particular forms of writing accompany some cultural hegemony, as they frequently do, we can not only explore the relationship between such literacy forms and practices and the privileging of particular linguistic and discursive forms, but also discern how varying degrees of access to those forms may impact on an individual's sense of identity, rights and opportunities. The particular crucial site of Aboriginal students engaging with the literacy practices of the Australian academy is significant for many such critical moments. But what is important is that the issues raised are not at all necessarily limited to the indigenous communities of Malcolm's research, but have universal relevance.

3 Explanation: focus on research

The purpose of Part III of the book is to provide examples of a number of relatable methodologies for research into academic, workplace and professional writing. The chapters focus on text-linguistic, discoursal/pragmatic and social-constructionist approaches to writing, with an emphasis, particularly in the contribution of Candlin and Plum, on the fruitful integration of different methodologies in addressing key issues of writing and literacy practices in what Fairclough (1992a) has termed a 'rational' research programme.

Text-linguistic approaches to writing research have been remarkably fruitful, not only in providing descriptions of textual products, but in seeing through them, as it were, the traces of communicative activity performed by writers. Texts thus serve as a point of contact between writers and readers but also, indirectly, offer evidence of the active discursive processes of construction and interpretation by writers and readers. Texts in this sense offer a means of admittedly speculative access to these processes. Put simply, the goal of this research has been to reveal 'what linguistically definable concrete features might help us to distinguish a text which works nicely in a certain situation from a text which does not' (Enkvist, 1985: 25). A multitude of analytic perspectives have been brought to bear on this enterprise, influenced, for example, by a clause-relation perspective (e.g. Jacoby, 1987), speech act theory (Beauvais, 1989; Eemeren and Grootendorst, 1984), genre analysis (Bhatia, 1993; Swales, 1990), systemic linguistics (Halliday, 1988; Martin, 1987) and varieties thereof (Coulthard, 1994; Couture, 1989).

While some studies have been content simply to describe the patterns of rhetorical structure or lexico-grammatical forms they find in texts, most recent research has sought to relate these to the communicative purposes of writers in particular contexts. This movement of research is significant in view of the integrative approach taken by this book. What is being evidenced is that textual regularities derive from the exercise of particular conventions, and that the description of texts offers insights on the purposive and often institutionally grounded constraints and choices which operate on the writer.

The chapter from Yu-Ying Chang and John Swales admirably reflects this transitional positioning of text-focused writing research. It does so by first subjecting a number of informal elements in academic writing – which the authors refer to as being 'of uncertain appropriacy' – taken from different disciplines, to detailed text-linguistic analysis. They relate these to advice about their use given in a number of manuals and handbooks concerned with stylistic choice, and further corroborate this analysis with interviews with a selection of experienced academic authors. Not surprisingly, there is a range of opinion expressed, from the more prescriptivist to the more descriptivist position. To facilitate the transition in research focus we refer to, though the use of this multiply sourced and corroborating evidence already signals this, the authors explore the impact of what they describe as an increasing licensing of alternative positions on the use of the elements; a situation, it turns out from their chapter, which is neither entirely helpful to, nor necessarily welcomed by, some aspiring academic writers. Thus textual analysis is linked to interpretative analysis and both are set against the wider social-constructionist perspective on academic writing.

The impetus has thus been given to signalling the importance of the second research methodology discussed in this collection, the narrowing of focus to the micro writing environment. As we have indicated earlier, such a focus is less concerned with the macro socio-cultural Context than it is with the possibilities open to writers in more local contexts. On this view, any writer works as a social actor immediately contextually located and engaged in interaction with specific readers. Now, while it would work against our central integrated theme to draw too firm a distinction between these little 'c' and big 'C' contexts, as broader issues of ideology and institutional practice clearly influence the exercise of action in local circumstances, factors such as the actual writing task, and the writer's perception of that task, and his or her readership, directly affect the execution of the task.

In such an analysis, research seeks to uncover the particular beliefs, perceptions and expectations brought by the individual writer to the writing task, drawing on experience of this wider context and of other texts. It is natural, then, that such research will rely heavily on the verbal reports and protocols of writers and readers themselves, either employing think-aloud methods during the composing process (Smagorinsky, 1994), or discourse-based ethnographic interviews focusing on written drafts (Cross, 1990; North, 1986). The value of this approach lies in its role in bridging the gap between the perceptions of writers and the constructs of analysts.

The contribution by Ivanič and Weldon not only has this focus as its mainspring, it also visibly manifests how such a process might be captured in the process of research. In their chapter, the authors engage in a dialogue, seeking to understand and explain how writers negotiate their relationships with their readers, and how they accommodate the dilemmas of self-representation they face as they write. Writers are engaged in sending messages, but these are as much messages about themselves and their readership, and thus the stance they are taking in their writing, as they are about the ideational content of the message. What is significant methodologically is the introduction of discourse-based interviews with writers and readers, focusing on the gradual unfolding of the text in response to these personal, social and content-directed pressures.

The final research approach, the social constructionist, has been extremely influential in both how we define professional, workplace and academic writing and how it is taught. Drawing on ethnographic and textual data, and informed by the work of writers such as Bakhtin (1981), Kuhn (1970) and Rorty (1979), this perspective views writing as both contextually constrained and context creating, emphasising the role of social relations within discourse communities in defining what can be said and how it will be received. Bruffee (1986: 774) defines social construction as the conception of 'reality, knowledge, thoughts, facts, texts, selves, and so on . . . as generated by communities of like-minded peers'. Textual conventions are seen here as deeply embedded in writers' and readers' cultural and rhetorical assumptions about what constitutes appropriate topic, argument and format, and these assumptions may both carry and maintain the power of institutional authority.

Bruffee (1986), Bizzell (1992) and others have therefore made the construct of 'community' an important element of professional writing research, situating it as a powerful normative force which constitutes the shared values regulating discursive practices. In doing so, they make explicit connection with the work of Lave and Wenger (1991) and their concept of 'communities of practice'. While there is some debate about the nature of discourse communities (Killingsworth and Gilbertson, 1992; Swales, 1993), a substantial part of the writing competence of a 'professional' or a 'legitimate member' of such a community is held to involve familiarity with its conventional discursive forms and the ability to exploit these effectively in his or her writing.

The view that communities' are defined and demarcated by their discursive practices, which enable them consensually to construct and justify their knowledge and beliefs, has had a considerable impact on the study of academic, professional and workplace literacies. Several of the chapters in this volume give evidence of this. As one example, academic communication is now widely regarded as a social activity which functions in disciplinary cultures to facilitate the production of knowledge through written persuasion (Bazerman, 1988; Berkenkotter and Huckin, 1995; Hyland, 1997; Myers, 1990b). The chapter by Barrett in Part IV, as we comment later, demonstrates the centrality of writing as a professionally defining activity in the community of practice of psychiatric medicine.

The chapter by Candlin and Plum, which concludes Part III of the book, has several purposes: it emphasises the need for, and the value of, an integrated research methodology involving the themes of writing as text, process and practice central to this book as a whole, but it also shows how such an approach offers a way to unpack and explain certain current and problematic issues in writing research, notably those surrounding the concepts of *generic integrity*, *apprenticeship* and *participant relationships*, all of which figure in the other chapters in this volume. In testing out the integrated model against these issues, Candlin and Plum's chapter makes the point that just as the objects of writing research are increasingly interdiscursive in their significance and intertextual in their nature, so this is also true of the research paradigms themselves. Here, as elsewhere, integration cannot be taken for granted, but needs itself to be negotiated among researchers from different traditions, and with different research objectives. The chapter works well to summarise the components of the research model this book advocates, but also shows its practicability, again focusing on disciplinary writing in the academy as its research site. As such, it also provides the important bridge between the chapters in the first three parts of the book and the case studies that follow.

4   Realisation: focus on praxis

We have argued earlier for the establishment of a discourse between research and practice, and have declared this to be desirably a relationship of mutuality and co-involvement. The purpose of this final part of the book is to present three case studies as examples of this discourse. In addition, the Part IV also seeks to display the relevance of the three key dimensions of research into the analysis of writing in real-world contexts, the focus on text, the focus on process and the focus on practice, and their associated methodological orientations.

The case studies have, however, two other functions. They serve, firstly, to show how the constructs and methodologies discussed earlier can apply in quite distinctive environments. In Milton's chapter, this environment is the computer-mediated training of novice writers drawing on extensive textual corpora to investigate the conventions of academic writing in a second language. In Barrett's study, the context is the way that professional writing practices in a particular institutional environment, that of a clinical psychiatric unit, act to construct patients and provide account-based definitions of illness. Here writing is most obviously social action, but it is quite characteristically in this context, also professional and public action. Finally, for Gollin it is the ways in which collaborative writing in an organisation offers evidence of the relationship between participant role, contribution and the developmental process undertaken in the gradual refinement of the written text.

A second function of these case studies is one that imbues, directly or indirectly, all the chapters in this volume. They all, we hope, illustrate the easy and convenient way in which the research-based analyses can offer recognisable opportunities for practical application, in writer training, in professional development of trainers and practitioners, in the evaluation of writing processes and products, and in the evaluation of quality in programme delivery and individual performance.

PART I

Expression: focus on text

1

Integrating products, processes, purposes and participants in professional writing

VIJAY K. BHATIA

Overview

Analysing text as a genre, especially in institutionalised contexts, whether academic or professional, provides relevant and useful information about the way that particular genre is constructed, interpreted and used by the established members of the disciplinary community in the conduct of everyday business. Genres are invariably situated in the contexts of specific disciplinary cultures (Berkenkotter and Huckin, 1995) and are shaped by typical discursive processes embedded within the disciplinary activities of the profession. The ultimate generic product also displays a recognisable integrity of its own (Bhatia, 1993). However, this generic integrity is often perceived in applied genre literature in terms of typical lexico-grammatical and discourse patterns, simply because these are the most obvious surface-level linguistic features of textual genres.

In applied linguistic studies, these linguistic patterns have often been used as a basis for many writing courses within English for Specific Purposes (ESP) paradigms for reproducing authentic-looking samples of professional genres. However, recent research on thicker descriptions of textual genres (Bhatia, 1993; Swales, 1990) has underpinned the importance of explanation in the act of discourse recognition, construction, interpretation and use, with the result that many genre-based innovations in the area of writing instruction in ESP and professional contexts have started considering factors other than the lexico-grammatical and discourse organisational to bring in the notions of flexibility, creativity and innovation in their writing exercises.

This chapter will argue for and illustrate a genre-based approach to writing which aims to integrate the discipline-specific discursive procedures and the communicative purposes which these generic constructs serve to help apprentice learners to maintain the generic integrity of their writing products on the one hand, and to manipulate their products to meet participant expectations on the other.

Professional writing differs significantly from academic writing often undertaken in the context of the classroom. Much of academic writing is an individual's response to somewhat predictable rhetorical contexts, often meant to serve a given set of communicative purposes, for a specified single readership. Professional writing, on the other hand, is a complex, dynamic and multifunctional activity. Any pragmatically successful instance of a particular professional genre can be typically characterised in terms of its generic integrity, in the sense that members of the relevant professional community can identify and interpret it in terms of not only the socially recognised communicative purpose(s) it often is intended to serve, but also the private intentions, if any, the author(s) might have intended to convey. Most professional genres also display, and expert readers can identify, the complex intertextual and interdiscursive relationships the genre might have with other forms of discourse, spoken or written. Besides, the whole process of genre construction might be, and often is, the result of a combination of a number of discursive practices that professionals are routinely engaged in, all or some of which might contribute to the construction of the generic artefact it shapes. It will therefore not be inaccurate to say that professional genres are increasingly becoming co-operative endeavours rather than individually undertaken discursive activities (cf. Gollin, this volume).

Genre as artefact

One can identify four major elements of, or contributors to, any successful construction, interpretation and use of a professional genre.

1   Generic integrity

The most important element is that it should look like a professional genre, in that the members of the professional community with which it is often associated should recognise it as a valid instance of the genre in question. Most successful constructions of professional textual artefacts have recognisable generic integrity (Bhatia, 1993). It may be complex, in that it may reflect a specific form of mixing and/or embedding of two or more generic forms, or even dynamic, in the sense that it may reflect a gradual development over a period of time in response to subtle changes in the rhetorical contexts that it responds to; but it will certainly have a recognisable generic character. This generic character is more easily accessible to the established members of the professional community rather than to those who have a peripheral involvement in the affairs of the professional community in question (Swales, 1990).

Generic integrity is a reflection of the form–function relationship that so often characterises a generic construct. On the one hand, this relationship between formal and functional aspects of language use reflects a specific cognitive structuring to the genre, on the other hand, it also reflects the communicative purpose(s) that the genre tends to serve (Bhatia, 1993). There are three major indicators of generic integrity: the rhetorical context in which the genre is situated, the communicative purpose(s) it tends to serve, and the cognitive structure that it is meant to represent. If, on the one hand, the communicative purpose of a generic construct is embedded in the rhetorical context in which the genre is often used, on the other hand, it is also transparently reflected in the cognitive patterning of the genre. It is hardly surprising that all the major frameworks for the analysis of genre are based on one of these indicators or a combination of them.

2   Discursive processes and genre

The second most typical characteristic of professional genres is that they often are the products of a set of established procedures that form an important part of the disciplinary culture within a profession. A generic artefact often acquires its typical identity as a result of a set of conventionalised discursive practices, both written and spoken, that professionals routinely engage in as part of their daily work (see also Chapters 3, 9, 11). Many of these discursive practices have distinct stages, with identifiable inputs and outputs. These discursive practices are often characterised by the involvement of more than one participant, which, to a large extent, assigns multiple authorship to the resulting artefact and reflects interaction with the reader (cf. Hyland, this volume). This also gives the resultant document a distinctly rich inter-textual and inter-discursive patterning.

A business client's request for a loan to fund a specific business proposition, for example, is part of a larger business activity, which can be characterised by several discursive processes and stages. A typical funding request made at the front-desk banking counter initiates a series of discursive activities, some of which may include detailed client consultation with a banking official, either in person or in writing, followed by a report by the banking official to the appropriate department for further consideration. The department may, if it decides to take the request further, involve the risk-evaluation department in the further evaluation of the request. On the basis of the report from the risk-evaluation team, the loan department may decide to proceed further, which might involve further negotiation within the bank or with the client, before any final decision is taken, either to grant the request or to turn it down; whichever way it finally goes, it is the result of a series of discursive procedures which are routinely undertaken by the professionals in the conduct of their business.

Although neither the final textual artefact(s), nor the intervening textual outputs (e.g. reports by the front-desk banking official to his superior, or those by the risk-management department, etc.), may directly reflect the involvement or contribution made by these discursive processes and procedures, these are very much part of the whole business activity. The emerging textual products, whichever generic form(s) they may finally take, are the outcomes of a range of diverse discursive processes and consultations engaged in by several professionals, rather than just the person who ultimately has the privilege or authority to claim the sole authorship. That may be one of the reasons why so many of these professional genres have a somewhat predominant impersonal quality.

3   Generic purposes and intentions

A genre is identified by reference to the typicality of the communicative purpose that it tends to serve. However, unlike academic genres, professional genres serve a variety of real corporate purposes, often associated with novel, flexible and changing contexts.

Although many of the genres employed in well-established professional contexts serve a recognisable and somewhat standardised set of communicative purposes, they rarely, if ever, serve a single purpose. If nothing else, they almost always combine the more immediate single purpose with the more standardised ones of maintenance and continuance of goodwill and a mutually beneficial professional relationship.

In addition to the socially recognised communicative purposes associated with a specific genre, expert writers also make sure that the intended readers construe and interpret these purposes in the way the writer originally intended. In the case of news reporting, for instance, experienced news reporters make sure that their readers see the events of the outside world in a manner they want them to. This is often achieved by giving what in journalism is known as a slant to the news story. In many other cases, especially in corporate discourse, it is becoming almost a standard practice to mix promotional elements within more information-giving genres. Company annual reports, for instance, are increasingly being used for promotional purposes, including the promotion of corporate image, and even for fund-raising purposes (see Bhatia, 1997; Hyland, 1998b).

It is not simply the promotional intentions that find expression within the established boundaries of informative genres; often, one may find other less compatible communicative intentions mixed to give expression to conflicting generic forms (see Bhatia, 1997). Instances of such tendencies to mix conflicting purposes may be found in the case of diplomatic genres, especially the memorandum of understanding or what is also known as joint declarations, where one is encouraged to mix legally binding provisions with more popular and promotional intentions (Wodak, 1996). This mixing becomes almost inevitable because the signing parties wish to signal mutual understanding and agreement, on the one hand, and maintain a sufficient degree of flexibility for any future manipulation within the terms of agreement, on the other (for a detailed discussion of this, see Bhatia, 1998).

4   Genre participants

Practising genre is almost like playing a game, with its own rules and conventions. Established genre participants, both writers and readers, are like skilful players, who succeed by their manipulation and exploitation of, rather than a strict compliance with, the rules of the game. This is what gives expert professional writers some freedom to exploit the tactical space available within the boundaries of conventional behaviour, pushing out the boundaries of the genre. As Bhatia (1993) points out, they often use this tactical space to mix private intentions with socially recognised communicative purposes, often giving rise to mixed genres. In a similar manner, genre readership may well be multiple or corporate, rather than individually identifiable, which tends to make the game rather unpredictable and interestingly complex.

Learning to write professional genres is more like being initiated into professional or disciplinary practices than like learning to write in the academy. It is not simply a matter of learning the language, or even learning the rules of the game, it is more like acquiring the rules of the game in order to be able to exploit and manipulate them to fulfil professional and disciplinary goals within well-defined and established contexts. The professional writing activity is thus inextricably embedded within the disciplinary culture it tends to serve. Acquisition of professional writing competence therefore requires a certain degree of pre-knowledge of the discursive procedures and practices of the professional community that the writer wishes to join.

An important aspect of genre construction is the awareness of other participants in the process, not only the other contributors and writers within the professional organisation, but also the multiple and varied audience the genre is likely to be aimed at. Audience characteristics in professional contexts can hardly be over-emphasised. It makes a good deal of difference if the document is written for subordinates rather than for superiors. It makes a lot more crucial difference if it is written for outside clients rather than for insiders. It is an entirely different matter if one were to write to an established corporate client as against an individual non-specialist client, especially in the extent to which one can afford to be explicit and detailed in transmitting technical and specialist information in the context of suggesting alternative solutions or options in client advising. Expert and established genre writers are well aware of the constraints that the nature, background knowledge, disciplinary expertise or immediate concerns of the intended readership may impose on the process of genre construction.

Generic versatility

In addition to these four important aspects of genre writing, which assign specific genres their essential generic identity, there are others which make them dynamic, creative and versatile rather than static or formulaic. These factors include the following:

- *Corporate and organisational differences*: Genres, in spite of being overwhelmingly conventional in many aspects, show considerable freedom in the way different institutions and corporations construct and realise individual generic artefacts. Many of the established organisations have their own preferred ways not only of conducting business but also of achieving communicative goals. Individual players within the organisation must learn to play the game according to such established organisational preferences. Any trained journalist, for instance, may be required to adapt his or her communicative strategies in the light of prevailing ideological constraints imposed by a particular news corporation.

- *Strategies to achieve similar generic goals*: Although genres are instances of conventionalised and somewhat standardised communicative behaviour, in that they often display regularities of discourse organisation (Swales, 1990), consistency of cognitive structuring (Bhatia, 1993), typical generic structure potential (Hasan, 1985), or stages of communicative activity (Martin, 1985), they are often flexible in terms of the strategies the individual writers may employ to achieve similar generic goals. Some of the prime examples of this communicative behaviour may often be found in the area of advertising and promotional discourse, where it is not very uncommon to find the same product or service being advertised using a number of different strategies, depending upon the target audience characteristics, medium, the immediate concerns of the advertisers, the competition the product or the service may be facing, or even the time when the advertisement appears. The use of different strategies also results in significant variation in the use of linguistic resources.

- *Specialist knowledge*: Two kinds of audience characteristics offer variation within a genre in professional settings: level of specialist knowledge and single or multiple readership. Level of accessible specialist knowledge is likely to influence two kinds of decision: firstly as to the technicality of the written content, that is, whether the genre should be encoded in predominantly plain language or in technical language; and, secondly, as to the degree of detailed specification of information necessary in a particular case. These influences may be most characteristically observed in unequal interactions, particularly between lawyers and clients (Candlin *et al.*, 1995), doctors and patients, civil servants and members of the public, and police and lay persons. Besides, knowledge of audience characteristics also helps the writer to use appropriately effective communicative strategies to influence the reader, especially in the case of persuasive genres where various kinds of appeals are chosen depending upon the analysis of audience characteristics.

The other readership factor, i.e. whether the reader is an individual or a group of individuals, is significant in that it helps the genre writer to use an appropriate interpersonal stance, crucial in some professional genres. In the case of promotional genres, for instance, it is often considered advantageous to address promotional letters to readers individually rather than generically. Similarly, it is considered tactically superior to submit job applications individually written rather than to send a duplicate copy of one application for several jobs. Even if a candidate is applying for several jobs, some more similar than others, he or she is advised to take special care not to give the impression that this is just one of several applications being sent by the candidate.

■ *Variation in linguistic realisations*:   One of the most fundamental assumptions in discourse studies is that there is no strict one-to-one correlation between any specific linguistic form and the values it can take in a variety of discourse contexts. Just as one linguistic form can assume a number of discourse values, similarly, a particular discourse value can be realised by several forms. It is more accurate to argue that in the context of professional genres, this relationship between a specific generic value and its linguistic realisations is relatively stable, rather than fixed. Promotional values across a variety of closely related professional genres, for example, are very likely to be realised differently in promotional advertisements, job applications, book blurbs, philanthropic fund-raising letters, and, to some extent, in book reviews and a number of other related genres, all of which form what could be designated as a colony of promotional

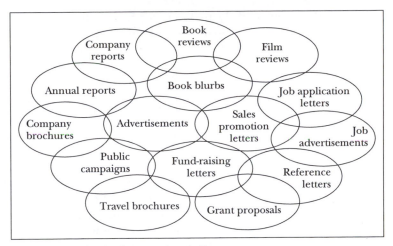

Figure 1.1   Colony of promotional discourse

discourse, which can be displayed as in Figure 1.1 (see also Bhatia, 1993, 1998, for a detailed discussion of this point).

■ *Genre mixing and embedding*:   The most interesting character-istic of professional genres is their versatility, in that they have a natural tendency to mix not only a variety of communicative purposes, but also private intentions within the context of socially recognised communicative contexts. This makes generic frameworks very versatile in nature. Within the notion of generic integrity, it accounts for a variety of levels of generic realisations (genres, sub-genres and sub-sub-genres), on the one hand, and mixed (Bhatia, 1997) or hybrid genres (Fairclough, 1995), on the other. It can account for the expression of socially sanctioned communicative purposes and the mixing of these purposes with private intentions (see Bhatia, 1993, 1995, 1997).

In the preceding sections, I have made an attempt to characterise the nature of professional writing as distinct from much of aca-demic writing. The main thrust of the argument has been dir-ected at two apparently conflicting issues, the generic integrity of much of professional discourse, on the one hand, and the versatil-ity in genre construction and interpretation, on the other. This raises a very important question: How does one resolve the ten-sion between these two conflicting constraints in order to acquire, practise and eventually claim ownership of some of the generic constructs that one is likely to interact with in the conduct of one's professional duties? In the rest of the chapter, I suggest a possible solution to some of these. But first I identify the nature and specification of some of the necessary writing competencies one may need to master to be able to claim ownership of a subset of professional genres.

Genre acquisition

Acquisition of professional genres involves two kinds of competency, one at the level of awareness and the other at the level of performance. The first is invariably acquired in the form of what Berkenkotter and Huckin (1995) call genre knowledge, and the second is often accomplished through practice and performance. Although in real-life professional situations the two are seen as rather indistinguishable, in pedagogic contexts they can be distinguished and prioritised as follows:

Awareness of:
- *Generic potential*:   Every instance of genre is endowed with a natural and somewhat restricted capacity to communicate an allowable range of meanings to achieve institutionalised goals within a specific disciplinary culture. In other words, every instance of genre has a potential to give expression to only some and not all of the communicative purposes that members of a particular professional community may determine. The very first requirement on the part of a professional writer is thus to be aware of the generic potential of the range of professional genres his or her community is routinely engaged in as part of their daily work.
- *Generic complexity and versatility*:   In addition to awareness of the potential of a range of genres, one also needs to be aware of the dynamic quality of each individual genre, especially the way a genre can be constructed and exploited, construed and interpreted, used and developed to express a range of purposes and intentions within well-defined rhetorical contexts, with eyes set on the eventual pragmatic success of the communicative endeavour.
- *Freedom and flexibility within allowable generic constraints*:   Most established practitioners of professional genres have a good

awareness of allowable generic constraints that operate on a successful generic artefact. The constraints may be operating on the communicative purposes and private intentions that can be legitimately expressed, the range of lexico-grammatical resources that can be employed to give expression to such intentions, on the way the artefact can be rhetorically structured, or a combination of some or all of these. In the case of promotional genres, for instance, it is always possible for established writers to choose from a range of strategies available to promote a particular product or service. Similarly, they have considerable freedom in the choice of lexico-grammatical features to realise established generic goals.

■ *Cross-cultural and intercultural sensitivities*:   Genres vary across cultures, languages and language varieties, especially in the choice of rhetorical strategies, cultural values, linguistic realisations and discourse structuring. Discourse communities react differently to these issues depending upon who controls the power to accept or reject such variations, or deviations. In academic publications, for example, it is still the generic forms of the Western world that often prevail, because the editorial procedures and norms are predominantly controlled by British and American academics. However, in advertising and business communications, there is a considerable amount of flexibility and accommodation, because successful communication in these contexts depends more seriously on the uptake on the part of readers, who are often situated in contexts outside the Western world. Any expert genre writer therefore needs to have sensitivity to inter- and cross-cultural constraints operating on genres across national, cultural or ethnic boundaries.

Some other contextual contributors to the construction of genres are:

■ *Audience characteristics*:   Expert genre writers need also to take account of whether the intended readership is real, perceived or invoked; whether it consists of a single individual or several individuals, a group or some combination of these; what level or degree of familiarity, especially based on past business or professional relationship, is anticipated; etc.

■ *Medium*:   Medium factors are playing an increasingly complex, dynamic and dominant role in professional writing. With the popularity of multimedia, especially the use of fax and electronic mail, professional genres have significantly changed the nature and form of professional activities. The traditional modes of variation in communicative practices (written, spoken, spoken to be written and written to be read) are still significant in genres such as advertising, where the choice of persuasive strategies depends largely on the choice of medium.

Writing competencies

In addition to the various aspects of genre knowledge, any ability to construct, interpret, use and exploit genres in professional contexts involves a number of competencies, some of which are:

- ability to select the right genre (generic potential);
- ability to identify and discern communicative purposes in writing;
- ability to identify, understand and predict cognitive structuring in genres;
- ability to decide which private intentions, if any, can be covertly expressed within a recognisable set of generic purposes;
- ability to predict rhetorical strategies associated with a range of genres: in writing a job application, for example, one should be able to realise that it is perfectly acceptable to transgress the Gricean Maxim of Quantity (Grice, 1975) in not telling the *whole* truth, but not the Maxim of Quality to say something which is *not true*;
- ability to choose the right kind of appeal, persuasive or any other, keeping in mind the nature of the genre in question and the understanding of and relationship with the audience (see Chapters 5 and 7);
- ability to choose suitably appropriate lexico-grammatical realisations of the communicative purposes (both socially recognised and more covert ones, including private intentions) (see Lea and Street, this volume).

Genre and writing instruction

Professional writing expertise essentially incorporates an ability to interpret, innovate, develop and exploit generic conventions to claim ownership of a specific set of genres associated with a particular disciplinary culture (Berkenkotter and Huckin, 1995).

Training in writing professional genres, therefore, may consist of a number of stages, some of which are the following:

- *Acquisition of the code*:   General writing skills include the ability to think, organise and write clearly, concisely and coherently.
- *Acquisition of genre knowledge*:   General generic skills: the standard forms of many workplace genres are important because they provide a quick, convenient and efficient template for cognitive structures, facilitating the transfer of professionally relevant information within specific disciplinary cultures.
- *Genre practice*:   Real professional writing also involves creative use of generic skills to mix, embed and create novel generic forms to respond to familiar and predictable, and not so familiar, rhetorical contexts.
- *Genre ownership*:   This final stage of genre acquisition enables writers to use standard generic procedures creatively to re-create novel generic forms, to develop predictable forms to communicate private intentions within the framework of socially recognised generic purposes.

1   Acquisition of the code

Although a control over the knowledge of the code is an essential prerequisite for the acquisition of any genre-writing skill, a complete and perfect control is neither a necessary nor a sufficient condition for any subsequent successful acquisition of generic skills.

2   Acquisition of genre knowledge

Ideally, one acquires genre knowledge by validly participating in the affairs of the professional community; however, such a process can be time-consuming and often frustrating. The most economical and effective way to acquire genre knowledge is through the analysis and interpretation of a specific set of samples of the genres in question. In most writing programmes, analysis has generally been given a very low priority and is rarely taken up with the same seriousness that goes with the production of written texts. Writing is often viewed as a productive skill. Analysis, on the other hand, has been regarded as a passive skill, and any mixing of the two is thought to be generally undesirable. However, since genre-based writing requires pre-knowledge of the conventions, conversations and procedures operating in specific disciplinary cultures, the importance of analytical skills can hardly be overemphasised.

What then is genre knowledge? Let me begin by citing Berkenkotter and Huckin (1995: 126), who define genre knowledge as a form of 'situated cognition', which seems inextricable from professional writers' procedural and social knowledge (Berkenkotter and Huckin, 1995: 13). Fairclough (1992a: 126) points out that

> a genre implies not only a particular text type, but also particular processes of producing, distributing and consuming texts.

Genre theory exploits the knowledge not only of the communicative goals of a particular professional community, but also of the discursive practices embedded in the disciplinary culture of that community. The other aspect of this genre knowledge is a sensitivity to generic form and content. In this sense, content is as important as the way it is structured (Johns, 1998). Almost all theories of genre have paid quite significant attention to structural form. Some even use this as the main criterion to identify genres, for instance Hasan (1985) in referring to generic structure potential (GSP), and Martin *et al.* (1987) in their definition of genre as a staged, goal-oriented social process. Others have also given the structural form an important status, though not so criterial, as in Swales (1990) in move-structure, and Bhatia (1993) in cognitive structures. Generic forms are also reflected, though not explicitly, in Miller's (1984) typification of rhetorical action. The main purpose of genre theory is to study how communicative goals of professional communities are achieved in specific rhetorical contexts using structural forms appropriate to specific content. Structural forms, therefore, assume an important status in the study of genre. As Berkenkotter and Huckin (1995: 43) point out,

> forms themselves have little meaning; it is only when they are seen as serving certain functions that they become meaningful. But often one cannot detect these functions without first noticing a pattern of forms, and often such a pattern cannot by itself be detected without looking across genres . . .
>
> (Berkenkotter and Huckin, 1995: 43)

The most important connection between the perceived world and the real world is the understanding and awareness of what could be called *generic potential*, after Halliday's use of the term in the context of 'meaning potential', which essentially is all that identifies a particular genre and in turn gives it its integrity. Genre knowledge, though recognised through typicalities identified in representative texts, is more than just that; it is an awareness of the power that lies underneath each generic artefact. It also represents the power to identify integrity of genres and to distinguish subtle relationships between familiar and not so familiar generic patterns. Genre knowledge provides the ability to recognise that the expression 'The sun never sets over Lufthansa territory' is a subtle exploitation of the cliché 'The sun never sets over the British Empire'. It allows one to use the known to respond to the unknown. Therein lies the power of the genre.

The essence of a genre-based analysis of linguistic behaviour in professional contexts is not entirely in the *lexico-grammar*, not even in the *structural form* that we perceive in the analytical exploits of one genre or the other; it is in the cumulative knowledge of the conventions that allows one to make choices in disciplinary content, lexico-grammar and generic form, among other things, to achieve a specific set of communicative purposes. In some cases, however, one may get the impression that structural form is assigned a rather more privileged position at the expense of other factors, as in Hasan (1985), but she also qualifies her statement by saying,

> To think of text structure, not in terms of the structure of each individual text as a separate entity, but as a general statement about a genre as a whole, is to imply that there exists a close relation between text and context . . .   (Hasan, 1985: 68)

It is often pointed out that generic structures constrain individual creativity. However, we tend to forget the fact that when we learn a genre we do not simply learn to acquire a generic form, or a way of achieving purpose, we learn, more importantly, to make sense of the conversations, discursive practices and above all the goals of the established members of a disciplinary community we wish to be part of. Generic structures, though they appear to be linguistic in form, are abstracted from authentic instances of genres used in actual practice and are essentially socio-cognitive in nature.

3   Genre practice

Having familiarised oneself with the knowledge of the conventions, conversations and discursive procedures engaged in by the members of relevant professional communities, one can be engaged in the practice of genre construction and interpretation. Here genre practice is seen as a goal-directed discursive activity, rather than as a purely textual one. Although genre practice will still be considered contrived and somewhat less than real, it will certainly be more than just putting sentences together to form a text. It will still be governed by the communicative purpose, whether real or imagined, of the genre in question, a valid and reasonable explanation for the choice of relevant lexico-grammatical and discoursal possibilities, a sense of exploitation of tactical space leading to the right choice of rhetorical strategies to achieve disciplinary goals, and some concern with the ultimate pragmatic success of the intended generic artefact.

4   Genre ownership

The final step in the acquisition of genre expertise is often considered to be the claim of genre ownership. One can claim ownership only to the extent to which one can display sufficient expertise not only in a dynamic use and exploitation of the available generic knowledge and resources to respond to familiar and not so familiar rhetorical contexts, but also to create, innovate and develop new generic forms to achieve novel communicative goals within the framework of socially accepted generic boundaries. One may often go beyond these accomplishments to create hybrid or mixed generic forms, embedded genres or, sometimes, novel generic constructs.

Integrating products, processes, purposes and participants

In this discussion of a genre-based writing approach, there exists a tension between the real world, which is complex, dynamic and somewhat unpredictable, often requiring experts to exploit generic resources to respond to novel rhetorical contexts, and the pedagogic one, which is simplified, static and largely predictable, requiring a somewhat standardised response to well-defined and often familiar rhetorical contexts. We teachers would often like to see a direct correlation between the two. We often find one of the most common manifestations of this direct correlation in attempts to equate 'input' to 'intake' in language teaching and learning. Another manifestation of this is found in the use of ideal or exemplary texts or genres as templates for practice and eventual acquisition of similar textual forms. Here the expectation is that by acquiring the use of one discourse or generic form the learner will be able to respond to similar rhetorical situations. Unfortunately, however, the correlation is not necessarily so simple.

Yet another kind of over-simplified and too direct a correlation can be found in attempts to distinguish genre either as a product or as a process, thereby overlooking perhaps the most important aspect of genre construction, namely, the purpose embedded in genre knowledge as part of the composing process. What makes the generic process and eventually the product possible is the conventional knowledge of the genre in question. The knowledge of generic conventions essentially shapes the act of communication to suit a specific rhetorical situation. It is this genre knowledge that the learner acquires and makes use of to respond to familiar and not so familiar rhetorical situations. Genres, therefore, are not simply meant to be used as templates within which novel rhetorical actions are supposed to fit; at the same time, they must be seen as socially constructed forms that are dynamic and can therefore be, and quite often are, reconstructed, reconditioned, revised to achieve quite explicit socially recognised communicative purposes. Moreover, these forms can also be exploited and even manipulated to achieve somewhat implicit private intentions.

Just as text and context are interdependent, in the sense that a text makes very little sense without its context, similarly any expressions which are entirely independent of generic expectations of the members of a relevant discourse community are unlikely to make a great deal of sense to these members as instances of effective professional communication. It is rather uncommon to find instances of successful communication, especially in institutionalised contexts, which are entirely independent of the generic expectations of the members of the professional or academic community to whom they are addressed. Success of any instance of communication, to a large extent, depends on the shared conventional knowledge of the genre to which the specific instance belongs.

We confront now the question of relationship between conventional generic form and individual expression, the so-called tension between generic integrity and individual freedom in the expression of private intentions. Bazerman (1994a) seems to understand this tension when he points out that genres rely on our being able to recognize them and to some degree understand the meanings they instantiate within the systems of which they are part. A textual form which is not recognized as being a type, having a particular force, would have no status nor social value as a genre. A genre exists only in the recognitions and attributions of the users . . .

Through an understanding of genres available to us at any time we can understand the roles and relationships open to us. An understanding of generic decorum will let us know whether it is ours to ask or answer, to argue or clarify, to declare or request . . .

This understanding of the way genres structure social relations could be highly conservative in that decorum would urge repeating only the familiar, reproducing old dramas, prompting only replayings of the old songs at the familiar moments. It can also give us the understanding to lead old hopes and expectations down familiar-seeming garden paths, but that lead to new places. Only by uncovering the pathways that guide our lives in certain directions can we begin to identify the possibilities for new turns and the consequences of taking those turns. When we are put on the spot, we must act generically if others are to understand our act and accept it as valid. Without a shared sense of genres others would not know what kind of thing we are doing. And life is mysterious enough already.   (Bazerman, 1994a: 99–100)

In the context of actual classroom teaching, the tension between *conventional form* and *individual expression* can be resolved by considering generic conventions not simply as a blueprint for further replication in similar rhetorical contexts, but more as resource to develop an understanding of the generic conventions which make the genre possible. The resolution of this tension can be understood with reference to the notion of *genre knowledge*, which will help the learner to examine text in context, on the one hand, and to help him or her to make textual choices informed by socio-cultural, professional and organisational frameworks, on the other.

It is the knowledge of the discursive practices of the members of the discourse community that these members draw upon in order to exploit and manipulate generic resources to achieve their own private intentions within the context of socially recognised communicative purposes. The two perspectives I have just alluded to are not the same. *One conforms, the other creates and re-creates.* One is a blueprint, the other is a resource. One constrains, the other liberates – within conventional boundaries, of course.

Conclusion

To conclude, I have highlighted the tension between linguistic description in genre theory and its application to professional writing and made an attempt to carry it to some conclusion. I have suggested that although generic description includes sensitivity to generic form and content, it should not be viewed narrowly to exclude other aspects of genre construction, interpretation and use. In fact, it should be viewed as a kind of generic knowledge that also explains why and in what way it is embedded in disciplinary practices. It should be seen more as generic potential, which helps a good practitioner to use, innovate and exploit this generic knowledge to respond to recurring and novel socio-cultural as well as professional rhetorical contexts.

As Coe (1994) points out,

> To learn a generic form without becoming aware of tacit strategies, purposes, functions and values is not so much to master the genre as to become subject to it . . . To help someone learn generic forms without helping them also to that critical awareness and mastery may subject them to the genre more than empower them.
>
> (Coe, 1994: 188)

In order to take full advantage of the potential of genre theory, it is necessary to view genre as a construct with a narrow focus but at the same time with a broad vision. Instead of focusing on individual texts and their surface-level textual descriptions, genre practice should be regarded as a resource to re-create, innovate, exploit and manipulate conventional practices to achieve individual expression. Genres are crucial to our understanding and practice of participating in the affairs of specific and individually relevant disciplinary communities. Ignoring the generic perspective on professional texts will turn writing instruction from 'what should be a practical art of achieving social ends into . . . [an] art of making texts that fit formal requirements' (Miller, 1994: 67). As Martin (1985: 250) points out, 'genres are how things get done, when language is used to accomplish them'; however, they ought to be done appropriately and in such a manner that they are seen to have been done so.

2

Interaction in writing: principles and problems

GREG MYERS

Introduction

It seems obvious enough to say that writing is used for interaction, like saying walking is used for locomotion, sexual intercourse for reproduction, and cooking for nourishment. As in these analogous cases, the most obviously functional aim of the activity is not all there is to it. Writing is not always or only a form of interaction: one may do it to record, to help one think, to pass the time at a meeting, or just to enjoy the way a new fountain pen carves black, flowing lines across a somewhat heavy and textured sheet of paper. But as in these analogous cases, the obviously functional aim of the activity is at times worth remembering. When one reads flat, impersonal, jumbled essays as a tutor, or incomprehensible software documentation as a user, or cruelly impersonal bureaucratic reports as an employee, or university prospectuses as a secondary school student, it may be useful to remind oneself of the relations between people embodied in even these least personal of texts. Similarly, it is useful to remind researchers, who may be analysing a text as part of a computer corpus, or a stack of photocopies, or a poem in an anthology, or an isolated paragraph, or a set of example sentences, that writers and readers think of each other, imagine each other's purposes and strategies rightly or wrongly, and write or interpret the text in terms of these imaginations.

Though it is obvious that writing is interaction, it is not at all obvious just what any particular piece of writing, taken just as a text, tells us about that particular interaction and the persons involved. One approach in applied linguistics has been to propose a simplified model of what people are like and what communication between them must be like, and then to look at how various linguistic features might work as these principles are followed or not followed. Then, if one finds these features working in this way in actual texts, one takes it as a confirmation of the usefulness of one's simplified model. This is the approach taken in a wide range of studies based on the Co-operative Principle (Grice, 1975, 1989), or Politeness Theory (Brown and Levinson, 1987), or the Reciprocity Principle (Nystrand, 1986, 1989). But even with all these studies to guide us, we are left with problems defining the way Readers and Writers (seen as abstract participants) act in a social world seen as a set of conventions.

In this chapter, I will review some of the assumptions of such principle-based models, how they might be adapted from conversation to writing, and how problems arise in applying them. First I review what may be familiar work on pragmatic principles, to bring out key assumptions relevant to writing. Then I apply these analyses to two texts, starting with politeness because that has been the area of some of my own work, and then going on to a range of other approaches based on communicative principles. Then I raise some questions about the theories of persons and actions implicit in such models. Finally, I will note how some researchers have dealt with these questions, either by limiting the sorts of questions they ask about texts, or by using texts as a basis for broader studies of interaction. My conclusion is that the analyst can learn about texts by studying social action, but cannot simply read off social action from the texts.

Principles and interaction

By a highway in the desert of Southern California is a billboard in white type on a green background, like an informational sign (which I saw in D. Bernstein, 1997):

Example 1

Food – 3 miles
Good Food – 30 miles

At the bottom it says, in another typeface:

```
Daily Grill
In Palm Desert at El Paseo
```

I would guess that no driver on Interstate 90 has any trouble interpreting this sign as an ad saying that it is worth driving a bit further to get better food at the Daily Grill. Yet it is rather difficult to trace this interpretation to the semantics of the words and constructions, partly because it is so elliptical, and partly because it depends on drivers' knowledge of some conventions and their inferences about why the sign was put there. It is worth reviewing here some of the work in pragmatics that has been enlisted to account for such interpretations, to bring out some of the underlying assumptions about interaction in general and writing in particular.

Paul Grice (1975, 1989) suggested a Co-operative Principle as a statement of what participants in interaction must generally assume each other to be doing:

> Make your contribution such as is required, at the stage at which it occurs, by the accepted purpose or direction of the talk exchange in which you are engaged.

When students first read this it seems both obvious and wrong – obvious because participants must be saying what is required at that stage, and wrong because participants often do things that seem distinctly unco-operative, joking or lying or being ironic. But of course the Co-operative Principle is not a statement of what participants *should* do, or even of what they actually do, but of what they must each assume the other to be doing, for the conversation to go on (Thomas, 1995: 62). When Hearers interpret Speakers, they assume that the Speaker must be thinking of what the Hearer needs next. So, for instance, we could note that the Daily Grill billboard does not actually say that the food in 3 miles is *not* good, but we infer that it is not. One part of Grice's Maxim of Quantity says that we assume our interlocutor tells us as much as we need to know; we draw the implicature that if the sign could tell us the food in 3 miles was good, it would. With such maxims in mind, we can then look at cases in which participants do not seem to be following the principle and its associated maxims, and reconstruct the kind of reasoning a Hearer or Reader might follow in interpreting this apparent breach. For instance, in this case, the sign also seems to violate another aspect of the Maxim of Quantity, in telling us more than such informational signs usually tell us: that the food in 30 miles is good. One implicature we could draw from this would be that the good food, though more distant, is worth waiting for.

Grice's work has been developed in a number of directions; for instance, Leech (1983) supplements the list of principles, and Sperber and Wilson (1986) reduce the various maxims to just one, the Principle of Relevance. Though the Co-operative Principle was developed to account for reasoning in conversation, it applies directly to similar reasoning about literary texts (Short, 1996), advertisements (Pateman, 1983), and even non-verbal texts such as illustrations in advertisements (Forceville, 1996, following Sperber and Wilson). (I am told that in the 1980s, every single course offered by my Linguistics Department, whatever the topic, worked in Grice one way or another.) For our purposes, the important point is that he based the whole sense of what a conversation is on the way participants in conversation attribute to each other the intention to communicate.

A similar style of argument characterizes Brown and Levinson's model of politeness (1987). They draw on Goffman (1967) for the concept of *face*, which they reinterpret as the desire to have others see one in a favourable light, and to act unimpeded. They propose a Model Person, like the sort of simplified model used in economics, that would be endowed with only the desire to protect their face and that of the other participant. Brown and Levinson suggest that interaction necessarily involves a number of Face Threatening Acts (FTAs), such as blaming, requesting or apologizing, and they use a range of anthropological data to illustrate a complex scale of ways of redressing these threats. Since their Model Person is a construct, a strategic calculator working out only this one set of motivations, it allows the analyst to reconstruct a possible line of reasoning that would lead to the selection of any given linguistic feature, and discuss possible differences between cultures. For instance, their model is one way of accounting for the way a Speaker might use a question form to make a command, or might weaken a statement of disagreement with a modal expression. In

Example 1, for instance, the FTA could be criticism of the food establishment in 3 miles. But this criticism is not directly stated; we infer it only from the contrast. This reminds us that Brown and Levinson's model is built on Grice's assumptions about co-operative communication; the default in their scale of strategies, the choice of not making a choice, is simply to follow Grice's principle.

The Brown and Levinson model is based on face-to-face inter-action, because it assumes an elaborate calculation of the weight of the FTA, the distance between Speaker and Hearer and their relative power. But it has been adapted for analysis of writing, either by focusing on texts such as letters for which the Writer and Reader are in an identifiable relation to each other (Cherry, 1988; Myers, 1991a), or by analysing the audience as a composite of several possible types of Hearer with different relations, as in academic texts (Myers, 1989, 1992; Hinkel, 1997), or defined relations, as in medical (Lambert, 1995, 1996), business (Bargiela-Chiappini and Harris, 1996; Pilegaard, 1997) or legal texts (Trosborg, 1997). For any feature of the text, such as the hedge *might*, these analyses reconstruct the sorts of reasoning that might lead a purely strategic Model Person to choose this feature for this act. The results of such an analysis are particularly striking with academic or bureaucratic texts that seem to be purely informa-tional; by identifying features associated with the redress of Face Threatening Acts, the analyst can bring out competitive and co-operative work being done in the text. So the applications of Brown and Levinson's model go far beyond the sorts of formulas of etiquette that most people think of as politeness, and far beyond their original application to conversation.

Martin Nystrand (1986, 1989) has developed an approach to interaction in writing that, while it resembles Grice's Co-operative Principle, arises from other controversies and leads in somewhat different directions. He criticizes both cognitive approaches to writing that focus only on the purposes and strategies of writers as encoded in autonomous texts (Olson, 1977; Flower and Hayes, 1981), and also what he calls Idealist approaches that locate mean-ing in the Reader's interpretation of an entirely flexible text (Fish, 1980). For Nystrand, we can see writing as interactive only when we recognize that both Writer and Reader approach the text with 'mutual co-awareness' of the other. He presents this as a Recipro-city Principle applicable to all social acts:

> In any collaborative activity the participants orient their actions on
> certain standards which are taken for granted as rules of conduct
> by the social group to which they belong.   (Nystrand, 1986: 48)

This way of formulating the principle directs the attention of analysts from the text itself to the 'social group' and its shared standards, and to ways these standards might be internalized, or not, by
writers and readers in specific interactions. From this principle,
Nystrand draws an axiom as the basis for a 'grammar' of textual
elaborations:

> A given text is functional to the extent that it balances the recip-
> rocal needs of the writer for expression and the reader for com-
> prehension. Communicative homeostasis is the normal condition
> of grammatical texts.   (Nystrand, 1989: 81)

For Nystrand, as for Grice, the starting point of analysis is the
assumption of a matching of the needs of Writer and Reader that
makes communication possible and that results in stability and
predictability of interpretation. As with the Co-operative Principle, the Reciprocity Principle may seem at first both obvious and
wrong – obvious in that we can see there must be some shared
standards, and wrong in that we can all think of communications
that do not involve 'reciprocal needs', such as a deceptive letter, a
reader skimming a textbook, or a billboard on a highway. But for
Nystrand, as for Grice, the statement of a general principle allows
the investigation of instances where there is possible trouble, in
terms of the reasoning that a strategic Writer or Reader would
make when faced with the apparent trouble. He develops from
this axiom a 'grammar' of possible elaborations in text, each elaboration responding to a different kind of projected trouble, and
indicating a different kind of reciprocal adjustment to the relation of Writer and Reader. For instance, he could categorize the
last lines of Example 1 as a 'genre elaboration'. Readers of the
billboard (who have only seconds) are puzzled by the deviation
from what they expect of highway information signs; the last two
lines redefine the genre (ads often do at the end) so that Readers
see a consistent purpose on the part of the Writer.

Genre analysis approaches (Bazerman, 1988; Swales, 1990;
Berkenkotter and Huckin, 1995) may not seem to fit with these
principles-based approaches, since they typically start with some
detailed analysis of a range of empirically derived textual features.
But they too depend on an assumption of what Nystrand calls

'communicative homeostasis'. One key contribution that genre analysts make is to locate various norms, standards and conventions, which tend to float free in some linguistic accounts, in what Berkenkotter and Huckin call 'community ownership': 'Genre conventions signal a discourse community's norms, epistemology, ideology, and social ontology' (Berkenkotter and Huckin, 1995: 21). Berkenkotter and Huckin are particularly interested in the relation between academic texts and disciplinary knowledge, but their points about the relation between textual form and action apply as well to the billboard in Example 1. As we have seen, we read it first in terms of our expectations of informational signs; these conventions 'signal' a community's sense of the relevant spaces and divisions of travel (for instance, eating places are interchangeable but exits are not). The logo at the bottom and the shift in typefaces are conventions that signal a shift to seeing the sign as an advertisement rather than a roadsign, with a different set of norms brought into play.

The principles of Grice, Brown and Levinson, and Nystrand all give discourse analysts a way of reconstructing interaction from specific features of texts. They take very different approaches, but we should note some of the assumptions they all make:

- Writers and Readers are strategic selves, calculating choices or interpretations of choices in line with singular aims, matching the form to given functions of the text, or functions to the given forms.
- Interpersonal elements are seen as modifications of a basic message or content for greater effectiveness, standing out against unmarked forms.
- Society or a given community functions as a body of norms to which individual Writers and Readers turn as a background for interpretation.
- The task of the analyst is to generate possible categories of forms and functions, and base interpretation on the relations between these categories.
- Explanations of these form/function relations may draw on social practices, cognitive processes, communicative efficiency, or institutional structures.

It is not fair to say that these approaches are inherently individualistic in their focus. But their use of the social world is complex, requiring us to take for granted links that are seldom made explicit. The discourse community provides a set of norms or conventions concerning textual forms, roles and acts. Writers internalize these norms, and draw on them and on their Readers' awareness of them, in producing texts, and Readers draw on these norms, and Writers' awareness of them, in interpreting texts. When they do this, the text reproduces the norms in the discourse community. Thus, they can argue that the study of texts can lead analysts to social norms and processes outside texts, without spelling out the links. We will return to these links after analysing some examples of textual features of interaction.

People and relations

To consider how these analyses might work with texts, let us look at two texts: one a leaflet that is clearly interactional, the other the opening of an academic article that may seem more of an impersonal and self-contained statement. I have chosen a leaflet because the genre poses the problem of Writer and Reader in a complex form: the Writer is usually an institution or collective, the Reader could be almost anyone, and the medium involves the erratic circulation in which the text may be available to be picked up with other leaflets in a shop display, sent through the post, or handed out at a stand in the market square. Example 2 comes in an six-page folded leaflet (the size of a sheet of A4 size writing paper folded in thirds) promoting membership of Friends of the Earth; it has a tree frog on the front staring out at us and if reads, 'Look forward to the future'. This is the last page before the form to send in money:

Example 2

[picture of sky behind trees]
Become a Friend of the Earth

Our supporters are to thank for every success we score on behalf of the natural world. They finance almost all of our work. When you consider what we are up against – government, powerful industrial interests, and the huge resources at their disposal – you can appreciate how important this funding is and how much it achieves.

   We use all our supporters' contributions wisely. Less than 8% of our income is spent on administration.

Continued

['handwritten' in blue ink:]
As the pace of environmental destruction accelerates, it's too easy
to get downhearted. Even to give up on it all! But we *are* making
progress, and a better future *is* possible. And that's where Friends
of the Earth comes in. Its track record in developing positive solutions to all those problems – internationally, nationally, and locally
– is second to none. It's a real force for change in a world that's
stuck in a dangerous rut. It's your support that makes this work
possible – and it's needed now more than ever before.
Jonathon Porritt
Special Adviser to Friends of the Earth

[182 words]

Example 3 is the opening of 'Unbounded dependencies and
coordinate structure', which is, as far as I know, the first published
appearance of a line of generative grammars that became known
as Generalized Phrase Structure Grammar (GPSG). The author,
Gerald Gazdar, now a Professor of Artificial Intelligence, was then
a very young linguist best known for his book on formal pragmatics. The article appeared in *Linguistic Inquiry*, one of the core
journals of generative linguistics, published at the Massachusetts
Institute of Technology, the leading centre for what was then
known as Transformational Grammar.

Example 3

Consider eliminating the transformational component of a generative grammar. In particular, consider the elimination of all movement rules, whether bounded or unbounded, and all rules making
reference to identity of indices. Suppose, in fact, that the permitted
class of generative grammars constituted a subset of those Phrase
Structure Grammars capable of generating only context-free languages. Such a move would have two important metatheoretical
consequences, one to do with learnability, the other with processability. In the first place, we would be imposing a rather dramatic
restriction on the class of grammars that the language acquisition
device needs to consider as candidates for the language being
learned. And in the second place, we would have the beginnings

Continued

of an explanation for the obvious, but largely ignored, fact that humans process the utterances they hear very rapidly. Sentences of a context-free language are provably parsable in a time that is proportional to the cube of the length of the sentence or less (Younger (1967), Earley (1970)). But no such restrictive result holds for the recursive or recursively enumerable sets potentially generable by grammars which include a transformational component.

My strategy in this article will be to assume, rather than argue, that there are no transformations, and then to show that purely phrase structure (PS) treatments of coordination and unbounded dependencies can offer explanations for facts which are unexplained, or inadequately explained, within the transformational paradigm.

[232 words]

An analysis of features associated with politeness would begin by asking what sort of Face Threatening Act is going on in each case. In the Friends of the Earth (FoE) leaflet, it is clear; they are asking for our money. The FTA in the *Linguistic Inquiry* (*LI*) article may be less obvious, since there is no explicit criticism of other researchers. But even those of us who are not formal linguists can guess that transformational generative linguists might feel threatened by a proposal to eliminate transformations while still producing a generative grammar, and might feel there was a considerable self-assertion in Gazdar's claim that, for this particular structure, he could do without them. In fact, there were massive changes going on within Transformational Grammar, with the development of Government and Binding (GB), but that is another story. What matters to us is that such an article could be perceived, and was perceived, as a strong criticism and a strong claim, and thus a weighty FTA.

These examples suggests that there are people and actions in these texts, even in apparently impersonal academic articles. But in these cases at least, focusing on explicit speech acts and on pronouns gives us a very limited analysis. Analysts working in Systemic Functional Linguistics have extended this basic approach to look in more detail at how the interpersonal is constructed. Geoff Thompson and Puleng Thetela (1995) have analysed relations between Writer and Reader, distinguishing between 'personal' aspects of interaction, such as modality and evaluation, and 'interactional' aspects, the ways roles are enacted or projected in texts.

They used print ads as their examples, and you will see that these work particularly well, since ads nearly always use the possible projected and enacted relations for strategic purposes.

If we apply Thompson's and Thetela's analysis to Examples 2 and 3, we will go beyond the *enacted* relations of the texts – the request in FoE and the hypothetical in *LI* – and look at the various *projected* relations. For instance, in the FoE text, we see

- modalization of statements (discussed below)
- embedded evaluations of their opponents (powerful industrial interests)
- naming of supporters and opponents
- assumptions about who is on whose side

In the *LI* text, there is representation of relations in the way two sides of generative linguistics are set up, one using transformations and the other not. The evaluations of the transformational position are only implied.

Theo van Leeuwen is working on an ambitious series of studies (1995, 1996) that have developed categories for the ways social actors and actions are represented in texts. The representations of actors and actions discussed by van Leeuwen position the reader by implication; in the example in van Leeuwen (1995), the implied reader aligns himself or herself with the white Australians depicted in the text, since it is their reactions that are predominantly represented. In his most recent study (1997), van Leeuwen extends these studies to present different kinds of evaluation in texts. His corpus of texts on 'the first day of school' is particularly interesting, because it includes such a wide range of different genres, from teacher training materials, to parents' handbooks, to children's stories.

If we apply van Leeuwen's analysis to Examples 2 and 3, for each action in the text we ask who is doing what. If we consider just the first paragraph of the FoE text, we have:

  our supporters are to thank
  success we score
  they [supporters] finance
  our work
  we are up against powerful interests
  you can appreciate
  how much it [the funding] achieves

'Supporters' perform a material processes, 'you' perform mental processes, while FoE is presented doing material and relational processes. But not all of these are main verbs of clauses. The effect is to embed the actions of FoE, while foregrounding the actions of supporters. The 'letter' from Jonathan Porritt encapsulates many important processes, especially references to time, as nouns:

the pace of environmental destruction
a better future
its track record
change
a dangerous rut

This is not to play down these processes, but to take them as given, the background the reader knows about. The reader is positioned at a crucial present moment, looking backward and forwards.

In Example 3, most of the important actions are, in van Leeuwen's terms, *de-activated*, that is, they are not the main verb of a clause:

eliminating
permitted class
generating

This is characteristic of the kind of argument going on here, in which processes are the very entities under discussion. Other processes are considered, not as having happened at a point in time, but as potentially possible; this is, of course, in the nature of the project of generative grammar.

learnability
processability
provably parsable
recursively enumerable sets
potentially generable

To unpack just one of these phrases: one could, if required, prove that one can, if required, parse a sentence of a context-free language in a time proportional to the cube of the length of the sentence, and both these processes of proof and parsing can be bracketed off and taken as given, in an adverb and adjective modifying 'sentences'. Doing the proof is Earley's problem, not Gazdar's.

Many writers have pointed out the role of modality in setting up a relation between Reader and Writer. Much of the analysis of hedging and modality focuses on how the weakening of statements can function in mitigating FTAs (Myers, 1989; Hyland, 1996a; Salager-Meyer, 1997). For instance, the *LI* text qualifies its claims:

we would be imposing a rather dramatic restriction
we would have the beginnings of an explanation

But both the FoE and the *LI* texts also use strengthened modality. In the FoE leaflet, the following sentence only makes sense with the indicated emphasis:

But we *are* making progress, and a better future *is* possible.

This is not just stating the progress, but asserting it against the justifiable downheartedness. And in the *LI* article, there are also unqualified statements that would be unusual in an academic article in another field, but that are presented here as matters of introductory background:

the obvious, but largely ignored, fact
facts which are unexplained, or inadequately explained, within the transformational paradigm

The first of these assertions is supported by a footnote, and the second is slightly softened by a parenthetical comment, but both assert categorically what is included and excluded in the argument to come. Such an opening may be more common in a field that models its argument on mathematics than in one that bases its argument on laboratory reports.

In this section, I have pointed out some of the approaches to identifying persons in texts, starting with the obvious – pronouns – and moving to the less obvious – process types and modality. In the next section, I will deal with ways that links between parts of the text, and between one text and another, may constitute interaction.

Linking

This section brings together two issues that are often treated separately: coherence (the semantic links between clauses) and intertextuality (the links between texts). What is different in current approaches is that analysts have come to emphasize that coherence is not just a property of a text, but is a social relation between Writer and Reader based on shared knowledge.

Nystrand (1986), Brandt (1989) and others have pointed out the implied rhetorical relations in coherence links between clauses within a text. One detailed analytical system that develops these rhetorical relations is that of Mann and Thompson (1986, 1988). They base their analysis on the identification of 'nuclear units' taking 'satellites' with about two dozen possible rhetorical relations such as Concession, Antithesis, Cause or Elaboration. This approach has many similarities to other analyses of clause relations, by Meyer (1985), Winter (1977) or Hoey (1991). What it has in common with the approaches I have been describing is the emphasis on shared knowledge between Writers and Readers, and a finite set of functions related to forms. Each relation is defined, not just in terms of what the Writer wants to do, but in terms of what the Reader recognizes as the effect intended by the writer. These relations are seen as structuring the text at all levels, from clause relations up to the major units of the argument as a whole. Teresa O'Brien (1995) has applied this analysis to students' writing on exams and coursework, showing how readers' evaluations of incoherence may be traced to breakdowns in rhetorical structure.

Consider these three clauses in the FoE leaflet:

. . . you can appreciate how important this funding is and how much it achieves.

We use all our supporters' contributions wisely.

Less than 8% of our income is spent on administration.

There is a link through this in the references to money, seen from different points of view as 'this funding', 'our supporters' contributions' and 'our income'. Then the third clause provides a specific piece of evidence to support the general assertion of the second clause: the small percentage on administration is an example of wise use of contributions. The relation of these clauses, taken as a unit, to the rest of the text is harder to analyse; one way of interpreting the link is through 'Our supporters' in the first paragraph and 'our supporters' contributions' in the second. The text assumes a sceptical reader for whom not all organizations receiving gifts are worthy, and this organization must rebut the unstated criticism that the money will be spent only on its administration.

An important part of the style of the *LI* article is the sense that all links are spelled out logically. So the first three sentences are presented as a progressive specification of the constraints on this grammar:

Consider . . .
In particular, consider . . .
Suppose . . .
Such a move would have . . .

The specialist reader can relate these three imperatives within each other, and then take them all together as 'a move' with the results in the rest of the paragraph, and the implications of these results. The enumeration of these results is particularly marked, 'In the first place' and 'In the second place'. Gazdar will claim that his grammar has the advantage of being fully explicit (unlike its rival); the underlying logic of the solution is projected in this stylistic sense of logical links.

The study of coherence tells us about links between sentences, but recently researchers have begun to look at other links, between verbal text and pictures, and between one text and another. One approach to what Gunther Kress and Theo van Leeuwen (1996) call 'multi-modal texts' starts by asking why these pictures are here, how they are relevant to the text, how they show enough and not too much for the communicative purposes. The leaflet is heavily illustrated, with 12 pictures and an FoE logo, but it makes no reference in the text to the purpose of the pictures, and there are no captions such as 'Amazonian Indians who have benefited from our programme' or 'This frog is threatened by rainforest destruction'. The relations are left for the reader to construct. So, for instance, there are Amazonian Indians in the FoE leaflet, one of them looking out at us, and in the text this gaze becomes a sort of appeal from them, or a symbol of the concern with humans as well as nature that is asserted by the FoE slogan 'For the planet for people'. In the page analysed here, a tiny picture of tree and sky comes at the top of the page, as a kind of bullet point, and thus can be seen as a kind of orientation, suggesting a set of qualities to be identified with the organization. Of course, divergent readings are possible, so a tree frog in FoE can be associated with wildlife photography, rather than with the rainforest as endangered. As it happens, the *LI* article has no illustrations, and they are very rare in this linguistics journal, but they are of course a key feature of many academic texts (Kress, 1998; Kress and Ogburn, 1998; Myers, 1990c, 1997; Lemke, 1998).

Another important aspect of the interaction of Writer and Reader is the representation of other texts as shared knowledge between them. In the FoE leaflet, the link is in the form of a message from Jonathon Porritt, formerly head of the organization but now a well-known independent environmental commentator. The shift in source is marked by having his words in blue ink, apparently handwritten. It is also marked by a shift in style, including an exclamation and sentences beginning with conjunctions. In the *LI* article, intertextuality is conveyed by citations, so that footnote 1 gives 'Marslen-Wilson (1970)' as support for the 'obvious, but largely ignored, fact', and the statement that context-free languages are 'provably parsable' is given with no proof, but with a reference to two articles. Note that researchers associated with rival views, the transformational approaches, are not yet cited; in academic texts, critical comments are often made in generalized form about an approach rather than a researcher. These references do not explicitly place the Readers, but implicitly offer them a particular alignment of the field (Bazerman, 1993). So the intertextual links, like the links within the text, and the links between verbal text and pictures, define a possible form of interaction.

What these textual analyses can tell us

The various kinds of systematic analyses proposed by Brown and Levinson, Nystrand, Thompson and Thetela, van Leeuwen and other linguists have several useful effects. They bring together features that are sometimes isolated under the headings of hedging, representation of speech, speech acts, cohesion or address. They treat all these features as related to some rhetorical link between Writer and Reader in which both Writer and Reader are aware of the aims of the other, and both share assumptions about how texts work. They direct attention from the text as a set of propositions to the text as the interaction of people.

Since these analyses start with assumptions about function and form, they allow for comparisons across genres and across time (Bazerman, 1988), so analysts can check in quantitative terms analyses based on close reading of a few texts. Perhaps they are most useful in pedagogical terms, in introducing students to academic texts, or outsiders to any new genre, such as grant proposals, software documentation or mission statements. They undo one's first sense, as an outsider, that these texts are formulaic, things to be filled with standard contents, and remind one how much is contingent, up for grabs, worked out moment to moment, in even the dullest text. Note that in all these applications, one is dealing with the Writer and Reader as entities projected in the text, in a social system bounded by our own analytical assumptions about the purposes of communication. One cannot criticize these assumptions for being over-simplified; Grice, Brown and Levinson, and Nystrand offered their models as useful analytical fictions that would justify themselves in the way they classified and accounted for linguistic data that are puzzling in other models. And that is what they do.

What these textual analyses cannot tell us

What these models cannot do is allow us to read texts in a way that tells us something new about society. Analyses based on these models can show that there *is* interaction in these texts, but it cannot tell us what kind of interaction, between what sorts of actors, because it starts with assumptions about what interaction is: the matching of forms to functions by strategic calculators sharing communicative goals.

The first problem arises at the beginning of analysis. Why, in the last section of this chapter, did I deal with some words and clauses and not others? As one includes more and more features under the heading of interaction, one might conclude that it is all interaction. But all the principles-based approaches assume that there is some neutral, ideational message that is then modified in various ways. More broadly, in assuming some function as the basis for choices, they take some choices as more basic than others.

The second problem concerns the kinds of actors constructed. As I noted in the introduction, these approaches assume strategic communicators making choices to achieve ends; that is why I have left the participants abstract as Writers and Readers. (It is also why these approaches work so well with ads, where there is a clear strategic purpose; but even in ads that is not all that is going on (Myers, 1998).) Analysts often want to go beyond this to say what real writers are like, to hear various voices. But this approach doesn't seem to give us a way of dealing with the messy composites that are behind texts. How does Friends of the Earth take on a voice and act like a person? How does GPSG become an approach? We have no way of seeing how a text *makes* an actor, because in this approach we have assumed a coherent actor there already.

The same problem applies to the relation between Readers enacted and projected in the text and any real readers. The multiple encounters with the text, and bizarre and idiosyncratic readings, are replaced with a rationalized and uniform interpretation according to principles. The FoE leaflet projects a sympathetic environmentalist; real readers will range from contrarians to animal lovers to deep green activists highly suspicious of FoE. The *LI* article projects a sceptical but collaborative generative linguist; real readers could be students, ironists, GB theorists looking for a mis-step, computer scientists. As with the writers, these actors are created by the text as it moves around in the world. They cannot be analysed simply by following out the rational calculations implied in the models.

Another problem concerns just what is being claimed about the relation of textual conventions to particular instances. We can start with a simple example; in focus groups, most British people who saw the FoE leaflet recognized the 'personal' message 'handwritten' in blue ink as a kind of convention. What happens when one knows a convention is a convention? Surprisingly, it can still have some effect. The same arguments apply to politeness conventions in academic articles, or the imperative in advertisements, or the disclaimers put on job references to avoid legal liability. The analyst is not revealing tricks, but is pointing to features that many readers know and expect, and then treating them as having a deterministic effect.

One approach to this issue of how the conventions relate to effects is to assume that skilled readers have internalised these conventions, and that they therefore have their effects, as analyzed, without readers necessarily knowing. This is the approach often taken, for instance, in dealing with novice and expert writers within an academic discipline. But this only raises the issue of what it means to internalize or naturalize such conventions, and how, in that case, there can be variation and change. Many analyses assume that each text that instantiates a convention reproduces that convention, entrenches it more deeply. But this assumes that readers are passive recipients or at least unreflexive users of the multiple imprints of texts, and this is again to confuse the many kinds of readers with the unified and simplified Reader or Hearer of principles-based models.

Stepping back, we can see that these problems arise with each of the assumptions necessary to link a principles-based model to a social interpretation. There is no unmarked background of message against which to analyse the interpersonal. Writers and readers may not act as strategic selves, but may take a number of relations to the text. The social world is not a stable background, providing conventions for interpretation, but is a set of complex relations that the text may or may not stabilize. Analysts cannot assume that their own processes of analysis mirror the social origins and effects of the text.

Beyond principles: dematerializing and rematerializing texts

Some current lines of research on written interaction go beyond, in one way or another, the kinds of assumptions I have described. I started by saying that one aim of research on interaction in writing was to get beyond the idea that texts were just things, to put the people back in. Current approaches take the analysis of interaction in one of two ways, dematerializing the text even more so that it is just a set of features in relation to each other, or rematerializing texts to insist on them as things circulating in particular places and moments.

The first of these approaches is perhaps best illustrated by the corpus analysis of variation by Douglas Biber (1988). He analyses the distribution of various features in selected texts from the Lancaster-Oslo-Bergen corpus of British English, and then uses factor analysis to group features that tend to occur with each other, or tend to occur in complementary distribution with each other. His first factor, with some of the strongest statistical indications of co-occurrence, he calls 'Informational vs. Involved Production' (1988: 107). Texts score at the high end of the scale on this factor if they have, for instance, private verbs (such as 'believe'), THAT deletion, contractions, present tense verbs, and second person pronouns; so, for instance, advertisements would score high. Texts would score low on this factor, or towards the 'Informational' end, if they were low on features such as these, and relatively high on the proportion of nouns, long words, and prepositions, and if they have a high type/token ratio (few repeated words). So, for instance, scientific research reports would score low on this dimension. Atkinson (1992, 1996) has used this scheme to trace changes in medical journal articles over decades and centuries.

Such approaches do not have the same problems as the principles-based studies I have described, because they are not necessarily saying anything about the social worlds in which these texts move. 'Involvement' for Biber is defined in terms of the occurrence of items from this set of linguistic variables and it need not correspond to any of the various ways we might mean 'involvement' in dealing with texts in society. (Similarly, 'Information' is close to an information-theoretical use of the word, but not necessarily to the other possible meanings it has for us.) And by abstracting away from any particular authors or readers, these studies can draw much more subtle relations between the various linguistic features than can be done in intensive studies of a few texts. In this volume, the approach through intensive textual comparison is exemplified by Hyland's chapter.

The second of these approaches, rematerializing texts, came home to me most strongly as Roz Ivanič, in a conference presentation (Ivanič *et al.*, 1997), lovingly displayed the binders and paper and illustrations that went into the grade school projects she was analysing. The material qualities – the size, shape and feel of texts – are usually ignored in analyses of writing. But it is the shiny paper that signals to us that the FoE leaflet is promotional material of some kind for an organization. Rougher or browner paper could signal environmental awareness (though the FoE leaflet says that it is, as one might expect, printed on recycled paper). The eight-page FoE leaflet leads the Reader through a complex case from threats, to achievements, to the organization, to the benefits of membership. One can, of course, read these pages in any order one wants, but the unfolding means that some pages are likely to come up first, while others are likely to remain concealed until the Reader shows enough interest to sit down with the thing. An academic text has different effects in one column or two, A5 size or larger, shiny or matt cover, or with different typefaces; the printed *LI* article has a quite different look and feel from the photocopied typescripts of its very widely circulated preprints.

In another way, it is brought home by Canagarajah's (1996b) poignant account of how academic publication in Sri Lanka depends on photocopiers, high quality paper, typewriter ribbons, and the always unreliable post. The relevant point here is that these material details take us from the general rules of interaction of principles-based approaches to the specifics of particular encounters of people with texts. A similar sort of move is made in ethnographic studies of academic writing (Prior, 1994; Haas, 1994; Ivanič, 1998), situated studies of texts such as manuals (Sauer, 1995), and simulation of professional tasks (Winsor, 1994; Freedman *et al.*, 1994). Charles Bazerman's new book (1998) traces the material paths of such texts as notebooks, patents, and newspaper articles that made Edison's career. There are similar situated studies in this volume: Street and Lea, Ivanič and Weldon, and Barrett.

What all these studies have in common is that they go back to the pieces of paper, as a way of focusing attention on particular writers or readers and what they do with the page. Some of these issues are also raised by researchers concerned with new media that shift the relations of writers and readers and call into question the assumptions about interaction (Bolter, 1991; Faigley, 1997; Snyder, 1998). Reading such studies of texts as things, we realize that writing is just one kind of textual interaction, and that interaction is just one of the ways people use texts. Analyses of language get tied up with analyses of pictures, movement, talk and spaces. Analyses of interaction get tied up with analyses of recording, noting, classifying. All these approaches take us out into the social systems we are studying, but leave behind some of the assumptions about what interaction is or must be, and which linguistic features define it.

In either dematerializing texts and pursuing interaction as a bundle of linguistic features, or rematerializing texts and pursuing interaction as a series of encounters situated in time and place, the powerful link between specific textual features and particular actions is made much more complex and less direct. Instead we have to make more tentative links, to say how this feature co-occurs with that one, or to say how this text works in this case. This does not leave room for some of the more sweeping claims made in principles-based pragmatics, but it opens up a number of specific avenues of applied research. In this somewhat more humble frame of mind, we might go back to the cases I mentioned at the beginning of this chapter, the coursework essay, software documentation, bureaucratic report or university prospectus. We have something to teach these writers about the complex interactions represented in texts, and such teaching may help them write considerably more readably and effectively. But maybe we need to learn from the apparently naive view of the text as a thing.

3

Writing as academic literacies: understanding textual practices in higher education

MARY R. LEA AND BRIAN STREET

Understanding texts and practices

We are interested in examining the underlying and implicit theoretical frames about writing that academic staff are using to inform their own practice and, specifically, their advice to students about how to write in higher education. In particular we focus upon the guidelines on writing that are provided for students in different fields and what they might tell us about such underlying models.

These we see as linked to three levels of practice in higher education: institutional, disciplinary, individual. We access these models through analysis of the ways in which they are embedded in written texts and via interviews. In the former case they are more likely to be implicit within accounts for students of what counts as writing, although we do have examples of memos that were circulated along with drafts of the guidelines that make explicit the underlying thinking and contestation. In the case of interviews, the commentaries on student writing in general and on the guidelines documentation in particular may involve either implicit or explicit models of the writing process. In both cases the accounts of writing cannot be understood solely in terms of the immediate situations or texts but rather reflect, and in turn constitute, social and institutional practices derived from the broader context. For example, academic knowledge is frequently represented as attending to transferable writing skills, whilst we would argue that it is always embedded in deeper epistemological frameworks that are frequently discipline specific. Hyland, and Candlin and Plum, in this volume, make similar arguments.

We focus on a range of texts concerning the writing process, such as 'guidelines for dissertation writing', 'advice to staff on assessing literacy', 'feedback sheets', 'student handbooks', 'assessment exercises', 'rules for writers'. This array of text types is presented to students in terms of transparent content, e.g. 'how to write', whilst we analyse them in terms of the models of writing implicit in them and the relationship of these to representations of practice. Faculty generally assume that the meanings of these texts will be apparent and attention is not drawn to their character as textual practices themselves, even though they are ostensibly about writing. We attempt to make the conditions for understanding these texts explicit by drawing attention to their textual and contextual features.

These texts were collected almost incidentally as part of a wider study into issues of student writing in higher education in the UK[1]. As part of our interviews with academic staff in this project we asked lecturers to outline what they were looking for in their students' writing; this was expressed as a mix of disciplinary genres, individual preference and departmental direction. At this point in the interview we were often given copies of the guidelines on writing that a member of staff would normally make available to students and this material provides the main focus of this paper.

Contrasting the texts provided in different fields and disciplines brings out both how different they are across these domains and how strongly they are rooted in implicit conceptions of what constitutes writing even whilst their authors represent this as transparent and 'common sense'. For instance, two documents that we examined, one provided by a tutor in English and one by a tutor in Social Sciences, addresses institutional, general and subject-specific aspects of the writing process, whilst the latter addresses more directly the institutional and formal levels with little attention to subject-specific features of writing. To understand how such texts must appear to students, we need to develop a language of description that sees the texts themselves as textual data and as evidence: we need to disrupt their innocence. As one reads each set of guidelines, it seems self-evident that this is what writing at the university should be about and there seems no great problem in responding to its demands. If students cannot do this, then there is a problem with them – or, as it is generally represented, with their 'writing skills'. But as one reads different sets, it begins to become apparent that the levels of thought on which they are based are quite different and the specific expectations not only differ but may be contradictory.

Students may well have difficulty coping with this variation when they may not even have the language of description that indicates that these are different 'levels' or genres (see Bhatia, this volume). Likewise, students are seldom given support in conceptualising the epistemological frameworks within which such documents are constructed or in recognising that they consist of contestable knowledge claims rather than given truths. As we indicate later, it is also apparent that the guidelines address only the presuppositions about writing embedded in the tutor's or department's field and do not address the assumptions and practices around writing that students themselves may bring with them. The possible consequences of this omission are dramatically illustrated by Malcolm's paper in this collection.

Mostly, the documents do not attempt to make a bridge between where the students are coming from and what the department is setting up as 'proper' writing; rather, they simply describe straight what such writing consists of. In contrast, we did examine some documentation that addressed the possibility of variation in understandings and expectations of students; in such instances it seemed as if students were being addressed as novice members of the academic community (Lave and Wenger, 1991). It is precisely because these documents embed such a variety of implicit contrasting and contradictory views of writing at a number of different levels that we suggest it is difficult for students to 'read off' how to make sense of these different forms of documentation about writing to which they are exposed.

The English Coursework Assessment Form to which we referred above explicitly addresses two levels of criteria for writing: 'general criteria' and what it terms 'literacy criteria'. The former consist of a list of characteristics that mix formal requirements – 'respect of word limit', 'referencing' – with essay-text conventions and expectations – 'coherent organisation', 'persuasiveness of argument'. These are seen to be 'general' across all essays, although, as we have indicated elsewhere (Lea and Street, 1997), what constitutes 'coherence' and 'argument' is in fact less transferable from one domain to another and less transparent than this suggests.

The other set of criteria on the English document are curiously referred to as 'literacy criteria' (as though the general set did not also involve 'literacy') and again encompass both formal technical features of writing at sentence level – 'grammatical structure', 'spelling', 'punctuation' – and more text-based features derived from linguistic terminology – 'cohesion', 'style', 'presentation'. The explanation for the choice of the term 'literacy' to describe these criteria is to be found not in the text itself but in a memo attached to a draft of the form as it was circulated around the department for comments. The memo indicates that there has been concern with students' 'poor formal language' when they arrive at university. The English department sees its main task as 'facilitating and developing students' critical and conceptual abilities', which might involve faculty in extending the 'descriptive' abilities students arrive with into more 'critical thinking and organisational skills' – a recognition that some 'bridging' will be necessary between the literacy students arrive with and that which is to be required of them at university. Unfortunately, the memo suggests, this work is interfered with by the 'poor formal language' that students arrive with – 'problems with syntax and grammar for instance'. Because of this, students'

> progress in relation to critical and argumentative skills is invariably hampered. If we received students who had a good knowledge of English language in its formal aspects, who could write clearly and precisely, our task would be considerably aided. It's not, of course, sufficient – some students have very good literacy but a poor sense of critical argument – but formal writing problems always hinder a student's progress.

This, then, is what is meant by 'literacy' in the 'literacy criteria' – the formal language capacities that are required as a necessary, though not sufficient, cause for critical argument. The thinking that lies behind the criteria is not always made so apparent in the guidelines and documents we have examined, and indeed even here the memo is for faculty and is not directly addressed to students so that they can identify the provenance of the guidelines they are being asked to meet. The level at which this text is addressed is more ideological and argumentative than the formal discourse of the 'criteria' suggest. The memo itself adopts a prescriptive discourse but it is evidently part of a larger debate, as the slightly defensive tone implies and as its 'deficit' view of student literacy indicates, a view that is highly contested in the literature on language and literacy in education (Street, 1997; Kress, 1997). But the document that the students see disguises such contested discourse and instead uses inventory style writing to indicate requirements, not to open up debate: the criteria are simply listed and numbered: '1 Knowledge of topic; 2 Coherent organisation'.

The issue here is not whether such documents ought to enter into explicit debate about their ideological and epistemological underpinnings, but the descriptive point that they do not, which has implications for how students receive them and may also offer some explanation for why students have difficulty with them. For the documents and the assumptions embedded in them are not as self-evident as their discourse suggests; they are always part of wider debate about the nature of language which the students themselves are likely to have encountered – especially in English. That such documents differ considerably amongst themselves also implies that they derive from implicit ideological and conceptual contests. Their tendency to disguise this may itself help to explain what has become characterised as students' 'problems' with writing.

One example of what could be considered as equivalent guidelines for Social Science students taking an interdisciplinary course involve a different discourse, different content and different assumptions about the nature of writing and about what constitute guidelines for students. The document and its assumptions derive from different debates within the field: although in this case we do not have access to such a clear associated memo as in the English case, the interview with a member of faculty does bear out the extent to which such documents rest upon institutional and departmental debates. The tutor in question had responded to such departmental and institutional directives requiring him to spell out word length, referencing conventions, etc., despite his own disquiet about the validity of such an approach towards student writing:

> They are being asked for fairly conventional forms of essays. Not that I particularly indicate the sort of word length that is expected. I don't think you can lay down precise word limits but we are meant to do this now. But I don't give handouts other than for the extended essay, telling them how to use references etc. I will comment on essays about bibliographies and what is expected of them but I'm not terribly fussy about references and footnotes. I think there is a great danger with students that you emphasise the things that are peripheral and on the whole fairly easy and not the core skills which are much more difficult but of greater value.

The heading of the particular document to which this tutor refers suggests that it applies to a number of contexts for writing: 'To all students taking inter-disciplinary studies courses with extended essays'. The document consists of a series of subheadings that lay out general prescriptions for essay production: 'Submission place and deadline', 'Essay length', 'Plagiarism', etc. These are all institutional requirements at the formal, prescriptive level and do not correspond to either the 'general' or the subject-specific requirements of the English document. These Social Science guidelines do correspond to the general criteria of the English guidelines when they address questions of 'references' and 'footnotes', and there is a section on 'essay plan' that includes not only issues of length but also a request to 'outline the ground' of the work. But this is the nearest that this document comes to entering into the detail of essay writing itself, of the kind evident in the English document. There is no reference here to cohesion, style or clarity. It is clearly written at a different level; a level that the tutor does not feel entirely happy with in relation to his own approach to essay writing.

For students, attempting to distinguish these levels so as to know how to interpret the different sets of guidelines they are issued with can be problematic. The documents themselves do not necessarily indicate that they are going to be 'institutional', 'subject-specific', about formal, legal requirements or about the nature of discourse and essay genre. No doubt students become accustomed to inferring the type of document and the nature of the guidelines in each case – but this developing skill remains hidden from institutional view and is seldom part of the teaching and learning process. Rather the documents are issued as though they are self-evident and – ironically in a context where writing is the subject under consideration – their character as texts, as genres of writing themselves, is not addressed.

As we illustrate above, we are particularly interested in examining what are the institutional dimensions embedded within these different texts and whether we can highlight how these may differ between university settings. There appear to be two contrasting approaches to students implicated in the texts that we have examined. The 'inclusive' approach draws in the student particularly at a departmental level – in a sense as a novice member of the university – attempting to address some of the difficulties that students might experience with their writing. In Lave and Wenger's (1991) terms, students are addressed in these documents as new members of a 'community of practice'. This we have referred to previously as an academic socialisation approach to student writing (Lea and Street, 1998). In contrast, the 'exclusive' approach evident in the texts appears to unwittingly operate to exclude the student through recourse to particular text types and configurations of textual information which suggest a deficit model on the part of the student writer. Although the interviews give us some clues to this distinction, it is in the texts surrounding student writing that we are able to identify more clearly these processes of inclusion and exclusion and to recognise attempts at academic socialisation or implicit assumptions of student deficit.

Case studies

We illustrate below two contrasting case studies to explicate in more detail the distinctions between the levels that we are making in the reading of these texts. Both Tutor A and Tutor B were long-term members of permanent academic staff teaching in interdisciplinary subject areas: in one case, Business Studies, and in the other, European Studies. During their interviews, both made available to us textual data in the form of standard feedback sheets being used at a departmental level and departmental handbooks for students which focused on learning to study within a particular interdisciplinary area. We consider these texts as evidence of particular genres and interpret them against the background of the interview data. We are interested in reading off from these texts contrasting and sometimes conflicting understandings of student writing. We make the assumption that these documents can be characterised as examples of written genres – for example, feedback sheets, handouts, guidelines on writing – and that they are read as such by students. However, our analysis of these texts suggests that we need to be guarded in this approach and that each individual document is tied to a particular context of institution: discipline, subject, course, tutor. However, as we suggest above, students, in trying to 'read off' the institution from different texts and documents, may be unclear within which context and at which level they should be interpreting such documentation. The written form is presented as self-evidently transparent and not as embedding a particular set of assumptions at whatever level – tutor, department or university.

Tutor A

We turn first to Tutor A, who discussed in detail the problems that he perceived with his students' writing and outlined his own particular criteria for assessment in a document he had written himself and made available to his students. The title, 'Coursework Criteria' indicated that this document was to be specifically understood as a course-based document, and the tutor's name at the bottom of the page indicated that it was written by this tutor for his students. The document consisted of seven numbered points of which the first five referred to the subject content of the written assignment: in Economics, for example, 'your discussion should include thoughts on the importance of the relationship to the world of Macroeconomic Management'. Number six made reference to the due date and number seven concerned assessment criteria as outlined below:

> 7. Assessment Criteria
> Students should avoid description. Marks in the 2.2 and 2.1. classification can be achieved if:
> a. There is an introduction explaining the purpose of the paper and the structure to follow.
> b. There is brief review of the literature and previous research findings.
> c. There is critical analysis of the theory and the resulting statistical output
> d. If the paper is summarised with concluding remarks.
> e. If the paper is produced in a professional manner.
> f. If the requirements outlined above are covered.

In his interview, he also described what he was looking for in his students' writing in the following way:

> I try to encourage them to not write an essay but to answer an issue in the way that they would expect to read it in the newspapers or in a journal. I don't want to be prescriptive. I say to my students, 'What you put in it is yours but there are certain things you have to do. I am looking for a paper that looks for a specific issue in Economics and then tries to take me through a background to it'. A good student will go away and do some reading that shocks me rather than going to the standard text. They actually go away and engage in some discovery for themselves drawing on some topical material.

This tutor uses his own individual interpretation of writing disciplinary knowledge, in this case Economics taught as part of Business

School courses. One can well imagine another description of writing for Economics within another department – even within the same university – which would not put such emphasis upon a journalistic style (see, for example, Candlin and Plum's paper in this collection). Indeed, the tutor quoted above in relation to the 'interdisciplinary Social Science document' described the influences on his requirements of writing as coming from an Economics model:

> My first degree was in Economics and my second degree was in Sociology. Therefore I tend to expect academic skills of argument. These are academic skills of argument, presentation of argument, reasoning, rationality, thinking, interpretation. . . . It's the discursive social science view. I'm not particularly interested in teaching students facts. I'm interested in developing their powers of reasoning, and in so far as I teach in a discipline, the paradigms and theories of what's called the discipline. So ideally speaking they should be able to use that language stroke framework in their essay writing as they progress. That's a part of the process of argumentation and discussion.

This offers a different, more discipline-based, interpretation of the nature of the requirements of student writing than that provided by Tutor A with his emphasis on 'journalistic style'. However, despite this particular lecturer's own disciplinary background, he in fact taught mainly on interdisciplinary Social Science courses where students came mainly from Business Management, and therefore attention to 'the way that they would expect to read it in the newspapers' might seem more appropriate.

Tutor A, in his written 'Assessment Criteria' for students, is drawing not only on his own individual understanding of a disciplinary model but also on a broader model of student writing in this context. The document, for instance, makes implicit assumptions about the meanings embedded in certain key terminology, e.g. 'critical analysis' in (c). Here there is less overt suggestion that the discipline itself, or this particular orientation of the discipline, might be implicated in the meanings that will be taken from this text by the student reader. His requirements for student writing are pitched at a broader, apparently generic level and explicated in his interview as an interpretation of his own practices. However, when we come to examine other documentation with respect to writing that is available to the same students, the criteria do not always fit easily with those the tutor explicates in his interview.

This additional documentation takes the form of a booklet concerned with studying in the Business School and the standard feedback sheet used for written assignments in the Business School.

We turn first to the booklet designed to support students with study skills. This booklet of 33 pages includes a number of different sections which are concerned with writing: 'Writing essays' (and avoiding plagiarism), 'Writing reports', 'Case studies', 'Written communication'. The implicit model in this document seems to be one concerned with teaching students at the broadest level about the features of contrasting written genres. So here we find an explicit acknowledgment at departmental level that within their courses students are writing across genres. However, the connections between these genres are not unpacked and there are no references in the document to students' experiences of other forms of writing. In the section on essays, writing is presented as an interactive and collaborative process and students are encouraged to adopt this approach to essay writing: 'Discuss the essay with others in your group' and 'Remember to keep in touch with the question'. Students are also encouraged to take a process approach to making drafts and editing their work. At the same time, however, technical skills are dealt with in some depth with sub-sections on references, quotations and bibliographies. Whilst some tutors see these approaches – interactive on the one hand, 'technical' on the other – as mutually reinforcing, others see them as contradictory, and certainly students have trouble interpreting what emphasis and priority a particular tutor gives to either.

There is less ambiguity, however, about the institution's view of writing, where legalistic and formal criteria receive a high profile. The chapter on essay writing, which consists of four columns of text spread over two pages, devotes one sixth of the document to warnings about plagiarism, under the heading: 'Plagiarism (some words of warning taken from the University's Assessment Handbook, 1992)'. Likewise, the standard feedback sheet, for tutors to comment on student essays, also highlights plagiarism. This sheet is used by Tutor A, amongst others, and the institution's emphasis here might seem to run counter to his own preferred view of writing – 'I don't want to be prescriptive'. The amount of space devoted to prescriptions about plagiarism is highly significant in a document that is necessarily constrained for space and where the choice of topic in relation to student writing is therefore indicative of priorities.

In this example, the feedback page is divided into four spaces: at the top is a space for the university logo and for entry of the course and module title; then there is a boxed space for the student's and tutor's name and the seminar to which the essay was relevant; there is, then, a larger boxed space for tutor comments, with typed requests for information on name, date and grade. Finally, beneath this box and in italic script reserved elsewhere in the document for imperatives (*Please complete...*) there are two procedural statements based on regulations imposed by the university or its Assessment Boards. The first, initiated by capitalised 'NB', states: '*A coursework assignment which is not submitted by the due date will normally be regarded as a failed assessment unless extenuating circumstances for late submission are submitted in the usual way and are accepted by the Assessment Board.*'

This statement makes clear that the feedback sheet as a whole is not simply to be construed as a personal relationship between tutor and student concerned with formative and supportive inter-action to help the student develop his or her essay writing skills – as the Business School study skills booklet is designed to be, it is, rather, more akin to a legal contract with rules and penalties that require the student to follow particular procedures as indexed by the quasi legalistic discourse ('normally be regarded as failed', 'extenuating circumstances' 'accepted by the Assessment Board'), and by the background knowledge assumed to be shared by all the parties ('submitted in the usual way') and indicated by ana-phoric reference to procedures ('the due date') and entities ('the Assessment Board'). This statement also sets the style and tone for the following note on plagiarism.

This note is indicated firstly by typeface and case, 'PLAGIAR-ISM' being written at the head of the sentence in bold capitals. This is followed by another statement in italics, now evidently the form to mark admonition and regulation: 'PLAGIARISM *is an assessment offence (see section 3.7–3.9 of University Assessment Regula-tions pp. 26–7 in Student Regulations). A student who knowingly allows his/her work to be copied, either verbatim or by paraphrasing, will be guilty of an assessment offence*'. Here the legalistic discourse is even stronger than before, contravening any lingering interpersonal equality that a feedback document might initially indicate in an educational setting. The use of numerical signs for sections and pages of the Regulations document evidently anticipates legal challenges and the discourse of a court of law where a litigant might have pleaded ignorance of procedures, rather than being simply a functional account of how the student may find out what to do to avoid problems in future. The second sentence is strange in focusing less on the student who plagiarises than on the one who 'allows his/her work to be copied'. This is presumably seen as a way of avoiding such cases by nipping them in the bud and ensuring that those whose work might be copied are equally deterred.

In this sense, then, both forms of documentation, the guidance on essay writing in the study skills booklet and the standard feedback sheet, highlight the institutional nature of the students' writing, and despite the more supportive tone of the advice on essay writing, students seem to be left in no doubt that certainly at one level their writing is to be construed within the legal requirements of the university's assessment system. We can identify here the contrast with Tutor A's own description of his criteria for writing in his interview, which is concerned with encouraging his students to develop a journalistic writing style, and with his own criteria, which seem to be more concerned with how students can achieve a second-class classification in their degree.

We may need to understand this variation of conceptualisations of student writing within the exclusion model at an institutional level that we suggest above. Tutor A's generalised description of the student body also reinforces the significance of the issue of exclusion and acts as his justification for adopting a deficit view of students' writing problems, in much the same way as the English department's literacy criteria cited above:

> We are in the bottom 10% of universities. 20 years ago only 1 in 8 or 20 went into education of the 18yr old cohort. They were a small elite, they were getting bad A levels but they could still write and think. They were used to writing essays. Now we are still at the bottom. Now the cohort entry is 1 in 3. The people we used to get have gone up the system. More and more are the people at the bottom of the one third entry. We are picking up lots and lots of people who have been given Access to education but they haven't got the skills we were previously assuming.

Yet at the same time, the university undergraduate prospectus openly welcomes the challenge of a diverse student body:

> The university embraces contrast and diversity. Staff and students bring together a variety of backgrounds and outlooks that enhance all aspects of study.

Whilst the institutional voice in this prospectus welcomes variety and diversity in the student body, the documentation concerned with writing does not appear to give credit to the variety of literacy practices which students might be bringing to the institution and the ways in which these might be implicated in their studies.

Tutor B

We consider now Tutor B, who teaches European Studies. Although she does not have individual guidelines that she gives to students on their writing, she does use a standard feedback sheet that has been agreed at a departmental level and students are able to benefit from an extensive document entitled 'Doing European Studies'. She makes quite clear in her interview that in her students' writing she is looking for a very particular epistemological orientation from students studying European Studies:

> What I mean when I say I want an empirical approach is that if somebody is trying to persuade me of something, and in some senses that is very largely what a student essay is very largely trying to do, I need evidence which has to be somewhat better than the student saying 'well I think this therefore you should'. I need argument. I need to have some reasons provided. Evidence and argument are the two things that matter. You want a student to say, 'I think this', but you want them to be able to tell you why they think this. You want them to be able to give you reasons that it's not a fantasy plucked out of the air. I am not suggesting that people who deal with non-empirical subjects fantasise. Supporting statements are based more on being subjective and finding the evidence within themselves and their reaction to the text. My students look to most of the evidence and argument outside themselves but in the end it leads them to say 'I think x'.

The feedback sheet that is used at a departmental level elaborates upon some of the categories referred to in her interviews, 'evidence', 'argument'. It is divided into ten sections as follows:

1. Identification and treatment of subject
2. Structure and organisation
3. Evidence and reading
4. Argument and conclusion
5. Coverage of subject
6. Style and grammar

7. Presentation
8. Other comments
9. Overall assessment
10. Suggestions for future development.

In common with other feedback sheets of this nature collected during the process of the research, distinctions are made between features of form and issues of epistemology, for example, 'style and grammar' are conceptually separated for the student from, for example, 'coverage of the subject' or 'argument and conclusion'. Despite the fact that present research points to epistemological contrasts in disciplinary requirements for the presentation of academic argument in student writing (Mitchell, 1996), the categorisation of feedback in this manner puts issues of argument firmly into a more autonomous model of writing (Street, 1996). Issues of academic argument are then separated both from those of style and grammar and those of structure and organisation. There is no indication for the student that grammatical and stylistic choices and ways of organising knowledge content are integrally related to the construction of disciplinary genres of writing (Bazerman, 1988; Berkenkotter and Huckin 1994; Hyland, this volume).

We learn from the interview that the adoption of this feedback sheet was a departmental initiative based on institutional moves, the idea being to speed up response time to students' work in the face of the increased pressure of student numbers. Its implementation did, however, lead to staff taking longer to mark student essays since the sheet is used by staff as additional to annotations being made directly on the student texts. The documentation therefore has implications at all levels of institution, department and tutor–student relationship.

Both the interview data from Tutor B and the textual data we analyse below suggest that she is making sense of her students' writing at a number of different and implicit levels. Although on an initial reading Tutor B appears to take an approach to writing which looks as if it is based on the traditional essay-type model of writing, her interview suggests that she is more concerned with the varieties of practices which students encounter during their interdisciplinary studies and the backgrounds that students bring with them to the university. In this way, both the data from her interview and the texts themselves illustrate a model of inclusion – supporting student writing through explicitly introducing them to both the genre of writing that they may be required to undertake throughout the course and additionally to some of the features of this genre, which at a departmental level staff have agreed to foreground as important. Despite the fact that we question below the apparently transparent nature of this particular genre model of writing European Studies, the approach in the documentation for students following this course does contrast quite markedly with the model of exclusion adopted by Tutor A, and some of the equivalent texts available for his students.

The document available for first-year undergraduates following a degree in European Studies is entitled 'Doing European Studies: a student handbook'; it is 188 pages long and of this the first 48 pages are concerned with issues of student learning and 'study skills'. In contrast to much of the documentation of this nature that we have analysed during the research, this handbook makes clear to students from the outset that their own identities and experiences of practices are implicated in the way in which they study, although in this case, not specifically in terms of writing:

> One reason why Universities can be difficult at first is that, academically, fields like European Studies rest on very different assumptions from A level, especially Language A level. To begin with they have a different focus, which is on public affairs which has its own vocabulary and concerns, which differ very much from those of imaginative literature. Coming to terms with such different ways of looking at things is important.

As with the Business Studies booklet, students are encouraged to take an interactive and constructivist approach to study of the kind that Geisler (1995) suggests is less often acknowledged by university tutors with their emphasis on subject content. She proposes a distinction between 'domain specific' views of student writing, where the emphasis is on students learning disciplinary knowledge, and those where the 'rhetorical processes' in which that knowledge is represented – the forms, styles and genres of writing itself – are made apparent. In reality of course all knowledge is constituted within such rhetorical processes, and development and change in disciplinary knowledge depend upon challenges to the schema and language within which it is represented. However, only an elite few students are permitted to see this feature of academic work and usually at later stages of their graduate studies. The document on European Studies that we are considering does in fact offer advice on reading that corresponds more to Geisler's 'rhetorical processes', perhaps because of the course location in literary and linguistic studies:

> You need to treat texts with a certain caution and probe for meaning. Ask what it is trying to say, why and how. Here you might think of starting by just reading a text through without taking notes in order to get a general view of its structure and message.
>
> Using books is not just a matter of reading and annotating words. It is, as already said, a matter of understanding. This means ensuring both that you understand the terms used and that you appreciate the meaning and significance of the material you are using. Some people, understandably, do not like 'jargon'. Nonetheless, concepts are a means of speeding up exposition and understanding. They can be a useful form of shorthand. Thus 'pluralism' is a useful way of describing western societies and politics without going into a great deal of description.

Unusually in such documents, the relationship of language, learning and disciplinary perspective is continually being made explicit to the student as he or she reads the text. The issue of learning is being addressed and introduced to the student directly in relation to issues of epistemology and what can be said to constitute the knowledge base of European Studies. The documentation applies this perspective to the advice it gives on writing itself, drawing upon a number of different implicit models of writing, such as genre, process, tri-partite essay structure. A section entitled 'The purposes of essays' leads the student through a way of developing argument implicitly defined as relevant for this subject area:

> As a learning process, essays force you to test your capacity for understanding in a specific area . . . Essays also help to structure your learning because they offer a sampling or test case approach, reflecting the fact that you can't go deeply into everything . . . They will bring you into contact with the way academics writing about Europe think and show what they think is important. This can help guide your own work . . . Above all they can help you to learn how to develop a coherent argument on the basis of your examination of the material. In an essay you have to come to a conclusion and present your knowledge and findings to the reader in a thoughtful, logical and coherent way. You are asked a question and your teachers really do want to know what *you yourself* think the answer is. As the notes have already made clear it is argument and your own contribution to the debate which counts most, not the amount of fact contained in the essay. This is also true of the report you may be asked to write once you are employed.

One interesting feature of this documentation – and perhaps to be expected in a document that addresses the student as a novice undertaking a process of academic socialisation – is that students are encouraged to 'write what they think'. Work by Ivanič (1998) would suggest that this is an area of profound difficulty for mature students; our research would support this and additionally illustrates how younger traditional students also find difficulties with the idea that the tutor really does want to know what the student thinks. The traditional essay, in which the student is supposedly required to argue a case from his or her own position, embeds inherent contradictions since as a genre it does not typify the spontaneity and individuality which is implied in the documentation. In other words, the essay is not merely an attempt on behalf of the student to communicate to the tutor his or her position on the question set. Evidence from our research suggests that across the university, students are attempting to unpack the ground rules underlying assignment questions set by tutors within different departments. It is this very gap between student and staff expectations of what is involved in answering the question which seems to result in the problems that faculty and students alike perceive around writing for assignments.

The following subsection (part of the section entitled: 'The purposes of essays') is headed 'Assessment and feedback'. This refers to the assessment criteria for essay marking:

> Generally, apart from presentational questions, like is the essay well written and expressed, so that its meaning is clear to the reader, in academic and intellectual terms, markers look for essays which meet the following kinds of criteria, e.g. of being:
>
> relevant: does the essay properly identify the subject and answer the question actually set?
> argument: is the argument supported by a clear structure which follows the argument through?
> informed: is the factual basis of the essay adequate and correct, and does it come from an adequate range of sources?
> argued: is the analysis carefully thought out and does it come to clear and reasonable conclusions?
> covering the subject: does the essay deal with all the relevant aspects of the question set or does it ignore things?
>
> The marker will try to address these issues in their comments and come to an overall assessment of the essay, using the normal marking conventions for Part I.

Previous sections of the booklet have unpacked some of the perceived requirements of writing in this interdisciplinary area. The
document now introduces students to assessment criteria and in
doing so makes reference to a number of categories which embed a
set of presuppositions we cannot assume are either shared or understood by the student reader. Despite the fact that the categories
are elaborated upon, the elaboration does not necessarily make
clear to the student what the criteria entail in this particular context.
The category 'relevant', for example, suggests that the essay should
'properly' identify the subject. Research with students suggests
that their understanding of the question and that of the tutors is
often at variance (Lea and Street, 1998; Lea, forthcoming). These
descriptive categories appear to be decontextualised and again
removed from disciplinary considerations, presented as if form can
be removed from epistemological perspectives, as in the feedback
sheet being used within the department referred to above. This
separation of epistemological considerations and definitions of
language form and structure appears to be an element of most of
the documentation that we have examined across institutions and
disciplines. They are frequently being presented as distinct and
autonomous categories although this document for European Studies goes to great lengths to introduce the novice student to different
ways of making sense of particular disciplinary knowledge.

Although, as with most documentation concerning student writing, reference is made to the issues of plagiarism, it is here deeply
embedded within a discursive text and, unlike the documentation from Tutor A above, goes some way to acknowledging student
confusion over plagiarism and the relationship of this to writing
knowledge:

> You do not need to give reference for well known facts such as the
> fact that the Second World War ended in 1945, but you do need to
> acknowledge striking instances and ideas or controversial arguments
> to which you refer. Acknowledging your sources is especially import-
> ant when you are quoting their actual words. Do not pretend that
> their ideas are ones you dreamed up. Do not plagiarize in other
> words. Plagiarism means trying to pass off somebody else's words
> as your own. It is something of which the University strongly disap-
> proves and can be heavily penalized. What teachers want is your
> opinions and not just those from a textbook.

However, despite an obvious attempt to clarify the issues at a subt-
ler level than the legalistic footnote on the standard feedback sheet

in Business Studies discussed above, the document does not address directly the worries that students themselves express regarding plagiarism. These involve issues of knowledge and identity (Ivanič, 1998) at much profounder levels than either legalistic prescription or 'somebody else's words'. Students, for instance, admit to finding that the texts they read come over as authoritative, so that it is difficult to re-present the meanings in their own words; in fact, they find it difficult to identify their own ideas separately from such sources, to distinguish between ideas they 'dreamed up' and 'somebody else's words' (Lea and Street, 1998).

Conclusion

By juxtaposing analysis of texts with commentaries on them, by both students and tutors, in both oral and written channels, we argue that features of the writing process that otherwise appear reified and universal, can be opened up to scrutiny and contest. Whilst the guidelines for student writing and the inventories of 'criteria' that we have been considering objectify and universalise the writing process, so that it appears to be a generic and transferable skill across different disciplines and fields, the commentaries upon them by participants – in this instance, university tutors – suggest that writing as a concept and as a process is more contested than this. Whilst the documents we analysed appear to merge a number of different elements of the process of student writing and make reference to these as if the relationships between the parts were in themselves self-evident, the problematic nature of these relationships and of the concepts that underpin them is brought out once we juxtapose sets of these documents, both to each other and to secondary commentary.

We believe that the reification of the autonomous model of literacy in which such documents are frequently constructed may be one reason why – despite a proliferation of such guidance documents in university settings – students have such difficulties in understanding how to deal with the variety of writing practices which we and others have documented. These texts embed different models and approaches to writing at all four levels – institution, department, course, tutor – and in terms of distinctions between features of form and issues of epistemology and between different levels and genres of writing within the university. Students are having to switch back and forth between these different genres and levels, not just between documentation but sometimes also within the same document. Like Candlin and Plum in this volume, we believe students struggle to read off the university and its requirements, to unpack the writing demands that are being made in different fields and environments in the course of their academic programmes. We would suggest that frequently such texts fail to recognise the variety of literacy practices that students encounter in the course of their studies or to make explicit at what level within the university the practices – appearing as self-evidently 'common sense' in Fairclough's terms (1992a) – underpin the writing of these documents. They remain embedded in an autonomous model of literacy.

Note

1. This was an Economic and Social Research Council funded research project entitled 'Perspectives on Academic Literacies: an Institutional Approach'. The study adopted a social practice approach; students' struggles with academic literacies were understood to result from a conflict between different and competing literacy practices rather than due to a deficit of study skills. The general findings of this research are reported in Lea & Street (1997).

PART II

Interpretation: focus on process

4

Writing and information design of healthcare materials

PATRICIA WRIGHT

Introduction

Few who study how written materials are generated think that the underlying processes correspond to a reverse play of the processes of reading. The levels of idea generation, choice of expression, revision of sequence and fine-tuning of detail have no counterpart in reading. This is particularly the case for materials sometimes referred to as functional texts (Pander Maat and Steehouder, 1992) because the communicative objective of these materials is to support readers in tasks such as decision-making or the following of procedures (Wright, 1988a). The present focus will be on the subset of functional texts that are concerned with helping people take decisions relating to healthcare (e.g. whether to have their children vaccinated or whether to undergo surgery rather than some alternative course of treatment). Healthcare advice also includes much procedural information, both on medicine containers (e.g. 'Dissolve in hot water and allow to cool') and in the leaflets distributed by clinics (e.g. recommending exercises to assist recovery).

Although the way people read these materials is very different from the way they are written, it is the central thesis of this chapter that writers need to be aware in detail of how people will read their material, because this knowledge can inform their own decisions and so result in written communications that achieve the goals of both writers and readers. This is not an entirely new thesis. Some of the broad issues raised by functional information design were aired twenty years ago by Waller (1979). Nevertheless, the way these principles apply in a range of healthcare contexts is only slowly being realised.

Most writing involves multi-level planning processes, a fact that has been recognised since the first detailed exposition of the cognitive processes in writing was articulated (Hayes and Flower, 1980; Flower and Hayes, 1980). Writing involves complex mental processes when the form of written expression is sentences and paragraphs. However, this complexity takes a quantum leap upwards when the visual arrangement of the information becomes critical (e.g. because of space constraints on a label), or when formats other than paragraphs, e.g. lists and tables, are included or when non-verbal representations, such as line drawings or photographs, must be integrated with the text.

In daily life, where functional texts form a significant portion of the reading that is done (Sticht, 1985), these visual presentation features are often major determinants of the success of written communications. When readers are checking the time of a train or a television programme, they find reference materials more helpful if the writer has given thought to the way the material will be used, the kinds of questions readers will be asking, and so provide an explicit visual structure that facilitates access to the answers (Waller, 1975). Similarly, when readers are trying to follow the instructions for microwaving lunch or getting the clock-radio to work, they will find this easier if the writer is familiar with, and able to apply, information design principles. Sless (1992) defines information design as 'managing the relationship between people and information so that the information is accessible and usable by people'. In order to attain this usability, writers need to make appropriate decisions about the choice of language plus any other representational forms adopted, and also glean information and feedback from the intended audience. It will be shown below that such feedback is needed before making decisions about content and presentation, as well as during the process of writing the draft, for the decisions made can be instantiated in alternative ways.

The appreciation of the importance of information from varied subgroups within the target audience generates a writing procedure that has been sometimes called 'reader-focused' (Schriver, 1989) and sometimes 'performance-based' (Shulman *et al.*, 1996). Both phrases serve to emphasise the need for the writers of functional materials to obtain information that is additional to the specification provided by the client, whether a drug company or a medical specialist. When the information must reach diverse ethnic and cultural groups, then these sources of additional information become key contributors to attaining a successful communication. For convenience, throughout the remainder of this chapter the phrase 'writing' will be taken to include these broader aspects of information design, the indispensability of which will be demonstrated for the domain of healthcare materials, although many of the points being made apply more widely to most functional materials (Wright, 1996).

Healthcare texts

As was indicated above, in their printed form, healthcare materials are diverse, ranging from the information on medicine containers to multi-page leaflets explaining medical conditions and available therapies. Even on medicine containers, the information is heterogeneous and includes specification of eligibility criteria, the procedures to be followed when taking the medication, and cautions concerning possible misuse or side-effects of the product. Visual and linguistic forms have to be chosen that will most effectively convey these different categories of message. The eligibility criteria must be attention-getting and forceful, whereas side-effects are usually low-frequency events and need to be couched so as not to arouse needless anxiety. In order to do this, the writer needs to be sure that readers accord frequency terms similar meanings to those intended by professionals.

There is evidence that this is not necessarily the case. Pander Maat and Klaassen (1994) studied common frequency terms such as *seldom, sometimes* and *regularly* by asking patients waiting in a Dutch Health Centre how often the side-effect described on these labels would occur in a group of 100 patients. They found patients often overestimated the frequency indicated by the label. For example, the professional body in Holland which is responsible for producing many drug labels (7,000) used the term *seldom* to mean less than 1%, but the average interpretation by the patients was above 6%. Varying the linguistic structure in which the quantifier occurred, suggested a tendency for people to assign a higher frequency to terms when they introduced a list of side-effects rather than when they occurred within a sentence frame. For example, the average estimate for the term *regelmatig (regularly)* was 47% when it was within a sentence frame but 56.4% when used as a side heading for a list. Such findings are not easily predicted from either linguistic or psycholinguistic theory, where the prominence accorded to terms encountered early might be expected to increase their polarisation, i.e. making rare events seem rarer. Rather it seems as though visual or linguistic prominence is linked by the reader to the interpretation 'more frequent'.

The sequencing of information was also found to be important by Berry, Michas, Gillie and Foster (1997). They contrasted the effects of having the procedural details of how the drug should be taken either precede or follow information about side-effects. The procedural information was remembered better if it came first, but the main determinant of whether side-effects would be remembered was their severity not their location in the text. However, readers' perception of the severity of any specific side-effect may vary with its personal relevance to their lifestyle. There is also evidence that perceived severity depends on how the side-effects are described. Pander Maat and Klaasen (1994) replaced the word *sometimes* with the word *seldom* in a leaflet accompanying a non-steroid anti-inflammatory drug. Through telephone interviews with patients who were using the drug for the first time, these researchers found that although there was no effect on patients' general attitude towards the medication, the use of the lower frequency term decreased the number of side-effects that patients recalled having been mentioned in the leaflet. More significantly, it also decreased the number of side-effects that patients reported as having personally experienced. This is strong evidence of the importance of the impact that small details within healthcare communication can have. It is also evidence for the need to check rather than assume readers' interpretation of the material. In this instance the term *seldom* had an interpretation by patients that was much closer to the professionals' intention when they used the term *sometimes*.

The importance of the reader's emotional response to the message is one of the features that distinguishes healthcare materials from other functional texts. Readers assembling flat-pack furniture may well be indifferent to the writer's tone, and require only that the procedures be understandable and easy to follow. In contrast, the reader of medical procedures may fully understand that the instruction says 'Take two tablets' but may feel that this is general advice for the average reader but that their own present need is greater. Hence compliance becomes a serious issue in evaluating the adequacy of healthcare information. Importantly, the term 'compliance' differs from the more conventional performance criterion for functional texts, which is whether the information can be accessed, understood and followed correctly when people are asked to do this in relatively artificial conditions. Such procedures yield an assessment of what readers can do with the information. Although this remains important, for healthcare advice it is not enough; the writer also needs to know whether the impact of the message is such that the recommended procedure will be adhered to. Assessing this may require some ingenious and sophisticated empirical procedures.

This distinction between assessing whether readers *can* and whether they *will* follow instructions correctly serves to emphasise how important it is for writers of healthcare information to have a detailed understanding of the ways in which readers will use and respond to what they write. From a detailed understanding of the cognitive processes that readers draw upon when using healthcare materials, it becomes possible for writers to select ways of supporting readers by reducing the demands made on attention, comprehension and memory processes.

How people read functional texts

As the time-line analysis by Schriver (1997) shows, since the 1990s there has been a steadily growing body of research concerned with how people read functional texts, whether computer manuals or bus timetables. The patterns emerging from this research strongly suggest that readers' interaction with such texts is akin to a dialogue in which the reader begins by asking a question. If there is no question, perhaps because there is nothing the reader thinks they want to know, then no reading takes place (Wright *et al.*, 1982; Wright, 1988b). It may therefore be necessary for writers to use attention-getting devices that alert readers to information that they did not realise they needed to know.

Because the readers of functional texts start with a question, their initial interaction with the document is to scan through rapidly looking for somewhere that may offer an answer. They do not usually read through the information in a linear manner but jump from section to section, sampling the content as their question changes during a single reading episode – e.g. from 'Will this help my headache?' to 'Can I take this as soon as I get home from the party or must I wait for the alcohol to metabolise?'

People have expectations about where information will be found. Rogers *et al.* (1995) observed that when a sample of 68 people between the ages of 63 and 68 were given medicine bottles with the label wrapped around so that some of the information was on the back, 18% failed to turn the bottle round and never encountered the information. For a label on a tablet box, the figure was 19%. It is not appropriate to dismiss these data as simply reflecting the vagaries of cognitive decline with advancing years. The elderly form a significant group of those taking medication. Hammond and Lambert (1994) estimated that two-thirds of the elderly use non-prescription drugs regularly. They are also a group where failure to comply is frequent and can have serious consequences. In the USA, it has been estimated that 125,000 deaths per year may be the result of non-compliance (Jackson and Huffman, 1990). Against this background, the contribution made by the written information accompanying medicines needs to be appreciated. Certainly some of the analyses of patient information leaflets have found these to be deficient in both content and presentation (Albert and Chadwick, 1992).

In healthcare materials, as in most other functional texts, it is important for writers to know about people's search strategies and the key ways of helping readers access the information they want. These techniques include the use of headings and the clear visual delimitation of different categories of information. This latter is particularly important for healthcare material because the questions readers ask will change with the context. Questions asked in the shop may be 'Is it suitable for my seven-year-old son?' whereas at the point of taking the medicine the questions become procedure-oriented, such as 'How much do I take?' or 'Should it be taken with food/water?'

Readers are economical with their time. If they suspect that they are not going to find the answer easily, or that they will not understand it when found, then they are likely to give up looking. This is one of the risks of putting the list of active ingredients early in the leaflets that accompany over-the-counter medicines, as is now required by the European Union. Readers may be put off by this highly technical listing and conclude that they will not understand any of the other information in the leaflet.

Assuming that the information for answering the question has been found, then readers' dominant cognitive processes become those of comprehension and inference. Problems of comprehension can arise from the jargon used, e.g. 'Irrigate the eye', as well as from referential ambiguity. An example of this category of misunderstanding is the instruction to take the medication '3 times a day at mealtimes'. The reader may infer that the writer is referring to approximate hours of the day, whereas the writer may have meant that the medicine should be taken with food. The phrase *at mealtimes* is being accorded a different interpretation by reader and writer. As was indicated earlier, frequency terms such as *sometimes* and *seldom* can lead to similar discrepancies.

Misunderstandings arising from the reader's inference processes extend beyond the initial interpretation of what the writer means. Readers will take decisions or create plans for action on the basis of their understanding. So they may correctly interpret what they read but nevertheless decide that they can behave in a way that does not fully accord with this understanding. The reasons for such behaviour can be diverse. Sometimes the readers see themselves as justifiable exceptions to the general audience they assume the writer was addressing ('I'm a much bigger and heavier person so I need to take more'). There may be important subgroups within the audience, perhaps culturally defined, perhaps related to medical history or medical knowledge, that will be particularly prone to misinterpretations. Sometimes they may believe that the information has been written solely so that manufacturers can cover themselves against claims for legal liability, and that it is not necessarily appropriate advice for their particular circumstances. In healthcare materials, the part played by the reader's inferences about the writer's agenda can be much more powerful determinants of achieving a successful communication than is the case in many other domains where the reading of functional texts has been studied (e.g. computer manuals – Wright, 1988c).

Similarly, readers will respond to their sense of the emotional tone of the message (Hayes, 1996). This will particularly be the case for longer documents such as leaflets rather than for the highly succinct information presented on medicine containers. There has long been good reason for expecting readers to be sensitive to the writer's tone. Fifty years ago, Rudolf Flesch devised a measure of 'Human Interest', based on 'personal words' and 'personal sentences', to complement his readability formula (Flesch, 1948). Yet few studies have explored how the tone of a healthcare message influences readers' behaviour in response to healthcare advice. Often readers form a mental image of the writer

(Hayes *et al.*, 1992) but it is not yet known which images promote compliance.

For the reader of functional texts, the finding and understanding of information is not the end of the reading process. The understanding has to be translated into decisions or plans for action. This translation activity can involve many processes, ranging from the seeking of further information, perhaps from other sources such as a pharmacist or a friend, to the creation and manipulation of plans for action. Again, there are ways in which writers can support readers in such activities. For example, making contingencies visually explicit (the dosage for adults/children) will aid decision-making. Setting procedural steps as bulleted items or numbered steps in a vertical list will help people follow procedures.

Table 4.1 summarises this account of people's activities while reading functional texts. The activities are grouped under three main headings: access, interpretation, application. One drawback with a representation such as Table 4.1 is that it implies a linear progression through the stages. As we have seen, this is not necessarily the case. The initial search may lead to reformulation of the question, and hence a new search; or the initial search may cause readers to give up before finding anything relevant to their question because they have doubts that they will be able to understand it even if found. So Table 4.1 fails to capture many factors that may lead people to stop reading. Nevertheless, it suffices to show how the reading of functional texts involves a wider range of cognitive activities than are normally encompassed by researchers who study reading in other contexts.

Even when writers have a good understanding of how readers interact with healthcare material, this of itself will not be sufficient to ensure that what they write, and the way they present it, achieves the intended communicative goals. There are so many opportunities for misunderstandings to arise, and it is so difficult for writers to divorce themselves from the knowledge that they already have about the topic (Hayes, 1986) in order to appreciate what those without this specialist knowledge need to be told. Consequently, it is necessary for the writing processes associated with functional texts, including healthcare materials, to incorporate data collection from the target audience as an integral part of the design procedure – not just as a final 'stamp of approval'. Following a study of the instructions for operating a video cassette recorder, Schriver pointed out that writers can gain substantially new insights from performance-based feedback, insights that relate not just to the text but to the interaction between the product and the text. She writes:

> Overall, the usability evaluation prompted document designers to attend to problems they would otherwise have missed or ignored . . . Usability testing provided document designers with a perspective that was simply unavailable when they drew on their years of practice in writing and graphic design.   (Schriver, 1997: 451)

Performance-based design

Once the need for performance-based testing has been acknowledged, it then becomes clear that writers will need access to special skills, either their own or someone else's, if they are to devise methods that give them the feedback they need to troubleshoot their draft materials. It is not enough to know that readers make mistakes, whether failing to notice information or misinterpreting it. If the mistakes are to be rectified, then their causes have to be accurately diagnosed. A failure to do this can result in revisions sometimes being worse than the original (Duffy *et al.*, 1983), or else offering negligible improvement. Shulman *et al.* (1996) contrasted the revision of medicine labels by guidelines and by performance-based testing. In a quiz testing readers' understanding of the label, those given the original design had 47% of the answers correct. This rose to only 48% for the revision based on guidelines, and to 68% for the performance-based revision. Perfect is hard to come by, but there can be no doubting the extra power given to the revision process by the feedback gained from performance-based testing.

Sless and Wiseman (1994) have demonstrated that a helpful general approach to evaluating healthcare materials is to set criteria for the constituent subgoals that readers have. They suggest that performance testing should ascertain whether information can be found within a specified time – e.g. dosage within 30 seconds. It is worth noting that this not only provides writers with current design targets but it may also provide a useful means of making comparisons across different products, and so may facilitate the aggregation of design expertise concerning potential pitfalls and how to avoid them. It is this level of synthesis that is badly needed in the field of information design at the moment.

The need for 'pilot testing' healthcare materials is increasingly appreciated but unfortunately such piloting does not always extend much further than showing the material to readers and asking them if they like it and can understand it. This approach is inadequate for several reasons. Politeness conventions make it difficult for many people to comment adversely on something they suspect the questioner has been involved in writing. This is especially the case when they recognise that the intent of the leaflet is to be helpful. Not only may patients or other members of the general public be unwilling to make negative comments but they may lack an appreciation that the information could have been presented in any other way. Consequently, they may accept as 'inevitably complex' some turgid and ambiguous writing. In a comparison of the feedback yielded by personal interviews and focus-group discussions, de Jong and Schellens (1998) reported that comprehension problems for a leaflet concerned with alcohol consumption were significantly more likely to surface in personal interviews, especially problems at the word level, but that queries about the credibility of the information were more likely to be aired in focus groups. Again, this is evidence that the answers obtained by asking questions depend heavily on the context in which the questions are asked. Performance-based testing may be less prone to such perturbations.

The second reason for the failure of this global or holistic approach to pilot testing is that many readers will blame themselves if they do not understand (Schriver, 1997). So rather than risk appearing stupid to their interviewer, they may say that they had no problems understanding the leaflet when this may not be true. Moreover, there is evidence that they may do this in postal as well as in face-to-face interviews. Livingstone *et al.* (1993) have reported an evaluation of a leaflet on cystic fibrosis (CF). Of the 312 people returning the questionnaire, 90% said they found it easy to understand. Nevertheless, when asked about the risk that they might be carrying the CF gene, a question which tapped a pivotal communication objective of the leaflet, more than one-third of the answers were incorrect. Indeed caution is needed in test construction because if questions can be answered with words or phrases from the written materials, this offers no indication that understanding has taken place. For example, after reading about an XYZ examination, you may be able to say that you think you should have it if you are in a high-risk category but you may not know what such an examination involves, nor what it achieves, nor what the parameters are that define high risk. As was shown earlier for the interpretation of *mealtimes*, readers may be completely unaware that their interpretation differs from that intended by the writer. Where the healthcare information reaches groups that differ widely in their cultural backgrounds or medical knowledge, there is an increased risk of miscommunications occurring. In contrast, when the assessment of the written material is performance-based, significant improvements can be achieved. For example, Morrell *et al.* (1989) asked people to write plans about how they would take their medicine. The misunderstandings detected by this procedure led to revisions which reduced errors among those over 70 years old by 21%, and among the 20-year-olds by 14%.

Another solution to the problem of ascertaining what readers believe is suitable behaviour after they have read the healthcare information, is to adopt a technique developed within the domain of human-computer interaction in which small 'scenarios' are developed that are used as the basis for evaluating specific aspects of performance (Young and Barnard, 1987). Unfortunately for health-care materials, this will sometimes necessitate readers commenting on how they think they would respond in hypothetical contexts. Nevertheless, many people are in the role of carers and many others intermittently assist people in purchases or in taking their medica-tion or when considering alternative therapies. So it is not alto-gether fanciful to ask a young adult, 'Would you take this medicine if you were a pensioner who took daily tablets for your heart?'

While one of the problems of this empirical approach can be the ingenuity required to devise the scenarios, one might hope that organisations within the healthcare industry could, in time, develop a set of core scenarios that applied across specific cat-egories of healthcare information. The synopsis of readers' activ-ities given in Table 4.1 offers a framework indicating the range of activities that a set of core scenarios would need to cover. The widespread adoption of such testing procedures would also facil-itate the accumulation of information about effective design for achieving these core objectives.

Shulman *et al.* (1996) have outlined some of the essential steps of performance-based design. These are expanded and modified slightly in Table 4.2. These steps that writers must take mesh with the above suggestions about supporting readers cognitive activities. The two perspectives converge on a common approach in which

Table 4.1   Summary of how people read functional texts

Access
- reader asks questions
- reader skip-searches for information likely to contain the answer(s)

Interpretation
- reader understands the verbal information
- reader understands the graphic information
- reader integrates verbal and graphic information
- reader infers personal relevance
- reader infers author's agenda

Application
- reader integrates understanding with personal beliefs and attitudes
- reader determines appropriate decisions and actions
- reader devises an action plan – i.e. subgoals and necessary steps
- reader carries out all steps in plan, monitoring outcomes
- if monitoring yields a mismatch between subgoal and attainment, reader formulates a new question and recycles from Access

Table 4.2   Steps in performance-based design (adapted from Shulman *et al.*, 1996: 15)

1. Identify audience and, in particular, the design needs of subgroups such as the elderly or visually handicapped or non-native speakers.
2. Specify the decisions or actions that readers should be able to take using the information. Include relevant performance parameters (e.g. search time).
3. Determine the document content and structure from an analysis of the full information needs of all subgroups of users, if necessary dividing the content across sources – e.g. label and leaflet.
4. Prepare a draft that meets the design constraints.
5. Performance-test the draft with members of the target audience, especially members of critical subgroups with special information design requirements.
6. Revise the draft in the light of insights gained from performance testing.
7. Performance-test the revision.
8. Iterate stages 6 and 7 until the criteria specified in 2 are met.

the writing process is tailored to the reading processes that need to be elicited by the text.

Healthcare materials may involve diagrams or other illustrative materials (e.g. explaining how to use an inhaler or apply a dressing). Wright (1998) reported that in a survey of patient information leaflets from 45 pharmaceutical companies, 45% included illustrations of some kind, with 84% of these being line drawings rather than photographs. There is a sizeable literature on the use of illustrations (e.g. Mandl and Levin, 1989; Lowe, 1993) but the ways in which readers integrate verbal text and illustrations has seldom been explored in any detail for healthcare materials. This may be among the reasons that Ley (1998) concluded with the verdict 'not proven' when assessing the usefulness of adding illustrations to patient leaflets. Another contributing factor may be the illustrations themselves. As was the case for verbal text, and for similar reasons, it is necessary for writers to evaluate whether the graphics are correctly understood by readers. Revision may be as necessary for a picture as it is for a sentence, and the contribution of prior knowledge or cultural background can be as influential for pictorial instructions as it is for verbal instructions (Zimmer and Zimmer, 1978).

Sometimes graphics may be used to emphasise a point in the text rather than to explain it. For example, in one graphic a cheerful set of vertical spoons were shown crossing the finishing line in a race. Here the writer's intention was to highlight the need to finish the course of medication. It would be interesting to know for what proportion of the readership this visuo-verbal pun was successful. Perhaps the author felt it did not matter. As long as some people got the point, then the graphic was useful. But information which puzzles readers may be counterproductive, perhaps undermining the authority of the writer, perhaps dissuading readers from bothering with the text. People's willingness to become nonreaders was mentioned earlier, so this is a risk that needs to be guarded against.

Even when the healthcare information is entirely verbal, we have seen that its visual display on the page/label may be critical to its success. So the question arises as to whether it is reasonable to think that a single author could be trained to have the requisite range of skills. Undoubtedly, any such individual will have needed to receive specialist training in information design. This is now available through some of the postgraduate courses in technical communication; lists of courses are available from several national societies (e.g. the Institute for Scientific and Technical Communicators – the British professional organisation for technical authors – issued a list of 22 courses in the United Kingdom in the latter part of 1997). Yet, in spite of this academic grounding, many professional technical authors feel that their skills and the need for specialist training go unrecognised (Davies, 1997). It is an international phenomenon. Casting an experienced eye over the Canadian scene, Blicq (1997) queried the apparent lack, or at least visibility, of centres of excellence in the field of technical communication.

Courses in technical communication clearly need to include training in the skills of developing evaluation methods that can be incorporated into the process of writing. There are several books giving advice on the conduct of performance-based evaluations (e.g. Dumas and Redish, 1993; Velotta, 1995). Nevertheless, from the preceding analysis of the wide-ranging communication skills required, it seems unlikely that subject-matter experts will be the most suitable people to write healthcare information.

Conclusions

It has been demonstrated that writing functional texts, especially for healthcare, requires special skills. These skills include and exceed those needed for other expository materials, such as textbooks. In particular, the contribution of readers to the control of their dialogue with the text needs to be taken into account in considerable detail by writers if appropriate decisions about language and layout are to be taken. These decisions may involve some tension. The layout may require a heading that is succinct, whereas expressing the concept adequately may require a fuller verbal description. These tensions often involve compromise solutions, so preventing algorithmic formulations being applied to such design problems. Hence the need for cultivating the techniques of performance-based design, techniques that require yet more specialist skills from authors.

When the need for this range of skills is fully appreciated, then it becomes apparent that either healthcare communication requires an input from a team of specialists, or it necessitates consulting someone who has been specifically trained in this range of skills, a graduate professional technical author or information designer. The cognitive processes of writing functional texts are too many and too diverse to be contained within one person's head. Writers need external inputs of many kinds in order to guarantee that their materials will achieve their communication objectives.

5

Disciplinary discourses: writer stance in research articles

KEN HYLAND

Academic texts are often seen as purely impersonal, objective and informative, merely faceless depictions of reality where words deal directly with facts. However, the persuasiveness of academic discourse does not depend upon the demonstration of absolute truth, empirical evidence or flawless logic. Texts are the result of actions of socially situated writers and are persuasive only when they employ social and linguistic conventions that colleagues find convincing. In this chapter, I explore a central dimension of these social interactions, examining the ways that writers represent themselves and their readers through the expression of author stance.

Basically, my argument is that in presenting informational content, writers also adopt interactional and evaluative positions. They intervene to convey judgements, opinions and degrees of commitment to what they say, boosting or toning down claims and criticisms, expressing surprise or importance, and addressing readers directly. I hope to show here that writers typically annotate their claims explicitly in this way and that controlling the level of personality in a text is central to successfully maintaining interaction with readers and building a convincing argument. Examining features of stance in a corpus of research articles, I suggest that choices of rhetorical strategy depend on relations between participants, and that the writer's stance is at least partially influenced by the social practices of his or her academic discipline. This preliminary characterisation of academic stance thus reveals some of the rhetorical knowledge needed for effective argument in different disciplines.

Writing as a social process

Work in the sociology of science has shown that academic discourse is embedded in the wider processes of argument, affiliation and consensus-making of discourse community members (Bruffee, 1986; Rorty, 1979). Rather than simply examining nature, writing actually helps to create a view of the world, influenced by the problems, social practices and ways of thinking of particular social groups (Hyland, 1997; Kuhn, 1970; MacDonald, 1994). Thus texts cannot be seen as accurate representations of what the world is like because this representation is always filtered through acts of selection, foregrounding and symbolisation; reality is seen as constructed through processes that are essentially social; involving authority, credibility and disciplinary appeals.

Writing is therefore an engagement in a social process, where the production of texts reflects methodologies, arguments and rhetorical strategies constructed to engage colleagues and persuade them of the claims that are made. Academic writing has therefore been seen as the use of various devices to enhance persuasiveness, drawing on either a rhetoric of impersonal objectivity, or one of reflexive awareness, to appropriately frame disciplinary submissions. Creating a convincing reader-environment therefore involves deploying disciplinary and genre-specific conventions such that 'the published paper is a multi-layered hybrid *co-produced* by the authors *and* by members of the audience to which it is directed' (Knorr-Cetina, 1981: 106, original emphasis). Textual meanings, in other words, are socially mediated, influenced by the communities to which writers and readers belong.

This emphasis on linking texts to the social practices of participants has extended the study of academic discourse beyond written genres to the circumstances of their creation and use (Bazerman, 1988; Berkenkotter and Huckin, 1995). Studies of scientists' accounts and practices, for example, have shown how research articles are constructed to downplay the role of social allegiance, self-interest, power and editorial bias to depict a disinterested, inductive, democratic and goal-directed activity (Gilbert and Mulkay, 1984; Myers, 1990b). Texts themselves remain important, however, as clues to the practices of their construction, to the social relationships between community members, and to the ways discourse conventions may serve to draw disciplinary boundaries and constrain the knowledge created.

A conception of stance

Stance refers to the ways that writers project themselves into their texts to communicate their integrity, credibility, involvement, and a relationship to their subject matter and their readers. It there-fore expresses a writer's socially defined *persona*, the 'created per-sonality put forth in the act of communicating' (Campbell, 1975: 394). I take it to have three main components: evidentiality, affect and relation. Evidentiality refers to the writer's expressed commit-ment to the truth of the propositions he or she presents, their reliability, strength and precision, or the strategic manipulation of these features for interpersonal goals (cf. Halliday, 1978). Affect involves the declaration of a broad range of personal and professional attitudes towards what is said or the person who says it, including emotions, perspective and beliefs. Relation concerns the extent to which writers choose to engage with their readers, their degree of intimacy or remoteness, and the ways they repres-ent themselves in the discourse.

Evidentiality entails a writer's assessment of possibilities and indicates the degree of confidence in what is said, ranging from uncertain potentiality to categorical assurance (Coates, 1983; Palmer, 1990). In addition, such epistemic uses of language have also been recognised as performing important interactional func-tions, marking informality, conviviality and group membership in conversation (Coates, 1987; Holmes, 1984, 1995). Consequently, epistemic comment is often seen as a principal means by which writers can use language flexibly to adopt positions, express points of view and signal allegiances (Lyons, 1977; Stubbs, 1996).

In academic discourse, the balancing of reporting objective data and signalling subjective evaluation is critical and the writer's assessment of the reliability of knowing can be a powerful persuas-ive factor (Hyland, 1996a; Skelton, 1997). Academic writers also manipulate commitment for interpersonal reasons and express con-fidence or scepticism to display interactive rather than propositional uncertainty (Myers, 1989; Hyland, 1996a, 1996b, 1998a). The use of certainty markers (emphatics) can mark involvement with the topic (Chafe, 1986b) and indicate solidarity with readers (Holmes, 1984), while hedges can signal the writer's admission of readers' face needs (Myers, 1989) and of community norms concerning rhetorical respect for colleagues' views (Hyland, 1998a). By marking statements as provisional, hedges may both seek to involve readers as participants in their ratification, and claim protection in the event of their eventual overthrow (Hyland, 1998a; Luukka, n.d.).

Affective factors reflect the writer's viewpoint or assessment of the state of affairs described in the discourse. Obviously, language can never be ideologically neutral, it serves to organise and express experience and so it always codes orientation and perspective, but I am referring here to the overt expression of a range of personal feelings and dispositions, often referred to as 'speaker attitude'. Affect has been held to influence a range of formal features from referential choice to case marking, although much of this literature has focused on non-Western languages (e.g. Chafe, 1994; Ochs, 1988). The expression of attitude has also been used as a means of investigating genre and register variation (Biber and Finegan, 1989; Crismore and Farnsworth, 1990; Eggins and Martin, 1997; Hyland, 1998b, 1998c, 1999) and has figured in the study of gender and cultural differences in student writing (Crismore *et al.*, 1993). Together this work has contributed to our understanding of how context can influence language choice and how differences in the expression of attitude can help specify variations between text types.

Relational elements refer to the discursive construction of relations with an audience and emphasise the ways that writers choose to either highlight or downplay the presence of their readers and themselves. The way authors represent their audience and their own involvement contributes to the level of engagement and detachment in a text (Chafe, 1982) and its interpersonal tenor (Halliday, 1994). The writer can create an impression of immediate contact with readers by commenting on their possible reactions or views (e.g. *as is well known, it is natural to suppose that*), directing them to particular aspects of the discourse (*recall figure 2, Now consider the case of*), and by asking questions (*but can this be taken further?*). In addition, writers can acknowledge the presence of both themselves and their audience to create a sense of disciplinary solidarity and shared endeavour by the strategic use of the pronouns *we, us* and *our*, and modifiers assuming common ground (Myers, 1989). Reference to the presence of the author can similarly be explicit or disguised, with the writer taking responsibility for actions, or avoiding agency by transitivity selections which favour the passive and non-specific subjects.

The rhetorical significance of these grammatical and lexical choices is in producing differences in the tenor of a text. For writers, they play an important part in anticipating the negatability of statements by alerting readers to their perspective towards both their propositions and their readers. Gaining readers' acceptance of claims is complicated by the fact that there is no independent, objective means of distinguishing the observational from the theoretical, and this means that the classification of each will change depending on what can be contested and what taken for granted (Longino, 1990). So, if the attainment of 'truth' does not lie exclusively in the external world, and there is consequently always more than one plausible interpretation of a given piece of data, the reader may be persuaded to judge a claim as acceptable, or may decide to reject it. The appropriate expression of stance is therefore an important response to the potential negatability of a writer's claims, acting to engage the reader and anticipate possible objections by soliciting support, expressing collegiality and displaying competence and reasonableness.

Corpus, taxonomy and method

The data for the study consist of 56 research articles. One paper from each of seven leading journals in eight disciplines was chosen to represent a broad cross-section of academic endeavour: microbiology (Bio), physics (Phy), marketing (MK), applied linguistics (AL), philosophy (Phil), sociology (Soc), mechanical engineering (ME) and electrical engineering (EE). The journals were nominated by specialist informants as among the most important in their fields, and the articles chosen at random from current issues, taking care to select only those based on original data to allow a comparison of linguistic features. The articles were scanned to produce an electronic corpus of just over 330,000 words after excluding text associated with tables, graphics and notes.

I developed a taxonomy of stance features corresponding to the characterisation sketched above, comprising five main functions: hedges, emphatics, attitude markers, relational markers and person markers:

- **Hedges** are items such as *possible, might, perhaps* and *believe* which indicate the writer's decision to withhold complete commitment to an accompanying proposition, allowing information to be presented as an opinion rather than as a fact (Hyland, 1996a, 1996b, 1998a).

- **Emphatics** such as *it is obvious, definitely* and *of course,* on the other hand, mark the expression of certainty and emphasise the force of a proposition. As noted above, the interactive manipulation of these features is a conventional aspect of academic discourse.

- **Attitude markers** express the writer's affective attitude to propositions in more varied ways than evidential items, conveying surprise, obligation, agreement, importance, frustration, and so on, rather than simply commitment. They are typically writer-oriented and are most often signalled by attitude verbs (e.g. *I agree, we prefer*), necessity modals (*should, have to, must*), sentence adverbs (*unfortunately, hopefully*), and adjectives (*appropriate, logical, remarkable*). In addition, writers can also signal their attitude to particular terms by including them in quotes or by typographical devices such as italics and exclamations.

- **Relational markers** are devices that explicitly address readers, functioning to either selectively focus their attention, emphasise a relationship or include them as participants in the text situation. Relational markers are essentially concerned with the writer's attempt to invoke reader participation, and I have focused here on the use of second person pronouns (*we find here, let us now turn to*), question forms (*why accept 2? where does this lead?*), imperatives (*consider, recall that, note that*), and digressions which directly address the audience (*this will be familiar to those . . .*) (e.g. Crismore *et al.*, 1993).

- **Person markers** refers to the use of first person pronouns and possessive adjectives to present propositional, affective and interpersonal information. The pronoun system is an important feature of stance as writers can present their material or perspectives subjectively (*we believe, my analyses involved*), interpersonally (*we can see from this, let us consider*), or objectively (*it is possible that, the data show*). There are clearly a number of ways available to academic writers to avoid direct reference to persons, and a number of reasons why writers might make use of them. Some journals, for instance, seek to editorially constrain authorial independence in this regard, interceding between author and product. However, the presence or absence of explicit author reference is generally a conscious choice by writers to adopt a particular stance.

Two comments need to be made about this scheme. First, I do not claim to have included all aspects of stance features in the corpus. Our knowledge of how evidentiality and affect are typically expressed in different registers is limited and the resources available to mark stance are extremely heterogeneous. Not only are many lexical items affectively loaded (e.g. *famous* v *notorious*), but community members often employ wordings that signal solidarity through a shared attitude towards particular methods or theoretical orientations which may be opaque to the analyst. Nor is commitment always marked by words on the page: a writer's decision not to draw an obvious conclusion from an argument, for example, may be read by peers as a significant absence. While recognising these secondary expressions of stance, however, this preliminary study is limited to more overt markers.

Second, there is obviously some overlap between these classes. The imposition of discrete categories inevitably conceals the fact that forms often perform more than one function at once. Thus items acting as hedges can also express affective meanings by signifying a position to the reader, and relational markers may additionally indicate the writer's attitudes for interpersonal reasons. Pragmatic congruence is a feature of academic writing because, in developing their arguments, writers are simultaneously trying to set out a claim, comment on its truth, establish solidarity and represent their credibility. The ways writers profess a particular relationship to their topic and their readers, then, often involve devices which solicit reader collusion on more than one of these fronts simultaneously. But, given the distinctions outlined above, it is generally possible to identify the predominant meanings expressed. The classification thus enables us to compare the rhetorical patterns of stance in different discourse communities.

To identify the stance markers in the corpus, I compiled a list of potentially important lexico-grammatical items from a survey of previous studies, particularly Biber and Finegan (1989), Hyland and Milton (1997) and Holmes (1988), from grammars and dictionaries, and from the most frequently occurring items in the articles themselves. As noted above, these were principally items such as pronominals, modal verbs expressing possibility and obligation, reasoning verbs, and adjectives and adverbs used to qualify statements and express attitudes. The corpus was then examined using a text analysis program to determine the frequency of these items. All target items revealed by the program were then manually examined by myself and a colleague working independently to ensure they expressed the writer's stance. This activity produced an inter-rater reliability of 0.88 (Kappa), indicating a high degree of agreement. I present the findings of the study below, and then go on to explore their significance for our understanding of social interactions among academic communities.

Findings

The quantitative analysis shows that the expression of stance is an important feature of academic writing, with an average of 204 occurrences in each paper, about one every 28 words.[1] Table 5.1 shows that evidential markers were the principal means of communicating stance and that hedges were by far the most frequent features of writer perspective in the corpus, comprising over 40% of all devices. This reflects the critical importance of distinguishing fact from opinion in academic discourse and the need for writers to evaluate their assertions in ways that are likely to be persuasive to their peers, presenting claims with both appropriate caution and deference to the views of colleagues. Attitude markers and emphatics had similar frequencies and occurred substantially more often than relational and person markers.

The disciplinary results reveal considerable variation in both the overall use of stance features and their expression. Table 5.2 shows the density of features in each discipline normalised to a text length of 1,000 words. As can be seen, philosophy, marketing and applied linguistics articles contained the highest proportion

Table 5.1   Stance features in academic articles (combined disciplines)

Category	Total no of items	Items per 1,000 words	% of total stance items
Hedges	4,787	14.60	41.92
Attitude markers	2,119	6.46	18.55
Emphatics	1,929	5.88	16.89
Person markers	1,422	4.33	12.45
Relational markers	1,163	3.54	10.18
Totals	11,420	34.81	100.00

Table 5.2 Stance features in academic articles
(per 1,000 words)

Item	AL	MK	Phil.	Soc	EE	ME	Bio	Phy
Hedges	18.0	20.0	18.5	13.3	8.2	9.6	13.6	9.6
Attitude markers	8.6	6.9	8.9	7.0	5.5	5.6	2.9	3.9
Emphatics	6.2	7.1	9.7	4.6	3.2	5.0	3.9	6.0
Person markers	4.8	6.2	6.5	3.5	2.6	1.3	3.3	5.0
Relational markers	1.9	1.3	11.8	4.6	1.2	1.8	0.7	1.6
Totals	39.5	41.5	55.4	33.0	20.7	23.3	24.4	26.1

of stance markers and engineering and science papers the lowest, corresponding to the traditional division between hard and soft disciplines. Hedges were the most frequent indicators of stance in all fields, although their proportions in different disciplines varied substantially, comprising 56% of items in biology and only 33% in philosophy. Writers in most disciplines were least inclined to use person and relational markers to convey stance, although scientists significantly under-used attitude devices. The philosophy articles contained over half the relational markers in the corpus and also the most emphatics, although the latter were proportionately much higher in physics and mechanical engineering where they comprised over a fifth of all stance markers.

The study examined over 300 items expressing stance and these were dominated by the person markers *I* and *we*, the hedges *may* and *would*, the emphatic predictor *will*, and *we* as a relational marker. The most frequent items, representing almost 50% of all the devices surveyed, are presented in Table 5.3. Within the hedges, probability items exceeded those expressing possibility, while usuality items (Halliday, 1994), such as *always* and *often* used to convey modality, were infrequent. Relational markers were dominated by the inclusive pronouns and the imperative *see*, and attitude markers by comments on importance and necessity. The largest differences between disciplines were in the use of inclusive pronouns (with 94% in the social sciences), inferential *must* and *possible* (34% and 41% in philosophy), and the attitude device *accurately* (40% in the engineering disciplines).

Overall, the results show that published academic writing is not the faceless discourse it is often assumed to be and that among

Table 5.3   Most frequent devices used to express stance
in the corpus

Device	Category	Frequency
may	hedge	646
we	person marker	623
will	emphatic	483
I	person marker	456
would	hedge	385
we	relational marker	372
possible(possibly)	hedge	306
could	hedge	269
might	hedge	265
suggest	hedge	258
see	relational marker	243
important(importantly)	attitude marker	239
our	person marker	233
even	attitude marker	203
should	attitude marker	185
simply	attitude marker	183
indicate	hedge	141
seem	hedge	138
our	relational marker	135
assume	hedge	128
in fact/the fact that	emphatic	123
show (that)	emphatic	117

the specialist terms, dense lexis, passives and nominalisations there
are conventions of personality. The extent to which writers represent themselves and their readers in these texts shows that stance
is not somehow peripheral to a more serious goal of communicating ideational content to colleagues. On the contrary, its frequency
suggests that it is central to academic argument, helping to facilitate the social interactions which contribute to knowledge production. More interestingly, the uneven distribution of stance
features indicates that these conventions may be to some extent
rhetorically constrained by the practices of different disciplines,
perhaps broadly reflecting the types of intellectual enquiry pecu-
liar to certain fields. This view is further elaborated, from a variety
of angles, in Chapters 1, 3, 7 and 9 of this volume. With regard to
stance, more research is needed to confirm these distinctions, and

more space to explore them, but it is possible to offer some tentative suggestions to help account for the more clear-cut preferences.

Stance and disciplinary style

One obvious point is that the distribution of stance shows a clear correlation with the traditional distinction between hard and soft disciplines, broadly corresponding to the sciences and humanities / social sciences (Becher, 1989; Kolb, 1981). Collectively, the journals in applied linguistics, marketing, philosophy and sociology contained almost 30% more stance expressions than those from the sciences and engineering, with hedges and attitude markers particularly strongly represented. This result perhaps coincides with our intuitions that the sciences tend to produce more impersonal texts. However, because the resources of language are used to mediate the contexts of their use, they might also reflect the characteristic structures of knowledge domains and argument forms of the disciplines that create them.

One major distinction between hard and soft knowledge areas is the extent to which succinctness and precision is valued, or even possible. Hard knowledge disciplines in particular often convey meanings in a highly compressed code impenetrable to the uninitiated, while knowledge-making in the humanities, despite the use of technical terminology, is often accomplished in apparently everyday terms (although frequently invested with discipline-specific significance). This is principally because what is considered the appropriate rhetoric for a discipline is tied to the purposes of that discipline. Natural scientists tend to see their goal as producing public knowledge able to withstand the rigours of falsifiability and developing through relatively steady cumulative growth, where problems emerge and are formulated in an established context (Bazerman, 1988; Becher, 1989). The social sciences, on the other hand, have produced interpretative discourses which often recast knowledge as sympathetic understanding, promoting tolerance in readers through an ethical rather than cognitive progression (Dillon, 1991: 109; Hyland, in press).

While there are clear dangers in reifying the ideologies of practitioners, these broad ontological representations have real rhetorical effects. One consequence is that in the hard sciences, to a greater extent than in the soft disciplines, current topics are determined by those of the immediate past, and these in turn serve to identify problems yet to be addressed. In many areas, research can thus be reported within a shared framework of assumptions and the accumulated knowledge of the field incorporated into a specialised language. In soft areas, however, the context often has to be elaborated anew, its more diverse components reconstructed for a less cohesive readership.

The suggestion that hard knowledge is cumulative and tightly structured not only allows for highly efficient communication, but contributes to the apparently 'strong' claims of the sciences. The degree to which the background to a problem and the appropriate methods for its investigation can be taken for granted means there are relatively clear criteria for establishing or refuting claims, and this is reflected in writers' deployment of evidential markers. While writers in all disciplines used hedges in the evaluation of their statements, they were considerably more frequent in the soft disciplines, perhaps indicating less assurance about what colleagues could be safely assumed to accept. There was also a significant quantitative difference in the type of hedges used, with writers in the hard-knowledge areas making over twice as much use of attribute hedges (Hyland, 1996a). These are devices such as *about, partially, approximately, generally*, and so on, which act less to proclaim uncertainty than to restrict the scope of the accompanying statement, mitigating the connection between reality and the language used to describe it:

(1) ... the LT50 for leaves of *C. megacarpus* are <u>about</u>
     −9 °C, which suggests that the latter ...   (Bio)
     The agreement between the measured and
         calculated performance is <u>quite</u> good and
         indicates ...   (EE)
     The literature on the urban drug scene in Britain
         <u>generally</u> shows a strange neglect of ...   (Soc)
     ... designs where the current is purely azimuthal,
         can be <u>largely</u> eliminated by ...   (Phy)
     ... for metallurgical coal is <u>usually</u> met by imports
         from the United States while <u>virtually</u> all ...   (ME)

The writer may therefore consider the claim to be true, but wish to specify how far results approximate to a conventional cognitive schema, enabling a situation to be construed in terms of variations from how the discourse community conventionally structures the world. Attribute hedges are thus not only a 'weaker' form of hedging, but also indicate the strength of community understandings by representing actual instances of measured behaviour in terms of their deviations from the discipline's conception of what reality is like. In addition, the use of these hedges in some cases appears to invoke a schema of relevant knowledge by marking certain details as non-salient, subordinating information by highlighting its generality or inexactitude and leaving precision for what is more important (Channel, 1990). Their greater use in the hard-knowledge papers may therefore suggest a more cohesive body of consensual knowledge than is typically found in the soft fields.

Shared perceptions and author presence

The use of a highly formalised reporting system to represent arguments relatively compactly also allows writers in the hard disciplines to minimise their apparent presence in the text. In contrast, soft areas employ a 'limited degree of standardization of cognitive objects and work processes' (Whitley, 1984), the under-determination of the code requiring greater personal intervention to reconstruct the intended meaning for colleagues and achieve a sympathetic reader-environment. Because of this, the writer in the soft disciplines not only relies more on overt intertextuality to construct a mutually significant context, but also relies more on creating an authorial self firmly established in the norms of the discipline (Hyland, 1998c). In other words, where problems are less clearly defined and demarcated, criteria for what counts as adequate explanation are less assured and interpretative variation increases. Writers thus have to work harder to engage their audience and shape their arguments to the shared perspectives of the discipline. They cannot assume an appropriate framework of knowledge, but must rely on a personal projection into the text to invoke an intelligent reader and a credible, collegial writer.

This is also illustrated in the greater use of hedging and higher densities of attitude and relational markers in the soft-knowledge texts. Writers not only hedge to convey propositional uncertainty but also seek to make their claims more acceptable to colleagues, expressing interpersonal meanings and displaying conformity to interactional norms. Distinguishing the precise function of a hedge is hazardous, as most forms carry more than one meaning. However, hedges were twice as frequent in linguistics, marketing and philosophy as in engineering and physics, and this suggested a greater orientation to readers and more sensitivity to the possible subjective negation of their claims. Typical hedges in the soft areas appeared to carry a strong interpersonal element:

(2) ... <u>one may suggest that</u> discussing the moral and
   social merits of ...   (Soc)
   <u>One could conceivably conclude</u> from this type
   of result that ...   (AL)
   <u>It is my contention that</u> conditional guarantees
   fall under category C.   (Phil)
   ... helps to retain existing customers and <u>may,
   possibly,</u> help to attract new ones.   (MK)
   However, <u>it seems likely that</u> the context in which
   these students study is important ...   (AL)

Similarly, writers in the soft-knowledge papers also showed greater efforts to engage readers in their discourse by the use of relational markers. While writers in all the disciplines used imperatives to some extent, principally *see, consider* and *note* (cf. Swales *et al.*, 1998), these mainly functioned to direct readers to a particular aspect of the exposition or help guide them through the text:

(3) <u>It is seen that</u> the measured port-to-port insertion
   loss of 1.7 dB is ...   (EE)
   To this purpose, <u>let the load vary</u> in a quasi-static
   manner ...   (ME)
   <u>Note the increase in power requirement and BE
   field compression</u> ...   (Phy)
   <u>Consider now</u> the simple conventional reflection
   effect ...   (Phy)

Apart from the citational use of *see*, however, the social and human sciences seem less impositional in their use of relational features as writers also sought to express a more personal style:

(4) He later lapsed into a less clear-cut (<u>but perhaps
   more authentic</u>) use of them as the following ...   (AL)
   <u>I must ask readers to trust me that</u> a viable syntax
   and semantics can be had ...   (Phil)
   ... behind the economics, <u>if you like</u>, is the valida-
   tion of an ethical orientation ...   (Soc)
   <u>Let me finally add that I do not know of any interesting account</u> of vacuous C-assertability.   (Phil)

The use of inclusive pronouns to engage readers rhetorically was largely confined to philosophy, where they comprised over 70% of the relational markers. Their use in engineering, on the other hand, was insignificant and they did not occur in the science articles at all. It is interesting to note that these disciplines cluster at the extremes of the abstract–concrete dimension of academic endeavour. The sciences and engineering typically value mathematics and symbolic manipulation, while philosophy values the humanities, intuition and the metaphorical representation of knowledge (Biglan, 1973; Kolb, 1981). Moreover, there is an important sense in which philosophical discourse differs from the sciences in that it does not seek to accomplish 'closure' by reaching consensus on a particular interpretation of a phenomenon. Rather, the discourse seems to be an end in itself, a continuing conversation in a spirit of contention between participants, without settling the points at issue (e.g. Rorty, 1979).

One important effect of this is that the philosopher's writing style is an important component of his or her reputation, and codification is largely personal. Effective argument relies heavily on hypothetical narrative strategies and game-playing, which entail a heavy element of humour, point scoring and positive face engagement (Bloor, 1996). Bloor refers to the essence of philosophical rhetoric as 'mind-to-mind combat with co-professionals' (*ibid.*: 34), and this is achieved by a high degree of personal involvement to create a sense of communal intimacy. A highly intrusive stance is imperative in this kind of discourse and the use of hedges, relational and attitude markers reflects this. Inclusive pronouns, in particular, work to create, or appeal to, a world of shared understandings which helps shape the author's view into appropriate disciplinary formulations:

(5) We seem to have here a kind of dicto-de-re
   ambiguity in the verbal form of . . .   (Phil)
   We cannot expect this paradox to confront us
   often, for the two usages that . . .   (Phil)
   Furthermore, we can perform the following
   algorithm by manipulating . . .   (Phil)
   . . . we still need to know why it has epistemic
   significance and we need to know what to . . .   (Phil)
   Closer to our concerns, Stalnaker explicitly
   opposes it for . . .   (Phil)

A sense of in-group solidarity in philosophy is also promoted by the high use of emphatics. Inferential *must* and the adverbs *clearly* and *obviously* were heavily used by philosophers and worked to invoke an intelligent reader in the text, a co-player in a closely knit community of peers. Emphatics were also relatively common in the physics, marketing and applied linguistics papers, but here they tended to stress the strength of warrants in establishing a correspondence between data and claims, predominantly with *establish* and *show*, and to express confidence in expected logical outcomes using *predict* and *will*:

(6)   However, <u>it is clearly</u> defective in some way.   (Phil)
       So it looks as if indicative conditionals <u>must be</u>
          material implications.   (Phil)
       <u>Obviously</u>, however, such a ground cannot obtain.   (Phil)
       Consequently <u>it is established that</u> such a
          configuration constitutes a . . .   (Phy)
       . . . in short, <u>we demonstrate that</u> what consumers
          know . . .   (MK)
       The causal-model <u>shows that</u> tolerating ambiguity
          strategists . . .   (AL)
       Listening <u>will continue to</u> play a large part in
          pronunciation training, . . .   (AL)

Talking to your audience thus appears to be accomplished in different ways, drawing on different criteria of appropriacy. The extent to which the author intercedes to urge acceptance or appears to withdraw to encourage cold judgement of the argument, is largely a disciplinary matter. It may be related to the fact that hard knowledge tends to be universalistic and driven more by conceptual questions than the interpretation of phenomena such as texts or human behaviour (MacDonald, 1994). The focus tends to be on the professional problem rather than the actual phenomenon under study, and the normal practice in such forms of knowledge-making consists of conducting experiments specifically to propose solutions to such problems.

   Hard disciplines are therefore predominantly concerned with quantitative model-building and the analysis of observable experience to establish empirical uniformities. Explanations principally derive from precise measurement and systematic scrutiny of relationships between a limited number of controlled variables.

This implies a very different authorial stance from that of the soft-knowledge domains, which are typically more interpretative and less abstract. Here variables are more heterogeneous and causal connections more tenuous, which means greater intervention in the argument is required and the writer's presence is necessarily stronger.

Stance and community values

These differences in authorial stance, however, do not only reflect disciplinary predilections for economy and variations in rhetorical style. Clearly, conventions of stance help instantiate aspects of a community's values and beliefs about knowledge and knowing. An important aspect of a positivist-empirical epistemology is that the authority of the individual is secondary to the authority of the text, and that the role of personal relationships is subordinated to the voice of nature. Researchers typically conceal their rhetorical identities behind a cloak of objectivity, masking their involvement with an array of linguistic detachment. The limited use of stance markers in the science and engineering articles studied here may therefore reflect the textual practices of the hard-pure disciplines in constructing a particular narrative of events. A low-key representation of self and other helps to reinforce the conceptual structure of the discipline by presenting science as 'collective, inductive and cumulative' (Berkenkotter and Huckin, 1995). Impersonality in knowledge creation emphasises a collaborative endeavour driven by the goal of helping nature to reveal itself more clearly. This reluctance to project a prominent authorial presence is especially evident in the far lower use of attitude and relational markers compared with those in the soft domains.

As I noted above, there were very few relational markers in the hard-knowledge fields (about three per paper), and they were particularly low in the sciences. Expressions of attitude were also infrequent in the sciences, where *important* and *essential* were common, and only slightly higher in engineering, where *accurately* and *simply* predominated. Additionally, necessity modals contributed heavily to this aspect of stance and almost a quarter of all attitude markers referred to the writer's view that something should be done or should happen. In sum, attitude markers in the science and engineering papers tended to reveal the author's opinions or character only through commenting on what readers should attend to, and how the writer would like them to respond to information:

(7)   . . . is <u>a difficult, but important and interesting</u>,
      subject of extensive study over the past . . .   (ME)
      . . . (DLTS) technique is a <u>more accurate and
      reliable</u> tool to get a quantitative measure . . .   (EE)
      <u>It is clearly necessary</u> to use improved device
      structures and to employ . . .   (EE)
      In simulation studies <u>one must check</u> any limiting
      case of calculations . . .   (Phy)
      . . . introduction RNA splicing, <u>an essential step</u> in
      MRNA synthesis, is a potential control . . .   (Bio)
      . . . <u>it is important to consider</u> the hydration of the
      plant, the minimum temperature and . . .   (Bio)

So while these devices subtly display affect, their principal role in the hard-knowledge texts is to persuade by communicating propositional attitudes and evaluation. That is, they tend to refer to issues the writer sees as important, interesting or necessary in order to fit claims appropriately into the anticipated background understandings of the reader. The soft/applied texts, on the other hand, tended to show far greater variability in the use of affective signals and were generally more opinionated:

(8)   . . . and <u>it seems sensible to assume</u> the men
      concerned were not unreflective . . .   (Soc)
      <u>I argue that their treatment is superficial</u> because,
      despite appearances, it relies . . .   (Soc)
      <u>It is my hope that</u> this model will facilitate further
      inquiry into . . .   (AL)
      Chesterton was <u>a serious and even excellent</u>
      philosopher.   (Phil)
      . . . <u>managers routinely simplify, or even oversimplify,
      complicated issues</u> to stimulate . . .   (MK)
      <u>Pomerance is just wrong</u> however.   (Phil)

The suppression of the acting subject in the hard-knowledge areas was also evident in the fact that writers were generally less explicit in the extent to which they offered an admission of personal judgements when hedging claims. Writers in the soft disciplines were more likely to indicate the subjectivity of evaluations with the use of verbs such as *believe, suspect* and *suppose,* which conveyed a sense of personal conjecture to the accompanying statement:

(9) I suggest that certain ways of thinking about
    social movements are likely to be very fruitful . . .   (Soc)
    Although further research is needed, we suspect that
    the type of new product used in . . .   (MK)
    I believe that these are different notions that may
    well involve different objects.   (Phil)
    On the basis of this pilot investigation, I consider
    the following implications relevant to . . .   (AL)
    We interpret most of the other significant
    interactions . . .   (MK)

In the sciences and engineering, on the other hand, a higher proportion of hedges were modal verbs, which are less specific in attributing a source to a viewpoint. In addition, these texts included more conventional illocutionary performatives such as *indicate, imply* and *suggest,* which emphasise the reliability of information over its degree of certainty (Hyland, 1998a). These forms also allow writers to distance themselves from their claims through the creation of 'abstract rhetors', which allow agency to be attributed to things:

(10) The results presented here suggest . . .   (Bio)
    Taken together, these data indicate that Tax1
    interacts with . . .   (Bio)
    The code equations imply that . . .   (ME)
    . . . hence, as the triangular sequence suggests,
    the rotation unravels the effect . . .   (Phy)
    . . . agreement between the measured and the
    calculated performance is quite good and
    indicates . . .   (EE)

Perhaps the clearest indication of the writer's self-presentation in the text is the use of person markers. The choice of first person helps writers to construct a more authoritative discoursal identity and to adopt an explicitly accountable stance. The suppression of personal agency is therefore often considered to be a means of concealing the social constructedness of accounts in academic writing, and scientists are generally seen as most guilty in this regard, concealing their interpretative practices behind a screen of empiricist impersonality. But while the engineering texts in my corpus contained very few references to the author, biology had similar figures to sociology, and the physicists used the first person more than either linguists or sociologists. In fact, the proportion of person markers was higher in the sciences than attitude or relational markers.

On closer examination, however, the use of person markers displayed the greatest intra-disciplinary variability of all the features examined,[2] suggesting that it may be an area where experienced users of the genre may be permitted a degree of freedom to manipulate discoursal conventions. The discursive practices employed by members of particular disciplinary communities are merely socially authorised conventions, not strict rules of conduct, and therefore constrain rather than determine linguistic choices. Within the boundaries of these conventions, there is clearly some leeway for innovation, allowing skilled authors to vary their expression of personal voice and mix what Bhatia (1993) calls 'private intentions' with the socially defined purpose of securing ratification of their arguments.

But although the frequency of person markers varied considerably within academic fields, there did seem to be disciplinary preferences for the authorial positions members take up (Clark and Ivanič, 1997). A concordance of the data showed that there were marked disciplinary differences in the main verbs most commonly co-occurring with the first person, indicating distinct representations of authorial presence in these texts. Broadly, these academic writers employed person markers for three main purposes – either to organise arguments and structure their texts (11), to introduce or discuss research activities (12), or to explicitly indicate their attitudes to findings or align themselves with theoretical positions (13):

(11) In this paragraph <u>we report</u> a comparison between
        the results obtained with our method ...   (EE)
      In this case <u>we rewrite</u> the former two expressions
        of equation (25) as ...   (ME)
      Lastly, <u>we draw</u> pedagogical implications from the
        study.   (AL)
      <u>We describe</u> two nuclear genes that behave
        genetically as activators of group 11 cis-splicing ... (Bio)

(12) <u>We also manipulated</u> the accessibility of corporate
     associations by including several . . .   (MK)
    <u>We acid shocked cells</u> in the presence of the
     non-specific CA2+ channel inhibitor La3+.   (Bio)
    In simulation <u>we set x=2</u>, about 1 as much as x.   (Phy)
    <u>Now we analyse</u> their kinematical meaning.   (ME)

(13) <u>I argue for</u> a modified essentialist account of
     spacetime points that avoids these obstacles.   (Phil)
    <u>I suggest that</u> this arises largely because of the
     extreme powerlessness of . . .   (Soc)
    . . . <u>we concur with</u> Baumgardner and Tongue
     (1988: 136) who call it . . .   (AL)
    <u>We believe that</u> the threshold force was not high
     enough to distinguish the difference between . . .   (EE)

There was an overall tendency in the disciplines studied for the first person to collocate with verbs conveying reasoning and possibility, or those describing research activities. There were broad differences, however. The fact that personal intrusion was more often associated with verbs such as *argue* and *think* in the social sciences and with *believe* and *propose* in marketing papers, demonstrated writers' decisions to place their claims in a framework of personal perception. Here, then, we find personal intrusion being used to refer more to perspectives on the object studied rather than to its manipulation or presentation. In contrast, in the engineering and science papers, person markers occurred more with verbs referring to experimental activities, such as *assay*, *measure* and *analyse*, and with verbs used to structure the text, particularly *note*, *discuss* and *refer*. Thus the first person was used mainly to construct the text and present decisions, rather than to take a personal stand on the object studied. Clearly the role of the first person is complex in terms of the ideological and interpersonal positions it offers the writer, but these preliminary findings suggest broad differences in the ways that academic writers employ it in adopting a discoursal stance, representing decisions to either foreground or downplay their involvement in creating a text and in creating knowledge.

A further interesting difference in the representation of person is the fact that philosophers and sociologists were the only writers in the corpus to occasionally present their actions using progressive aspect:

(14) I am only claiming that they do not have good
     epistemic reasons.   (Phil)
    I am not merely asserting that probabilistic
     methods can provide good reason to believe . . .   (Phil)
    I am arguing that PDP does not have particular
     epistemic drawbacks . . .   (Phil)
    I am not using very cognitively disabled people
     as a mere example for a broader purpose.   (Soc)
    In this way I am confronting fundamental issues
     of critical social science practice.   (Soc)

The progressive form suggests an action in progress, and its effect here is to move our attention from what is 'argued', 'claimed' or 'confronted' to the performance of the activity itself, positioning an active writer in the text. Its use therefore implies the presence of a conscious subject over simple inert perception or cognition, more vividly depicting the expressed action and projecting the writer's participation into the event in a more immediate and direct way. This marked form thus seems to be a further resource for the expression of authorial stance in disciplines which license a more narrative exposition, allowing writers to intrude a dialogic practice into an academic presentation.

Taken together then, these observations suggest that the use of stance is an important aspect of professional academic discourse, conveying the field-specific expressive and interpersonal meanings which help readers to evaluate information and writers to gain acceptance for their work. I have also argued that the choices made by individual writers not only help create an authorial style but represent an awareness of the conventional socio-discursive practices of their disciplinary communities.

Conclusion

I have tried to show that effective academic writing depends on rhetorical decisions about interpersonal intrusion and involves writers' selecting and deploying community-sensitive linguistic resources to represent themselves, their positions and their readers. This creation of an authorial *persona* is to some extent an act of personal choice, and the influence of individual personality, confidence, experience and ideological preference cannot be completely disregarded. However, writers do not act in a social vacuum and knowledge is not constructed outside particular communities of practice. Such communities exist in virtue of a shared set of assumptions and routines about how collectively to deal with and represent their experiences. Membership is at least partly a function of one's ability to employ these conventions appropriately. How language is used on particular occasions cannot, of course, be seen as completely determined, but the participation of individuals in disciplinary cultures demands an understanding of how to construct and interpret key genres. In this way, independent creativity can be shaped by accountability to shared practices.

This chapter has merely scratched the surface of a large topic and much more needs to be done to describe stance: how it is used, expressed and distributed in different disciplines and genres, and how it might be variably received by disciplinary in- and out-groups. I have, however, found sufficient differences to suggest a clear relationship between stance and its rhetorical contexts. Writing as a physicist, applied linguist or an engineer means being able to construct an argument that meets the field-specific standards of these respective disciplines, not only in terms of relevance and plausibility, but also of the social relationships that can be appropriately appealed to. Rather than thinking of academic discourse as impersonal, then, we need to think of it as reflecting the different social practices of disciplinary communities in constructing knowledge. Simply, some fields permit greater authorial presence than others. The results emphasise the point that social relationships within discourse communities exercise strong constraints on a writer's representations of self and others. Equally, however, an analysis of stance markers also reveals a great deal about the norms and epistemologies of those who use them.

Notes

1. Stance features often have clause-level realisations. Presenting results as word counts is therefore not intended to convey the proportion of stance features in a text but merely to enable a comparison of their occurrence in corpora of unequal sizes.
2. The average standard deviation for all disciplines was 14.5, being highest in marketing and applied linguistics and lowest in the science papers.

6

Writing as an intercultural process

IAN G. MALCOLM

In its broadest sense, culture embraces everything people learn and do as members of a society. The way we write, like the way we speak, is an expression of our enculturation, as well as being an expression of our individuality. The cultural knowledge which we display in writing is a product of historical and social formation, some of which we hold in common with other groups, yet some of which differentiates us from other groups. This chapter takes a perspective on writing which highlights its characteristics as a part of culture, operating as an agent of individual and social change and also as a means of identification, expression and negotiation of cultural distinctiveness in the context of a culturally diverse world.

Writing and culture

Writing is inherent in cultural self-perception, maintenance and transmission. In some societies writing is an area of cultural focus or *core value* (Smolicz and Secombe, 1985; cf. Wooden and Hurley, 1992). As such, it forms an important part of institutional practice and, inevitably, for purposes of cultural maintenance, an important part of education. Within a culture, different sub-cultures may develop different writing practices and different genres which may require quite different treatments. This can be seen in other chapters in this volume, particularly Chapters 3, 5, 7 and 9 (which examine diversity in academic disciplines), and in Chapters 11 and 12 (which examine institutional cultures). Studies in contrastive rhetoric (e.g. Kaplan, 1966; Connor, 1996) have revealed the extent to which preferred conventions in one culture may run counter to those in another, and Lea and Street (this volume) document how such differences can operate in university settings.

Since the written form of a language may be kept constant, while its spoken form is in a process of ongoing change, many societies use written language as a tangible link with their past. Ferguson (1966: 432) has noted how in Greece the H variety *katharévusa* is identified with the New Testament and when a translation of the New Testament appeared in the L variety, *dhimotikí*, in 1903, serious rioting broke out. In many cases the identification with a valued past lies not only in the variety but in the orthography used to put it into writing. Although the linguistic differences between the language spoken by Serbs and that spoken by Croats in the former Yugoslavia are minimal, the Serbs write with Cyrillic script, underlining their identification with Byzantium, while the Croats use Roman script, stressing their identification with Rome, and it was seen necessary in the Yugoslav constitution (Article 246) to recognize the right of citizens to different alphabets (DEYA, 1983: 8). On the other hand, other cases have been documented where one writing system has been replaced with another for political purposes (Stubbs, 1980: 82; Smolicz, 1995: 154).

In Adelaide, the Nunga people, among whom there has been significant language shift to English, have shown a preference for orthographies which will make their languages look different from English (Gale, 1992: 43). There have been a number of attempts to introduce Romanized spelling for Chinese, but the attraction of the logographic system, which identifies all Chinese as one, has meant that the alternative scripts have not gained widespread acceptance (Stubbs, 1980: 85–86). It is clear that written language is significantly used by many groups as a means of asserting or maintaining cultural differentiation.

Writing and the linguistic ecology of indigenous cultures

Writing is not an area of cultural focus in all societies. Some societies have had little significant contact with writing, and others with the opportunity to adopt the written word have shown little desire to do so. Street (1993) and Lewis (1993) cite, for example, the case of the Somalis, who, exposed to Arabic as a written language through the Islamic religion, did not seek to extend Somali to written functions. Even after the introduction of widespread mother-tongue literacy, they maintained a strong oral tradition.

Languages have been compared to natural species in that their ongoing existence is dependent on the maintenance of a balanced 'language ecology' or socio-cultural environment in which they may carry on the functions to which they are adapted (Haugen, 1972; Smolicz, 1995: 155; Mühlhäusler, 1996). In the case of the Somalis, the maintenance of a range of oral forms has been possible because of the resistance to the encroachments of written language on domains which are traditionally oral. In many other cultures, significant erosion of traditional culture has occurred following the adoption of literacy. This has been documented in particular with respect to the Pacific, where up to 4,000 languages are spoken (Mühlhäusler, 1996; Topping, 1992).

The terms *oral cultures* and *literate cultures* may be used in a number of ways. The terms are used here to distinguish those cultures which are oriented primarily towards the use of oral language, either because they do not possess a written form (i.e. what Ong, 1982, calls *primary oral cultures*) or because they retain an oral orientation while still having access to the written form and existing within the wider context of complex literate societies (i.e. what Ogbu, 1987, calls *residual oral cultures*). A number of writers have suggested that oral and literate cultures are associated with different values and different associated social practices. For example, Eggington (1992: 92–93) has suggested that communication carries different 'power values' depending on whether it takes place against the background of an oral or a literate culture. He argues for example that, in literate cultures, decision-making power rests with institutions whereas in oral cultures it rests with people, and that in literate cultures the truth value of the spoken word is not as high as in oral cultures because the final message is that which appears in writing. Topping (1992: 29) has contrasted literate and oral (or, non-literate, as he calls them) societies on a list of traits with respect to which they have contrasting values, including religion, history, literature, law, information storage and modes of thinking. Oral cultural values inevitably are threatened when a culture is introduced to writing for the first time.

In 1972 the Australian government adopted a bilingual education policy for Aboriginal schools in the Northern Territory. This decision led within ten years to 12 Aboriginal languages becoming media of instruction in primary schools which had been hitherto operating monolingual English programmes. Some, though not all, of the schools in the bilingual programme adopted a model of bilingual education which included the establishment of initial literacy in the Aboriginal language, followed by the transfer of the literacy skills to English (while the others involved only oral use of the vernacular). The impact of the introduction of these programmes on the primary oral cultures into which they were introduced was wide-ranging. It entailed intensive involvement of community members with linguists and educators in developing linguistic descriptions of the languages (where such descriptions did not already exist), working on the conceptual development of the indigenous languages to enable them to be used in the educational domain, agreeing on the ways in which concepts not common to the indigenous languages and English should be approached, determining orthographies, developing literacy materials, developing bilingual/ bicultural curricula and teaching approaches and training teachers and support workers for their roles in implementing the programmes. A new range of roles emerged, as many as possible of which were to be filled by community members: teacher-linguists, linguistic and cultural consultants, Aboriginal teachers and assistant teachers, literacy workers, community developers and specialist teacher educators.

Apart from the social impact of the modification of occupational roles within the communities and the intensive involvement of Aboriginal workers alongside non-Aboriginal personnel in teaching and production teams, these developments had a linguistic impact. Language is highly sensitive to setting and function, and the introduction of indigenous languages into the school setting meant that certain functions were extended, others displaced. The development of literacy materials commonly involved the gathering of oral literature from within the community and the transfer of this into written mode. But written literature is not simply oral literature written down. Commenting on the use of oral literature for literacy materials in another, but parallel, context, Nichols (1996: 209) has noted:

> When such differences in oral styles are transmitted into written form, the patterns of the European-American child will be 'privileged' in the typical classroom environment. His distanced, public discourse, which relies on less interaction and less prior knowledge of persons and places known to the storyteller, is topic-centered and thus in the style preferred for most formal classroom writing. He will have an easier time transferring his oral style to the preferred written style than will the African-American boy, whose approach to

his story is more personal and requires greater audience participation and knowledge of the characters involved. More important, the African-American boy reflects a preference for narrative discourse that leaves the audience to draw its own conclusions about the meaning of the narrative . . .

The artistic productions of oral and literate cultures are different, and although oral genres yield material which meets the requirement of relevance for students in a literacy programme, they may lose their authenticity and power when transferred to writing and fail to take advantage of the different possibilities of expression which are specific to the written mode. Eckert (1982), a linguist working with Wik-Munkan speakers, has described a methodology which was developed to overcome the problem of the stylistic differences between oral and written texts. It involved the bilingual literacy worker in separately orally translating a story to a live audience of children, then, later producing a written translation of the same story and comparing the two versions. On the basis of this comparison, the literacy worker progressively built up a version which combined the requirements of the written form with the need to capture some of the 'aliveness' of the oral style.

Although bilingual education programmes may be agreed to by indigenous communities as a means of supporting and lending greater status to their languages, they may in fact be seen to have the opposite effect if, as is the case in the programmes we have been discussing, the intention is to facilitate transfer to literacy in English as soon as possible (Folds, 1989: 43).

Groups whose language has no tradition of use in the written form may have an ambivalent attitude towards the introduction of literacy. While the written form of the language has no part in their cultural tradition, they may yet see it as a necessary part of the assertion of the parity of their language with those which *do* have a written form. On the other hand, they may be wary of the power of the written word to be destructive of their traditional values. It is useful to distinguish between the *adoption* and the *vernacularization* of literacy (Carrington, 1997: 83–84).

The adoption of literacy by a group may mean that their language will be used to serve purposes other than their own, whereas the vernacularization of literacy implies that the group acquire literacy for their own purposes. McKay (1982) describes a study of the attitudes towards literacy of members of an Australian Aboriginal community in Maningrida when the possibility of the introduction of bilingual education into their schools was being explored. Reporting on the views of speakers of the language Kunibidji, McKay notes that 85% of the population wanted to see literacy developed in the language, but their reasons were ' "intrinsic" or "affective" rather than "extrinsic" or "instrumental" or utilitarian' (McKay, 1982: 111). Being able to write their language was associated by them with enhancing the power and prestige of the language, rather than fulfilling any of the practical purposes which might be relevant to users of other written languages. They were, then, in favour of the vernacularization rather than the adoption of literacy. It has been suggested that often indigenous minority groups within modern nation states may see the written word in their own vernacular as incapable of achieving what can be achieved through the dominant language and that 'lack of hope of sovereignty and resignation to the adoption of an alternate tongue would inhibit the pursuit of literacy through their vernacular' (Carrington, 1997: 86).

Another problem arises where literacy is being imparted to speakers of a non-standard dialect. Because of the low prestige of the dialect in the wider community, its representation in written form may be interpreted as undignified, or even as a put down. Such may be the stigma associated with the dialect that works using it may be denied publication, or, if published, they may suffer censure from reviewers (as in the case of Shaw, 1984). This being the case, the use of the dialect in written form in school contexts may be discouraged, not only by teachers but by community members who speak it on the assumption that the school's task should be to eradicate it rather than build on it to extend the child's repertoire.

Some communities, while valuing their languages and seeing the importance of reading and writing, may give little support to bilingual programmes. It has been reported that Kriol speakers in the Northern Territory, although having access to bilingual education, may still identify written communication with English (Rhydwen, 1993: 161). Similarly, in homeland schools in central Australia, despite the provision of bilingual education, community members have expressed the view that English competence is the responsibility of the school and that Pitjantjatjara can be learned by their children in the community. In this case, the dissatisfaction with the literacy programme in Pitjantjatjara stems from concern that the language has been taught to their children by non-indigenous teachers whose teaching, because it derives from an inadequate cultural background, actually results in a breaking down of socio-cultural domains maintained in the community:

> Usually it was the Pitjantjatjara language that was placed in an English context sometimes producing a situation where languages were not only intermixed but cultural differences between *anangu* and whites were ignored.   (Folds, 1989: 41)

One of the main dangers seen by communities whose languages are being included in literacy programmes is that they may lose control over those languages. For example, the Kriol-speaking people at Ngukurr in the Northern Territory had not introduced a literacy programme although one had already been developed in Kriol in Barunga. The community's reason was that the differences between the variety of Kriol spoken by them and by the people in Barunga, while minor, were to them significant markers of identity and they did not want a literacy programme in which they would not have control over the production of literature. The idea of standardizing written Kriol was strongly opposed. The view was that a standardized Kriol would be nobody's dialect yet everyone would be able to read it (Rhydwen, 1993: 162). It is clear that non-literate communities may be well aware of the problem attributed by Street (1995: 135) to the idea of an autonomous model of literacy, that is, that some literacies become dominant and others are marginalized.

The effect of writing upon language

The introduction of writing into a society not only changes the culture: it changes the language as well. Writing, to be sustained, makes different demands on the linguistic system than speaking does. It requires devices for overcoming the absence of situational and paralinguistic cues to meaning; it requires the means to make meanings accessible to an audience the degree of whose knowledge shared with the writer may be unknown; it requires appropriate ways of exploiting different kinds of interpretative skills which come into play when the receiver of the communication is able to recover the text from means other than memory. Written language is language adapted to different circumstances of production and to different functions, therefore it constitutes a different variety of the language from the spoken form.

Interestingly, however, access to the written form brings about changes in the way people behave even in oral communicative settings. Many of us in a literate society depend on writing to 'catch' new words (like names) which we have heard orally. Until we see them in writing, we are not sure that we know them. Similarly, when we want to be absolutely sure that we have an agreement with another party, our society, if it is literate, expects us to trust the written rather than the spoken word. The written word tends to carry authority over the spoken in a number of respects: we turn to books (dictionaries and usage manuals) to settle arguments over how people should speak or write; we even sometimes adjust our pronunciation to make it conform to the way we write, as in the case of words like *often* and *forehead* (Stubbs, 1980).

It has been suggested that 'writing systems provide the concepts and categories for thinking about the structure of language rather than the reverse' (Olson, 1994: 68). Often, too, we regulate our speech intertextually, bringing our ways of speaking into line with authoritative written sources, as when, for example, expressions such as *value added* and *quality control* are adopted from commercial contexts and used in motivational oral discourse by leaders in non-commercial areas. A similar tendency is the move towards expressing dates orally in the way they occur on the page in official documents, e.g. *July 31*, instead of *the 31ˢᵗ of July*. The written word also enters profoundly into how people entertain themselves (Willinsky, 1991: 257) and how they carry out corporate worship. As Stubbs (1980: 30) has put it, 'in a literate society, the written language takes on a life of its own'.

The differences between spoken and written language have been related by Chafe (1982) to basic differences in the processes of speaking and writing. The first of these is a difference in the speed of production. Chafe points out that we write more than 10 times more slowly than we speak, so, unlike speech, which is comprised of idea units produced in spurts and bounded by pauses, writing uses many devices which have the effect of moulding a succession of ideas into an integrated whole, such as nominalizations, participles, attributive adjectives, sequences of prepositional phrases and various kinds of clauses. The effect of this is that there is more information per idea unit in writing than in speech. The second important difference is in the fact that the process of speech involves more obviously direct interaction with an audience. Hyland, in this volume, shows why we might not wish to distinguish too rigidly between 'impersonal writing' and 'interactive speech' – spoken language tends to be characterized by features which emphasize greater involvement and self-reference than writing.

It is, however, possible to overemphasize the differences between oral and written language, especially if we focus purely on structural features. Reading and writing, as Roberts and Street (1997: 168) have stressed, are not so much technical skills as 'social practices embedded in power structures.' In many ways, in the context of social life, the 'great divide' between oral and written language, sometimes assumed by educators, may not be in evidence. Rather, oral and literate modes may be characterized by overlap and interaction (Street, 1995: 29). As Edwards and Sienkewicz (1990: 6) have observed,

> the written word does not divide so much as the spoken word unites the aliterate and the literate; that is, the presence of literacy does not remove all trace of orality, nor must an oral culture always function independently of literacy.

When a culture has developed over many millennia as a context in which all communication is oral, it can be expected to have built up a repertoire of oral expressive genres and communicative behaviours of considerable subtlety. Muecke (1983: 76) has illustrated from Aboriginal men's narratives from the Kimberley region, Western Australia, how dialogue in the narration (which typically occurs without introduction) functions to achieve two ends:

> A listener of Aboriginal stories is positioned in at least two ways. Firstly as a new person following a retelling of a 'true' story where the narrator retraces once more the words of the original participants, and secondly as a participant who must respond actively during the telling of the story . . . The listener is thus linked, personally, via previous narrators . . . to the actual event.

The written form loses the immediacy which this kind of dramatic exploitation of the relationship between speaker and hearer achieves. Shaw (1984: 48), also working on recording Aboriginal narratives from the Kimberley region, has discussed something of the complexity of the stylistic conventions employed, and pointed out that to attempt to reproduce the stories in a fully explicit way would result in a translation looking 'not unlike a radio or television script'. Some of the conventions include 'hand movements, the making of non-verbal sounds (e.g. rasping) . . . the "silent language" of unspoken cues and gestures or the markers in speech of tone, inflection, exclamation, etc. . . . tongue clicks, hand claps, dramatic pauses, interrogatives, eye and body contact, mime, tapping with the finger or a twig for emphasis, drawing lines in the dust, and indications of direction and distance'. The translator, or the narrator, if seeking to employ the written mode, is faced with a diminished repertoire of expressive devices. It is questionable whether such communication as this can survive translation into the written mode.

A similar view was reached by Cataldi (1994) in reviewing a collection of transcriptions of Aboriginal song poems. The words in isolation seemed no longer to communicate, because the communication was inherently oral and holistic, involving music, dance and a living context. The songs, as Cataldi saw them, were not separable from the wider text of which they were a part, the text of the Dreaming, which the song evoked but could not contain.

Ariss (1988: 139) has used the expression *fixation into writing* to refer to the process whereby oral literature is qualitatively changed and, we might say, fossilized, when divorced from the interactional nature of its performance. He has also noted how the oral style, if reproduced with minimal change, yields printed text which can be subject to criticism by readers as rambling, repetitive and confusing.

Another of the effects of writing upon language is that it is associated with standardization. If a language is to be used as a written medium of communication, much of its variation must be lost or suppressed. Oral societies, as Mühlhäusler (1996: 214) has pointed out, 'can tolerate any amount of dialectal variation, [but] literacy requires the standardization of "languages" with preferably above 1,000 speakers'. Standardization, then, is destructive of some of the richness of linguistic variety. It does, however, give hope of maintenance for languages and may lead to other action in the interests of language maintenance on the part of speakers of endangered languages (Gale, 1992: 45).

Extending a language to written mode also involves the determination of an orthography. The most important consideration in determining an orthography is that it be acceptable to the community who use the language. If possible, it should also be compatible with orthographies being used for closely related languages, since it is likely that speakers may be, or become, biliterate in their own and related languages. It should also, as far as possible, provide for the expression of as many as possible of the relevant variants (McGregor, 1988). Decisions on orthographies need to be made with due consultation. Once an orthography is fixed, it is likely to exercise a powerful influence over the speakers of the language. (See, e.g., Widdowson [1994: 380]).

The development of orthographies and the standardization of one variety lead inevitably towards inequality, because, of necessity, not everybody's variety becomes standard. Literacy, then, brings selective benefits to members of formerly oral cultures. As Mühlhäusler (1996: 213) has pointed out, it privileges those who know metropolitan languages and the local language varieties which are made literate, and in so doing, it also helps to create communicative inequality and breaks down the natural linguistic heterogeneity of societies.

One of the losses brought about by reducing speech to writing is that of the individuality of the speaker. This point was made by Haugen (1972: 164), who argued that the process of editing, analysis, delay and stabilization which would accompany the process of reducing even one person's speech to writing would transform it into another medium which could be used in a wider public domain. This process is multiplied many times over when the language of many speakers is reduced to writing. The written form which results was called by Haugen the grapholect, and this pervades both written and oral varieties of English, particularly in educational contexts.

The relationship between written and spoken language and thought

Do members of oral and literate cultures think differently? It has been widely argued that, in keeping with the linguistic differences which separate them, members of oral and literate cultures have different characteristic thought patterns, the former favouring particularism and the latter, abstraction. A more recent view (Connor, 1996: 102–104) would be that such a designation of oral and literate cultures risks stereotyping them and is not consistently borne out by research, although it is arguable that written language, with the devices it provides for talking about text, does facilitate certain kinds of text-based talk and thought (Olson and Astington, 1990: 712).

Mühlhäusler (1996: 213) has claimed that, with respect to the Pacific, the introduction of literacy 'led to a conceptual restructuring as evidenced, for instance, in societal views of time. Instead of cyclic concepts of time, the metaphor of time as an arrow and the associated notions of progress began to emerge. Human actions, consequently, were not determined by seeking harmony with natural cycles but by emulating artificial, human-made goals or utopias'. However, Street (1995: 109) has drawn attention to ethnographic work from many cultures which have long possessed systems of writing outside of the Western context and which have taken advantage of introduced literacies to add to their repertoire for their own purposes. He has also suggested that the introduction of modern literacy may weaken, rather than strengthen, certain 'kinds of sensibility and scepticism that may have been fostered in oral tradition'.

Whatever thought-related differences may exist between oral cultures and literate cultures may equally well distinguish groups speaking the same language within the same society, as Connor (1996) has pointed out with reference to the work of Heath.

The effect of writing upon the individual

Newly literate groups do not necessarily take on board with literacy the goals and values of the literacy providers. Rather, 'as literacy is added to the rich communicative repertoire that already exists in the receiving societies, they adapt and amend it to local meanings, concepts of identity, and epistemologies' (Street, 1995: 109). Some groups may give evidence of a whole repertoire of literacies of which the kind acquired through the school system is but one and perhaps not the most central (cf. Gee, 1990). Others, having acquired literacy through formal education, apply it in distinctive ways. For example, Goddard (1990) analysed the uses to which Pitjantjatjara-speaking adults put their written language and concluded that the effect of acquiring literacy had been quite different from that anticipated by school planners. He described the kind of writing which was commonest in the community as *message-based writing*, and observed that, for these people, the proper medium for traditional literature and knowledge remained oral, while the written form was valued principally as a 'technology of communication' (Goddard, 1990: 31).

In particular, he observed that, as community members contributed to newspapers and magazines which had sprung up in response to community need, they were creating new written genres to serve their purposes, in particular genres of *reportage* (distinctive for their personalized and involved style and their integration of fact and comment) and *advocacy* (distinctive for their two-part structure, didactic approach and employment of particular rhetorical strategies). Another central Australian group, the Diyari, were reported by Mühlhäusler (1996: 232) to be using the vernacular literacy which Lutheran missionaries had introduced to them principally for the message-based forms of 'sending messages and writing letters', as well as (by native catechists and evangelists) for religious purposes.

The need to be able to read and write one's language may not be the most urgent language-related need recognized by many indigenous groups. The primary need is to maintain one's identity, and, with the loss of indigenous languages occurring at an alarming rate such that perhaps only 10% of those currently spoken will survive to the year 2100 (McKay, 1996: xxv), the first priority of many groups may be to *keep* their language rather than to extend its functions to writing. McKay (1996: xxvii), in a recent survey of Australian Aboriginal language maintenance, protested that there is 'too much emphasis on literacy in the indigenous language and, even worse . . . too much reliance on vernacular literacy alone to achieve the goal of language maintenance'. Sadly, there is evidence that the introduction of vernacular literacy has further endangered the indigenous language in some places in that the shift to literacy in the vernacular has been followed by a shift from literacy in the vernacular to literacy in the dominant metropolitan language (Mühlhäusler, 1996: 228).

Although there is not a necessary link between writing in the vernacular and identity maintenance, there may be a perceived link, and, where this is the case, the community may well embrace vernacular literacy for this reason rather than for the reasons put forward by political or educational administrators (as exemplified, in Northern and South Australia, in Gale [1992: 42]).

It is possible to distinguish two kinds of writing, each of which may have contrasting effects on the life of the individual. One kind is described by Willinsky (1991: 256) under the name *popular literacy* and is characterized by sharing the written word as a social experience, focusing on expression rather than correctness and emphasizing performance and publication. This approach to writing, which Willinsky sees as having long-standing cultural roots in English-speaking society, contrasts with that which he associates with public schooling and which, perhaps by implication, could be seen for many as *unpopular literacy*!

The first kind of literacy is controlled by the participants and operates on principles of inclusion. The second kind of literacy is controlled by institutions and operates on principles of exclusion. The latter is associated primarily with languages of wider distribution and commonly performs a *gatekeeper* function (McKay and Weinstein-Shr, 1993: 401–402). In recent times it has been used to regulate immigration and citizenship, movement through education systems, and access to employment. It gives selective recognition to people's ability to read and write, since these skills may be regarded as irrelevant unless in the standard or official language. It tends to be offered within education systems in the language of the state rather than the language of the learner, leading, for many second language learners in school systems, to what has been described as 'semi-literacy' (Smolicz, 1995: 161). It associates writing with success or failure in relation to externally prescribed norms rather than with the functions which it can perform for the individual.

These two perspectives on writing have been reflected, especially in the Australian scene, in two opposing traditions with respect to the ways in which writing should be taught in schools. These can be represented, perhaps rather starkly, as oriented towards facilitating either authentic expression of personal meanings (the *process approach*), or as equipping students to communicate with the gatekeepers of society (the *genre approach*). (See further, on this debate, e.g. Richardson [1991], Walton [1990] and Edwards [1992]). A more recent development has been the focus on 'multiliteracies' (e.g. van Harskamp-Smith and van Harskamp-Smith, 1994), which shifts the perspective more to the indigenous persons' assessment of the roles which literacy performs in their contemporary lives and raises the question as to why non-acquisition of literacy may be 'an act of resistance on the part of the indigenous student' (p. 107).

Writing and the negotiation of cultural identity

Writing, as we have seen, when introduced into a society, changes it and its language. In a study of numerous non-literate communities into which writing has been introduced in relatively recent times, Mühlhäusler (1996: 234) identified five effects which could be expected to ensue:

1. Linguistic diversity is lost.
2. Vernacular literacy is transitional.
3. Literacy brings about conceptual change.
4. Literacy leads to social restructuring.
5. Literacy is seen to reflect truth.

From the point of view, then, of members of non-literate communities, the prospect of adopting writing is associated with a significant threat to cultural identity. The benefits of writing may be less tangible to them than the potential it brings for destruction of what they value. Where communities have not yet encountered the written form, at least in their vernacular languages, they may seek to maintain the status quo. In the case of residual oral cultures, where the written form has been acquired, there may be strong community-based norms which influence the ways in which written language is interpreted and used.

The established norms of written discourse, as indigenous and other people of minority culture encounter them in educational institutions and in the media, may often make it difficult, if not impossible, for them to participate in that discourse. The perspective is one in which they become invisible. The *subject position* in the narrative is always assumed by the other party (Muecke, 1983: 72). A similar experience has been reported by English-speaking members of post-colonial societies in Asia: the discourse of education and learning is colonialist discourse (Yahya, 1994). The '"grand narratives" of Eurocentric discourse' (Morgan, 1993: 4) position them on the margins, or else ignore them altogether.

In the face of this situation, one option might be to withdraw from the discourse of the written word altogether and to identify only with the local group. However, this becomes difficult when compulsory education, mass communication media and necessary interactions with public service providers bring this written discourse regularly into the lives of most families. Alternative strategies are, then, called for, which will enable the discourse to be resisted and used at the same time.

One way in which this may be done is through adopting the written genres in existence in the dominant society and using them to express views which do not resonate with that society. Thus we may have a situation described by Morgan (1993: 5) as 'hybridity' or 'syncreticity', where 'the suppressed knowledge of a subordinate group infiltrates and alters the discourse of a dominant group'. Alternatively, an oppositional discourse may be developed which openly reinterprets the dominant colonialist or exclusionist discourse (Yahya, 1994). Members of the 'object' group may, through the written word, assume 'subject' position and review the ways in which their history or their cultural and artistic products have been dealt with in the words of the dominant. This may sometimes involve putting people right as to how written discourse should be used to treat cultural subjects, as, for example, in the following closing words of a review by Rankine (1994: 73):

> One thing I have found wrong with the book is that I do not think personal stories should be printed; for example, the story on p. 92 – 'Birth in the bush', told by Daisy Thompson. This is because it is against our Kaytetye law for women's business to be told to men, and any men can pick up this book and read about this women's business.

Another strategy, especially in the context of education, is to negotiate more equal terms for the social construction of knowledge. Educational failure is perhaps commonly attributed to factors relating to the mechanics of teaching and learning when it is not failure at all, from the point of view of the learners, but successful resistance to learning packaged in an unacceptable cultural frame. If learners have, or are treated as if they have, a 'castelike minority' status, they cannot be expected to learn (Ogbu, 1987). An alternative to this is to give equal respect to the cultural frames which the learners, on the one hand, and the school, on the other, have an interest in maintaining.

It is possible to illustrate some of the points we have been making by reference to a project which was carried out in 1995–96 at Edith Cowan University in Perth, Western Australia (Malcolm and Rochecouste, 1997). The project, which was concerned only with Aboriginal and Torres Strait Islander students, formed part of a national study looking at the framing of literacy in higher education. Over a period of a year a researcher spent time as a non-participant observer with Aboriginal students in classrooms and in their Student Centre. All 359 indigenous students enrolled in the university were invited to participate in the project, which involved, in addition to the observation of literacy events, the analysis of writing samples and the elicitation of data on attitudes to literacy by questionnaire and interview.

A major objective of the study was to enable literacy events of the university to be described both with respect to the way in which they were structured by lecturers and with respect to the way the indigenous students participated in them. The concept *literacy event* was interpreted, after Anderson *et al.* (1980: 59), as referring to 'any action sequence, involving one or more persons, in which the production and/or comprehension of print plays a role', and thus it embraced both interactional events such as tutorials and lectures and individual events such as the writing of essays and examination papers.

It was observed that the educational experiences in which the students participated were characterized by pervasive use of the grapholect, synchronization of participation, decontextualized language and assessment, all of which conflicted with features of community-based communication among Aboriginal people, which is, characteristically, oral, communal rather than dyadic in inter-actional patterns, contextualized and designed to avoid causing people 'shame' or conflict by overtly evaluating their contributions.

In class, students frequently showed resistance to the language they were expected by the lecturers to use, for example sometimes 'translating' from the grapholect into their oral-based register, sometimes failing to respond to lecturer elicitations, sometimes switching from decontextualized to contextualized language and sometimes simply refusing to express things the way the lecturer wanted (as, for example, in the comment 'I don't like that word. I don't use it').

Interpreting the behaviours of students and lecturers accord-ing to Frame Theory (MacLachlan and Reid, 1994), it was observ-able that the framing of the literacy events was constantly under negotiation between lecturer and students. The lecturers, through the way in which they patterned the discourse and worded their speech acts, would set up what they saw as an appropriate frame for the event. However, the students frequently called the frame into question, either by querying or rejecting the expectations the lecturer was making of them, or by counter-framing by imposing community-based (as opposed to institution-based) expectations on the event, either by marked style shifts, or by non-compliance with the discourse role allocated to them.

The comments of the students in interview frequently revealed the cross-cultural linguistic conflict in which they were engaged in the lecture or tutorial setting:

(a) 'it took me a fair while to come to grips with all the talk and all that sort of stuff'
(b) 'It is a totally different language from what you use outside, the campus, to what you use inside. Um you can't, you have to learn to live 2 different languages, one when you go outside and when you are at home and one when you are here.'
(c) 'Yes, I don't like writing a lot. When I say I don't like writing, I don't like writing the Wadjela [non-Aboriginal] writing. It's too long and it gets boring. And there's too many whys, and whom and where and whens all in there.'

Some of the comments also reflect the students' school experiences, which, it seems, they are determined not to have occur again at the university:

(d) 'So you were a Nyungar kid you sat at the back at school, you kept your mouth shut. At home because there was a whole heap of us, a whole heap of kids, we weren't encouraged to study.'
(e) 'I liked history but I had a lot of conflict with the teacher because we were learning European history and nothing that related to me as an Aboriginal person. I grew up not knowing anything about Aboriginal history and I didn't realise I was Aboriginal until I went to high school.'

The students' writing was interpretable on the basis of the same analysis as their participation in the oral (but grapholect-based) discourse of the lecture room. The frames which academic writing imposes on the student were frequently contested in the ways in which the students expressed themselves. Chafe's linguistic markers of written language (referred to earlier) were taken as contextual cues which specify the frame expected of the writer. Rather than complying with the requirement to frame their written discourse this way, the students frequently either negotiated or imposed alternative frames. For example, students tended to resist the requirement to reduce ego involvement and use detachment strategies and they frequently made intratextual switches to non-academic discourse.

Despite the resistance of students to the use of the grapholect in speech and in writing, a comparison of written work over the three years of university study showed that on most of Chafe's identifying features of written discourse the second- and third-year students were significantly ahead of the first-year students. This encouraging sign must, however, be interpreted in the light of the fact that there is considerable student attrition from year to year. Many students, rather than acquiring the accepted discourse of academic writing, made a premature exit from their studies.

Writing and the maintenance of cultural diversity

Writing is, then, we conclude, many things for many people. It is, for some, a bridge between mutually incomprehensible forms of speech; for others it is a means of emphasizing the differences in identity between people who speak much the same way. Writing can improve people's life chances: it can also destroy people's cultural identity. Writing is an instrument of empowerment; it is also a tool for discrimination against the powerless. Writing is a contested human resource and needs to be equitably managed.

Where diverse cultures come together within one society it has been the practice to identify the language of the more powerful group as the standard and expect speech and writing to conform to it. Increasingly in the present day, the legitimacy of this practice is being questioned. Vested interests are threatened when it is suggested (as in a debate which captured national attention in the USA in 1997) that the dialect of English spoken by a group which has inferior access to power is a 'language' in its own right. However, there is much evidence that, unless education in the written language is made more accessible to non-standard dialect users without doing violence to their linguistically based sense of identity, it will not succeed.

A fair way of dealing with cultural and linguistic diversity will acknowledge the value of such diversity and find ways of providing for cross-cultural communication without cross-cultural domination. Writing does not have to confront a person's linguistic variety or culture, although in schools and universities it often does. The principle of 'both ways' education (see, e.g., Eggington, 1992), applied hitherto mainly to education in remote settings where indigenous people have the numbers to demand a degree of control over the education system, should be applied more widely to replace the view which tacitly assumes that the normative educational environment is monolingual and monocultural. A similar concept, again deriving from indigenous sources, is that of *coming up together*, applied by Folds (1989: 45) to a genuinely balanced bilingual education in which one knowledge base is not allowed to proceed faster than the other. Writing can coexist with the maintenance of cultural diversity if the principle of coming up together can be followed and differences can be negotiated rather than denied. Until this can be done, the costs associated with the acquisition of writing skills will be greater than people of subordinated cultures will be likely to pay.

PART III

Explanation: focus on research

7

Informal elements in English academic writing: threats or opportunities for advanced non-native speakers?

YU-YING CHANG AND JOHN M. SWALES

Introduction

Anglophonicity has become a hallmark of the contemporary academic and scientific world. Many journals that used to publish in major languages such as German, French or Russian have been converting to English; the great majority of the many new journals are unabashedly anglophone; and in many countries tenure and promotion is increasingly tied to English-language publication. This trend toward English dominance has recently been both celebrated (Crystal, 1997) and critiqued (Swales, 1997). Irrespective of the merits of these arguments, most non-native speaker (NNS) academics and faculty are fully aware of the encroachment of English on their national academic cultures and of its consequences for them as individuals. However, there is another, if more patchily distributed, less recognized, contemporary trend that may further add to the compositional burden of the non-native speaker of English. This is the shift away from standard formal and impersonal styles of academic writing to ones that allow more personal comment, narration and stylistic variation. It is with this latter development that this chapter is concerned.

We first attempt a detailed but circumscribed linguistic analysis of certain 'informal elements' in academic writing, such as using imperatives, employing *I* or starting sentences with *but*. We then study NNS reactions to these usages. Like our colleagues elsewhere in this volume, especially those in Chapters 3 and 9, we draw upon a range of methodologies for these connected tasks. The stylistic investigations in Section I involve not only textual analysis, but also surveys of writing manuals, as well as face-to-face text-based interviews with research article authors and e-mail interviews with their journal editors. The data source for Section II consisted of 37 NNS graduate students, visiting scholars and an associate professor taking either a Research Paper or Dissertation Writing class at the University of Michigan in 1997. Informant reactions to the stylistic features discussed in Section I were elicited through a combination of recorded class discussion, e-mail follow-up interviews, and questionnaires. The fact that most of these NNS informants expressed considerable sensitivity to English-language grammatical and rhetorical choices once again points to the social constructionist nature of academic writing, as also discussed in Chapters 2, 5, 8, 9 and 12.

I   Stylistic investigation

Motivation and background

We approached the issue of 'informal' style from somewhat different perspectives from each other. The first author, an NNS doctoral candidate in linguistics, often finds that stylistic appropriateness rather than grammatical correctness is more of an issue for her as an academic writer in English. She was also confused by the discrepancies she found between the prescriptive advice contained in writing manuals and textbooks and the actual language usages detected in her academic reading. She further discovered that other NNS, often from different academic disciplines, shared her perplexity. The second author, the instructor for the two advanced writing courses, was dissatisfied with the teaching materials that dealt with such matters as the appropriateness (or otherwise) of using certain verbs in the imperative form, or when and where it might be appropriate to begin a sentence with *but*.

Moreover, we both found that the literature in applied linguistics and English for Academic Purposes (EAP) is not very helpful. Apparently, few investigators have attempted to explore discrepancies between prescriptive rules and descriptive practices in scholarly or professional writing. Among the traceable studies, two focused on macro-level investigations, i.e. the introduction (Swales and Najjar, 1987) and the organization of research articles (Harmon and

Gross, 1996). All the others provided justifications of the use of *a single* linguistic feature which had been discouraged or castigated in most writing manuals and handbooks (Huckin *et al.*, 1986; Huckin and Pesante, 1988; Rodman, 1991; Meyers, 1990).

It thus seems that no researcher has so far attempted to study how scholars in different disciplinary communities might violate, on suitable occasions, one or more of *a cluster of* prescribed lexico-syntactic 'stylistic rules'. If patterns of non-compliance could be found, this might provide useful information about the stylistic conventions deemed acceptable in particular disciplines (cf. Chapters 5, 6 and 9). Therefore, it was our hope that, through a careful and integrated examination of the handbooks, corpus and interview data collected from manual writers, journal editors, and research article (RA) authors, we could not only detect some mismatches between the prescriptive rules and expert practices, but, at the same time, reach a more appropriate understanding of disciplinary stylistic preferences. It was not our intention, however, to provide an in-depth analysis of the rhetorical functions of these features in this investigation.

Manuals survey

To compile a list of the most frequent *rules of appropriateness*[1] for English scholarly writing to be used as the basis of data analysis in this study, a survey of 40 style manuals and writing guidebooks was conducted. We focused specifically on what the guidebooks teach about how to employ *specific grammatical features* to attain an appropriate degree of formality. The sample surveyed covered manuals and guidebooks published from the 1960s to the 1990s. Roughly speaking, ten works from every decade were located. Among them, 3 were written for all varieties of formal writing; 7 were designed for student writers; 12 were style manuals for journal publication; the others (i.e. the majority), aimed specifically to serve professional or professorial writers of technical, scientific or academic English. Of the 40 texts examined, only 25 (7 in the 1960s, 7 in the 1970s, 5 in the 1980s and 6 in the 1990s) made some mention of writing style. (The other 15 covered only rules pertaining to the mechanics of writing, such as rules of punctuation and citation.)

We put aside rules which are more trivial, such as the ones regulating only the usage of certain individual lexical items (e.g. *that* vs. *which, as* vs. *like*), and focused on more general rules which represent certain broad grammatical patterns or regulate specific groups of lexical items. We thus obtained the following list of the ten most frequently mentioned features (the numbers shown in the parentheses indicate the numbers of manuals or handbooks which commented on each given feature):

1. the use of the first person pronouns to refer to the author(s) (*I* and *we*) (15)

    e.g. '*I* will approach this issue in a roundabout way.'

2. broad reference (11) – anaphoric pronouns (namely, *this, these, that, those, it,* and *which*) that can refer to antecedents of varying length

    e.g. 'The artist composes, writes, or paints just as he dreams, seizing whatever swims close to his net. *This*, not the world seen directly, is his raw material.'

3. split infinitives (8) – an infinitive that has an adverb between *to* and the stem of the verb

    e.g. 'The president proceeded *to* sharply *admonish* the reporters who asked unanswerable questions.'

4. begin a sentence with ~ (conjunctions and the conjunctive adverb *however*) (5)

    e.g. '*And* I will blame her if she fails in these ways.'

5. end a sentence with a preposition (5)

    e.g. 'A student should not be taught more than he can think *about*.'

6. run-on sentences and expressions (4)

    e.g. 'These semiconductors can be used in robots, CD players, *etc.*'

7. sentence fragments (4) – sentences which miss an essential element (i.e. subject, verb or object)

    e.g. '*But not for want for trying.*'

8. contractions (3)

    e.g. 'Export figures *won't* improve until the economy is stronger.'

9. direct questions (2)

    e.g. '*What can be done to lower costs?*'

10. exclamations (2)

    e.g. '*So it turns out that the author is telling the readership (for now) to ignore the author's objections rather than any they might have of their own!*'

Scrutiny of these ten items reveals that they are all features associated with informal speech style. As many contrastive studies of spoken and written language have pointed out, the use of personal pronouns, direct questions and exclamations is frequent in spoken language because they can invoke personal involvement among participants (e.g. Biber, 1988; Chafe, 1982; Nash, 1986; Tannen, 1982). Sentence fragments and initial conjunctions, on the other hand, probably reflect the spoken language characteristics of fragmentation (e.g. Chafe, 1982, 1986; Lakoff, 1982). In addition, according to Chafe (1986a: 31), in speaking, 'speakers' lack of time to choose words carefully appears also in their use of inexplicit pronouns, usually "it", "this", and "that", referring not to a specific referent but to a vague complex of ideas'. Further, run-on expressions/sentences and contractions are also found to be typical in speaking (e.g. Chafe, 1986a; Nash, 1986).

Given the association between these ten features and informal language use, it is not surprising to find disagreement over the usage of several of these items among the authors of manuals and guidebooks. Depending on their personal perception of 'objective style' and formality, authors often take different positions with regard to the usage of certain grammatical constructions.

The results of the survey show that, except for the use of first person pronouns, there is no clear indication of any diachronic change. In general, although disagreement still existed among the manuals published in the 1960s and 1970s, those which were published after the 1980s tended to encourage the use of first person pronouns more overtly and rigorously. These authors concurred that the use of *I* and *we* does not itself make a piece of writing less formal or less objective. Similarly, the authors who commented on the ban of initial conjunctions all intended to free their readers from these shackles. At the present stage, it seems that, among the ten features, only the use of first person pronouns and sentence-initial conjunctions have already been 'legitimized' in English scientific/academic writing. On the other hand, run-on sentences/expressions, sentence fragments, contractions, direct questions and exclamations are still regarded as features that a careful writer should avoid. As for the usage of broad reference, split infinitives and final prepositions, disagreement still exists among those writers of manuals and guidebooks who commented on them.

Procedures

In Swales *et al.* (1998), we studied the use of imperative sentences in ten academic disciplines. In the conclusion, we suspected that the use of this linguistic feature might plausibly be connected with the contemporary trends toward informality in scholarly writing. We further suggested that the imperative sentence is only one element of a cluster of linguistic features which enable academic writers to decouple themselves from an 'objectivity-reifying impersonal style' (Swales *et al.*, 1998: 118). These speculations then led to the thought that we would be most likely to find various other kinds of informal features in those disciplines that used the most imperatives. Therefore, the scholarly disciplines selected for examination are the three disciplines where the highest frequencies of main-text imperatives were originally found: Statistics, Linguistics and Philosophy.

Ten papers,[2] all from the same journal, from each of the three disciplines[3] were scanned for imperatives and for the ten informal grammatical features listed above.[4] In each case, a single recent issue, in which at least one of the articles was written by a faculty member at the University of Michigan, was first located. The inclusion of the local authors facilitated follow-up interviews probing into their individual and disciplinary textual expectations. In addition, to uncover the extent of the probable editorial influences in the use of these features, several e-mail interviews with the editors of the three journals were also conducted.[5]

Results and discussion

An overview

The imperative sentence, whose use was acknowledged in only one of the 40 writing manuals and guidebooks surveyed (cf. Swales and Feak, 1994), was marked as acceptable by all the journal editors interviewed (Table 7.1). As Table 7.2 shows, it was also the only grammatical construction of those studied which was employed by all 30 authors, with a rather high frequency (639 occurrences in total). As for the other ten informal features, three of the four most often mentioned ones in our manuals survey – *first person pronoun, unattended 'this'* and *sentence-initial conjunctions* – were also found to be the most pervasive in the current corpus, all with a

Table 7.1　Editors' comments on the use of the Eleven Features

	Statistics	Linguistics 1*	Linguistics 2*	Philosophy
imperatives	o	o	o	o
personal pronouns				
(*I, we*)	o	o	o	o
unattended *this*	Æ	Æ	Æ	o
split infinitives	Æ	o	o	x
forbidden first words	o	o	o	o
final prepositions	x	o	o	x
run-on	Æ	Æ	x	o
sentence fragments	x	Æ	Æ	o
contractions	x	o	o	o
direct questions	o	o	o	o
exclamations	x	Æ	x	o

o = acceptable
x = unacceptable
Æ = allowable to an extent (depending on the context)
* Linguistics 1 was the editor of *Language* before 1995. Linguistics 2 is the current editor of *Language* (since 1995).

rather large number of occurrences. In contrast, the features tabulated in the lower part of Table 7.2 (i.e. features discussed less often in the manuals and textbooks surveyed) occurred far less frequently. *Final prepositions* and *sentence fragments* were used less than 50 times; the frequency of *exclamations* was especially low, only 6 occurrences in total.

The above results show that, except for *split infinitives* and *direct questions*, in general, among the ten infomal features, those which were mentioned more frequently in the writing manuals and guide-books also tended to have higher frequencies of total occurrences. This finding seems to reflect the tension between linguistic prescript-ivism and authorial practice. On the other hand, the reason why *split infinitives*, one of the four most frequently discussed features, appeared in the data only once is probably because of the editor-ial control in the Statistics and Philosophy journals (Table 7.1).

Interdisciplinary differences

Table 7.2 shows that Statistics was the field which had the highest frequency of the occurrence of main-text imperatives; Linguistics

Table 7.2 The use of the 11 grammatical features in the three disciplines

	Statistics		Linguistics		Philosophy		Total		
	No. of uses	No. of persons	No. of uses	No. of persons	No. of uses	No. of persons	No. of uses	No. of persons	% of persons
imperatives	285	10	264	10	90	10	639	30	100
I/my/me	29	4	307	9	684	10	1020	23	77
unsupported *this*	97	9	316	10	230	10	643	29	97
split infinitives	1	1	0	0	0	0	1	1	3
forbidden first words	57	7	229	10	446	10	732	27	90
initial *and*	1	1	16	6	120	10	137	17	57
initial *but*	15	5	102	8	232	10	349	23	77
initial *so*	14	3	21	4	44	8	79	15	50
initial *or*	1	1	3	2	24	8	28	10	33
initial *however*	26	7	87	7	26	6	139	19	63
final prepositions	3	2	20	8	21	9	44	19	63
run-on	6	2	28	8	21	5	55	15	50
sentence fragments	0	0	4	4	11	6	15	10	33
contractions	0	0	21	5	71	6	92	11	37
direct questions	9	3	62	8	153	9	224	17	57
exclamations	0	0	1	1	5	3	6	4	13

was second and Philosophy third. When these frequencies of imperatives were compared with the other grammatical features listed in Table 7.2, an intriguing correlation between the use of imperatives and the other ten grammatical features emerged. Philosophy, although it had the fewest occurrences of imperatives, was the field where the other ten informal grammatical features were used the most frequently. On the other hand, mathematical statisticians, who used the most imperatives, used the other ten features *far less frequently* than the authors from the other two disciplines. A further text analysis, however, reveals that although these philosophers used fewer imperatives than the statisticians and the linguists, they exhibited a higher degree of rhetorical flexibility in their use of imperatives: they manoeuvred more different types of imperative verbs (e.g. *concede, like, accept,* and *agree*), and embedded these verbs in more various, syntactic and textual contexts (cf. Chang, 1997).

Comparison of Tables 7.1 and 7.2 might initially suggest that the philosophers' greater 'license' could simply be a reflection of a more liberal editorial style, and the converse for Statistics. However, although editorial style can be shown to be a factor in the acceptability or otherwise of certain grammatical features, it does not account for all the data. A first sign of *intrinsic* disciplinary preference is the attitudes of the two editors of *Language* (Table 7.1). Although (at least to our knowledge) they had no previous discussion about the use of these grammatical items in their journal, they provided very similar responses to every one of the 11 features.

The other obvious phenomenon is that even when we focus only on the use of the features which all the journal editors considered to be quite acceptable in their journals – i.e. *first person pronouns, sentence-initial conjunctions* and *direct questions* – the previous frequency order remains. The scholars in Philosophy used them far more frequently than those in the other two disciplines; Linguistics was the second, but with a frequency much higher than that in Statistics for any of the three features. The distinction between the two extremes – Philosophy and Statistics – can be best seen from the large differences in their use of two linguistic constructions associated with degree of involvement – *I* and *direct questions* (cf. Biber, 1988; Chafe, 1982; Tannen, 1982; Hyland, this volume).

Given these results, it appears that the philosophers, by employing almost all the ten features the most frequently and manipulating imperative sentences in the most varied ways, exhibit a more informal and interactive writing style (cf. Bloor, 1996). They achieve their intended rhetorical purposes through the alternation of linguistic moods (the interchange among *imperatives, declaratives* and *interrogatives* in a paragraph, for example), and through the manipulation of overt personal pronouns and sentence rhythm (e.g. *initial conjunctions, sentence fragments* and *contractions*). Our Philosophy informant, as a senior member in the Philosophy discourse community, provided us with a probable explanation of this writing style:

> Philosophy has to be more rhetorical in a way because it's dealing
> with issues where there isn't an established way of settling . . . There,
> if you want to give demonstrations in philosophy, you would have
> to be doing something more like therapy to get people over philo-
> sophical confusions.   (Gibbard, interview, 1997)

Therefore, this stylistic choice of contemporary philosophers could be considered to be the closest reflection of a postmodernist view of knowledge: 'Our certainty will be a matter of *conversation* between persons, rather than a matter of interaction with nonhuman reality' (Rorty, 1979: 157; our emphasis).

On the other hand, researchers in Statistics seem to continue to believe in the empiricist and positivist assumption that scientific studies are factual, and hence best designed to be faceless and agentless; their insistence on formal style thus still remains (cf. Biber, 1988: 192–195). To be prudent scientists, the statisticians avoid using features which reveal personal involvement or emotion (e.g. *first person pronouns, direct questions* and *exclamations*) and features which are claimed, by some authors of writing manuals and guidebooks, as reflecting incomplete thought and poor knowledge of grammar (e.g. *run-on expressions* and *sentence fragments*). The rather formal and impersonal tone in their textual presentations therefore serves to maintain an *appearance* of objectivity and neutrality since they seem to believe that knowledge is an *accurate* representation of the real world (cf. Hyland, this volume). As for Linguistics, its status as a field not comfortably categorized as either humanities, sciences or social sciences seems to be well reflected in its textual presentations. In general, the linguists also use all the features employed by philosophers, only that they use them less frequently, and hence exhibit a writing style less saliently informal than the philosophical style discussed above.

Conclusions of the stylistic investigation

The overall use of the cluster of linguistic features investigated in this study seems to reflect tendencies towards informality in current scholarly writing, thus confirming the observations of writers such as Canagarajah (1996a), Halliday and Martin (1993: 20–21) and Pennycook (1996). However, as we have already seen, the extent to which researchers in different disciplines exhibit such tendencies seems to vary. The different distributions of these linguistic features found in this study can therefore be said to mirror different contemporary stylistic preferences in the three disciplines (cf. Chapters 5, 6 and 9).

From the manuals survey, we can also see that many of the more recent manuals and handbooks already display a somewhat changed attitude about stylistic rules. As Huckin (1993: 15) noticed, these more recent manuals, 'instead of striking the traditional absolutist tone, are more temperate in their language'. For example, instead of saying 'the use of the indefinite pronoun *this* should almost always be avoided' (Linton and Trafton, 1972: 30), they may instruct their readers: 'be sure that the antecedents of the pronouns *this* and *that* are clear. If there is a chance of ambiguity, use a noun to clarify your meaning' (e.g. Dodd, 1986: 101). However, what does 'the antecedent is clear' mean? As Geisler *et al.* (1985) indicate, judgments regarding which referent is clear and which is not may be a problem in itself for many novice academic and scientific writers.

Therefore, however careful these manual/textbook writers might try to be in modifying the tone of their instructions, they still have understandable difficulty in capturing the complexity of the rhetorical choices involved in selecting and employing many of these grammatical features. For instance, although some manual/textbook writers suggest avoiding direct questions in formal writing, we can still see, from the results, that they are common in Linguistics and Philosophy (especially in the latter), but are rarely used in Statistics. And there remains the odd situation of imperatives. Although we have seen that this form is universally used by scholars in the corpus, it is discussed in only one of the 40 textbooks and manuals surveyed.

II   Non-native speaker reactions to issues of academic style

Informant demographics

In the remainder of this chapter, we investigate the verbal responses of 37 non-native speakers of English to most of the informal elements variably displayed in published academic and research prose and discussed in Section I. The 37 informants were drawn from two advanced writing classes for NNS offered by the English Language Institute at the University of Michigan: *Research Paper Writing* (ELI 520 Fall Semester 1997), 21 participants; *Dissertation and Prospectus Writing* (ELI 600 Winter Semester 1997), 16 participants. Both courses receive graduate credit, are entirely voluntary, and are not open to first-year graduate students. Of the informants, 25 were male and 12 female; the average age was probably around 30. Thirty-two of the class members were enrolled in graduate programs in the university, four were visiting scholars or researchers and one was an associate professor. Countries of origin were China (8), Korea (8), Thailand (7), Japan (5) and Taiwan (5) plus single individuals (all students) from Albania, Ecuador, Germany and Yemen. In consequence, the findings that follow primarily reflect the views, opinions and reactions of (mostly) junior scholars from Asia, but all with some US academic experience.

These courses are open to students from any unit in a large and complex research university. As a result, area of specialization can range widely; those for the 1997 participants are shown in Table 7.3.

Table 7.3   Interest areas of the informants

Health Sciences	7
Social Sciences	7
Science	5
Engineering	5
Architecture and Urban Planning	3
Humanities	3
Natural Resources	3
Business Administration	1
Law	1
Library Science	1
Social Work	1

A second broad characteristic of the informant pool thus emerges – it is most strongly representative of science, social science and technology. In the light of the linguistic sophistication shown in what follows, it should also be noted that none of the three Humanities students in the 1997 pool came from the Department of English or the Program in Linguistics; in other words, none of the informants had a primary research interest in *language* per se.

There is one further characteristic of the participants that is relevant to what follows: the academic writing tasks they were primarily engaged in during the time they were taking one of the two courses. Eight of the ten Master's students were writing theses, while the other two were writing weekly or fortnightly 'reaction papers' or 'critiques' on assigned readings in advanced courses. The one faculty member (the associate professor from Engineering) was mainly engaged in writing grant proposals, and three of the four visiting scholars were writing for publication, while the fourth (from law) was composing a long, commissioned book review. The situations of the 22 PhD students, as is common in US doctoral programs, were typically rather more complicated. The students' *self-declared* writing objectives, as written on the beginning-of-class questionnaires, broke down as follows: 5 were writing dissertations, 8 were writing for publication and 9 were attempting to satisfy program requirements (prospectus, third-year research paper, etc.).

This picture is, however, complicated by the contemporary preference, especially in science and engineering areas, for an 'anthology' dissertation, the central chapters of which consist of a small number of papers published, in press, or accepted for publication. Even in areas where the traditional synoptic monograph prevails, there is now strong pressure for doctoral students to graduate with a useful accumulation of presentations and publications to their credit so that they can be competitive on a very tight job market. Thus it transpires that much of the doctoral-level writing is avowedly or prospectively multi-purpose in the sense that a particular piece might serve to satisfy a program requirement (such as Preliminary Examination), set the groundwork for a publication, or be projected to form part of the dissertation. Indeed, according to their curricula vitae and self-reports, just over half of the 37 informants already had publications to their name, even though not all of these had been written in English and many had been co-authored.

To sum up the informant demographics, we can say that we find here a sophisticated group of junior scholars, most of those beyond the Master's level with one or more publications in English to their credit, who come predominantly from Asia, who have mostly entered highly competitive graduate programs, and who are mostly active researchers or research assistants in some (broadly defined) scientific field. As far as we can ascertain, all originally learned English as a foreign rather than a second language, and quite a number had previously taken several lower-level EAP courses at Michigan, going back as far as 1991.

Investigative procedures

Based on the informal features discussed in the earlier part of this chapter, in March 1997 we prepared and arranged for a two-hour in-class discussion – with a short break – on these issues. The discussion was recorded and later all recoverable utterances were transcribed. Extracts from this exercise are indicated by the letters CD (class discussion) in the following 'Findings' section. After studying the transcripts, we decided that it would be useful to follow up certain aspects of CD data, especially to gain further clarification and amplification. In June and July 1997, e-mail exchanges were initiated and eight participants (50%) responded substantially to this initiative. This data is subsequently coded as E (e-mail). In October 1997, a 50-minute class discussion with the participants in the fall *Research Paper Writing* course (520) was organized, but few disparities with, or points additional to, the transcribed earlier discussion were noted. Toward the end of the course a short questionnaire was distributed, asking for comments and reactions (of any kind) to a number of items that exposed the participants to a range of stylistic variations. Here is a typical example:

B. There is a small possibility that the results may be due to chance.
(1) This, however, is unlikely.
(2) However, this is unlikely.
(3) But this is unlikely.
(4) But probably not.

Although only 11 questionnaires were returned, several participants being away at conferences or on research trips, a number of these contained interesting and substantive comments. This third kind of data has been coded S (survey).

As far as we can ascertain, the three data types (oral group discussion, e-mail interview and written questionnaire) produced the same *substantive* findings; in other words, nobody very obviously contradicted themselves as they responded to the three different kinds of elicitation format. However, the three formats did produce differences in perceptual salience. The class discussions were undoubtedly the best vehicle for eliciting disciplinary disparities, presumably because participants could easily react to what other people from other areas had said about a particular element. On the other hand, the other two investigative modes produced more finely tuned and considered linguistic responses, again presumably because in these formats participants had much more time to reflect upon the issues or linguistic examples presented to them.

Findings

We offer here reactions and responses to only a selection of the 11 informal features discussed in Section I. As it happens, there was wide agreement among the informants that *contractions* (except in quoted material) and *exclamations* are not part of the academic writer's repertoire. The limited discussion of the *split infinitives* was further obviated by the opinion that, irrespective of personal preferences, its acceptability would be determined by editorial interventions and rules. There was no S data for *unattended 'this'*, while much of the class discussion was taken up with us trying to explain the point at issue. The findings for *run-on expressions* and *final prepositions* were not very revealing. The remaining five features (*sentence fragments, direct questions, sentence-initial conjunctions, imperatives* and *first person pronouns*) will be considered in this order since this reflects the approximate order of their increasing salience and concern for the informants.

Sentence fragments

As Quirk and Stein astutely observe, 'Serious discursive prose can be enlivened by the occasional, startlingly short verbless sentence' (1996: 27). Indeed, they go on to show that such sentence fragments occurred around 300 times in a 100,000-word corpus from *The Economist*, that is, roughly once per 1700 words of text. Examples they quote include:

Fine words.
Not this time.
Why?
Quite possibly not.

However, with one exception, our informants were nervous about this stylistic opportunity (and indeed it occurred only 15 times in the corpus results shown in Table 7.2). Here are three comments from the E data:

> I have seen it sometimes. I have never used it. Probably I would never be able to use it effectively.
>
> > (Visiting medical researcher from Japan)

> It is not common to see sentence fragments in my field . . . it requires more knowledge of English to use fragments than fully structured sentences.   (Ecuadorian Natural Resources MA student)

> I feel that it makes academic writing even more complicated since to put these informal features nicely in the formal writing might require an even higher level of English language skills. I don't use it.
> > (Senior PhD student in Chemistry from Taiwan)

In the S data, all but one strongly rejected the *But probably not* fragment illustrated in the previous section as being 'not formal', 'not a complete sentence', 'not written English' and so on. One partial exception, from a Korean third-year Psychology doctoral student with a keen and sensitive interest in academic English, shows affinities with the position adopted by Quirk and Stein. Jun wrote:

> Very colloquial. However this kind of strategy may work, when the author has a very plausible argument supporting this line.

However, there was one participant who, both here and elsewhere, expressed a radically different set of views. This was Yao, a Humanities-oriented third-year PhD student in Architecture from Thailand, who was writing a narrative account, much influenced by hermeneutics, of her experiences of being inside a traditional Thai house, based on her notes, journals and sketches. In the short class discussion on this features she maintained that she used it 'when writing informally', and confirmed this in the E data with 'Yes, but not so often'. The highly personal nature of much of her academic writing appears to have set her apart from the other informants, although it does align her with some of the philosophers in the Section I text analysis.

Direct questions

As might be expected, informant reactions to this element were much more mixed, and in a show of hands at the end of the class discussion on this issue, about half the participants recognized that they could and did use direct questions on occasion in their formal academic writing. However, Dr Sun, the associate professor in Engineering, was alone in acknowledging their use as a strategy for criticizing the work of others. (And here it can be noted that this strategy was quite common in the text samples from Linguistics and Philosophy.) The contrasts come out clearly in this fragment from the CD (Tak, like Yao, is a female Thai student, but this time from Engineering):

> YAO: I found them in my field all the time. I can find start the first sentence of a paragraph with 'What does this mean?' and then the paragraph will explain the answer.
>
> TAK: I don't think so . . . I think the literature in my field is very very formal, very old-style, nothing elaborated.

One of the most interesting responses came from Hideki, the Japanese visiting researcher. In the CD data, he observed:

> I think it is very common in my field, and I appreciate that kind of expression because it is easy to follow . . . but I will not use it myself because I don't have the courage to try it.

However, three months later in the E-data, he was beginning to change:

> I have never used it. However, I would like to try using it because the impact is strong.

A number of other informants also commented on the 'impact' of direct questions and on how indirect questions can be conservative and 'boring' (S data). Although there were a few students, such as Tak above, who expressed reservations, in general the comfort level with this feature was considerably higher than in the previous one. As the Korean urban planner wrote on the survey form, 'Although direct question is sometimes avoided, it can give strong message'.

'And' and 'But' in sentence-initial position

In the CD and E data, there emerged a fairly sharp difference in attitude towards these two sentence-opening conjunctions. Many more informants recognized that they had encountered in their readings more sentences beginning with 'but' than those opening with 'and'. Indeed, the most experienced academic in the group, the associate professor, observed:

> I don't think I can ever remember a sentence beginning with 'and' but I do think there is sometimes 'but' at the beginning of a sentence.   (CD)

These responses were interestingly similar to the Michigan professors who were interviewed: the linguist observed, 'I use "but" very often . . . "And" is strange, usually I don't use "and" in the beginning of a sentence.' The Statistics professor was also sensitive to the use of such sentence-initial conjunctions, 'It immediately made a signal to me that somebody is trying to make a persuasive argument, and that would alert me to be careful'.

A number of the class participants noted that in their early days of learning English, they had probably opened sentences with conjunctions, but had in graduate school learned to avoid them in academic writing, and now seemed to be facing a new challenge. Yao, the humanist from Architecture, was again the most forthrightly experimental, saying that she had 'borrowed' the usage because 'it puts more emphasis on what you are going to say . . . it makes it more dramatic, more active' (CD). Later she wrote, 'Although I am not sure it is grammatically correct, but since many authors use it effectively I feel it is quite tempting to follow' (E). Some others felt that their fields did not accept initial conjunctions, while others adopted a middle position. A Chinese Economics student felt that initial 'but' would be possible for him but 'risky'; a Taiwanese science student said she had herself no problem with such openings, but that her advisor would edit them out. Several, including the associate professor, complained that they did not know *when* might be an appropriate moment to begin a sentence with 'but'.

The relevant survey item had two variants beginning with 'moreover', followed by two variants beginning with 'and':

(3) And, as we have seen, they are not without educational indications.

(4) And they are not without educational implications.

Interestingly, all nine respondents rejected (4) as being 'too colloquial', etc. but only six rejected (3). Jun commented on (3) that

'It's not typical to start with "And". But "as we have seen" relieves my discomfort a little', whereas (4) 'looks much worse than (3)'. We, in fact, share Jun's perception here and note in passing that this is another area where further research is needed so that we can begin the process of offering more nuanced advice to advanced NNS writers of academic prose.

Imperatives

There was little disagreement in the CD and E texts that certain imperatives such as *consider, assume* and *note* were appropriate to formal academic style and could easily be incorporated by these groups of NNS informants, even though there was more uncertainty about the appropriateness of other verbs such as *notice.* Only one participant in the CD, a female Chinese dissertation-writer in Astrophysics, expressed a clear preference for replacing 'Assume . . .' by 'Assuming that . . .' when guiding the reader through formulaic mathematical material. In his e-mail responses, Hideki remained true to his cautious form:

> In legends of figures, it is commonly used (e.g. 'Note the relatively strong reflex in the chloroid.') Otherwise, I think it is uncommon. I often use it only in legends, never in the text. I feel it is risky to use it in text.

The crucial remaining issue, of course, is not the permissibility of the syntactic structure per se (even though 'bibles' such as *The APA Publication Manual* are silent on this possibility), but which lexical verbs are acceptable in which contexts. Although Swales *et al.* (1998) provides some useful data from a limited number of fields, there is clearly more work to be done before NNS scholars can be presented with the information that they need.

First person pronouns

The causes and consequences of using or avoiding first person pronouns (*I, we, our,* etc.) in academic writing would seem to be perennial topics of debate among scholars, their students, manual writers (e.g. Day, 1988), sociologists (e.g. Gilbert and Mulkay, 1984), linguists (e.g. Tarone *et al.*, 1981) and composition experts (e.g. Cadman, 1997). The salience of these choices presumably derives for the most part from their close association with authorial identity and authority (Ivanič and Simpson, 1992a). Since feelings and reactions can be both strong and unpredictable on this issue, current advice given to participants in ELI 520 and 600 is little more than the simple and possibly lame 'Find out what your advisor prefers and respond accordingly'. It is not surprising then that a full 25 minutes of the class discussion was absorbed by this salient topic.

It is not easy to summarize succinctly the diverse information contained in the three data sources, but some trends do emerge. Several e-mail respondents confirmed that first person pronoun usage was indeed increasing in their fields. Here is the Ecuadorian:

> Lately is common to find articles using I and We in journal publications. I have seen the change from a passive (Three 10m reaches were selected . . .) to I or We on new publications.

Even so, in the S data, all nine respondents preferred:

(6) In this study, the same method of analysis has been adopted.

to:

(1) In this study, I (single author) have adopted the same method of analysis.
(2) In this study, we (single author) have adopted . . .
(3) In this study, we (multiple authors) have adopted . . .

Most seemed to agree that 'we' as in (3) above was an acceptable choice in multiple-authorship contexts. Jun commented (S data), 'One good thing of having co-authors is that I can use "we" as many as I want', and Sun (CD) remarks, 'Well, when I am writing a paper with others I don't care about "we" or the passive, but when I am writing a single-authored paper, I stick to the passive'.

The use of 'I' and the use of 'we' for a single author proved, as might be expected, highly controversial. The MA thesis writers, in particular, were not happy at the thought of referring to themselves as 'I', except perhaps when describing their field experiences, even though they came from the Humanities. Other comments included 'nobody likes to use it in a formal paper!' and 'only usable for senior scholars'. The use of 'we' in (2) above emerged as being particularly contentious; it was depicted by some as 'nonsense', 'illogical', or 'confusing' or 'inappropriate', while others noted their advisors used this strategy or that it was an acceptable convention. An interesting reconciliation was offered by the

Astrophysics dissertation writer: 'Even though I am writing it, I think I am doing it with my advisor, so "we" is what I should use'.

As a coda to this discussion, we can contrast these concerns with the greater equanimity expressed by two senior native speaker professors in the text-based interviews. A liberal view could, of course, be expected in Philosophy:

> It seems awkward that if you don't use personal pronouns, and that it gets even more awkward if you don't use the personal pronoun 'I', especially since in philosophy, one's arguing a position which others may not share.   (Gibbard, interview, 1997)

Rather more surprising is this from a well-known professor of Statistics:

> I think it's true when you make major steps in any field, the individual person is more involved, so then . . . you wanna emphasize that it's you that's asserting it . . . and you're asserting that it's you, you're doing it.   (Hill, interview, 1997)

Thus, seniority has to be added to the complex mix of factors that influence stylistic choices in the contemporary academic world.

Implications for teaching academic writing

On several occasions throughout this project we asked the informants whether the informal features this chapter has discussed made academic writing in English easier or more difficult. Three, including the Albanian biostatistician and a Korean electrical engineer, felt that informality was a bonus. Of this group, Yao, the humanist Architecture student, was the most supportive of the trend and the most eloquent:

> In general, I think legitimizing these features makes it easier for non-native writers, since personally, it has been quite confusing for me to see how many reading materials in my field are done in some different manners from what was taught in writing classes. Sometimes, I think I unconsciously learn things through examples.

However, a clear majority of those who responded to our inquiries were concerned about the greater flexibility that greater informality might offer. The visiting medical researcher from Japan probably spoke for this majority when he wrote, 'I think these informal features make academic English more complicated'. Perhaps the shrewdest comment came from the third-year Economics student from Mainland China:

> In general, I think the use of informal language makes expressing yourself easier, because sometimes it is most natural to begin a sentence with 'But'. But it makes good writing more difficult, because it's hard to mix formal and informal language nicely.

Overall, the project reveals some palpable sense of unease with regard to potential breaches of strict formality in academic writing. And here it is useful to recall that none of the informants was a language specialist, and most were intent on developing academic careers for themselves in which English would loom large as their main language of publication. In effect, they argued that learning the rules of formal academic English was already a considerable challenge and one that did not need to be further complicated by having to learn how 'to mix formal and informal language nicely'. They preferred not having to decide whether putting a particular verb into the imperative at a particular juncture would be considered 'short and snappy' or 'heavy and bossy', or whether using 'I' might or might not be considered as authorially intrusive.

The work we have presented in turn raises challenges for all those of us who work in EAP writing for graduate students, faculty and researchers, and for those who study academic discourse and academic literacy acquisition. Obviously, we need further research into the kinds of stylistic phenomena sketched out in the first half of this chapter and into the kinds of response discussed in the second. Another obvious prospect is to hope that reference and style manuals will become more cognizant of contemporary academic literacy practices in their guidelines, as indeed advocated by Huckin (1993) and others. Rather less obvious is the preferred stance of EAP materials writers and writing instructors. On this, our provisional position is that the rhetorical consciousness of the academically inclined non-native speaker needs to be raised with regard to the more widespread of the informal elements, perhaps indeed by exposing them to selections from the material we have presented. Beyond that, we do not feel we yet have a sufficiently solid basis to offer class advice on these stylistic 'niceties', thus leaving for now their negotiation to individual consultation.

Notes

1. We distinguish here rules of *appropriateness* (i.e. rules which condition degree of formality in writing) from *rules of correctness* (i.e. rules which regulate aspects of basic English grammar and are never violated by educated writers; for example, 'Verbs must agree with their subjects.' and 'Use the correct case form.').
2. For our previous imperatives study (Swales *et al.*, 1998), only five papers from each discipline were studied; these papers were also included in the current corpus. In addition, to avoid inconsistency of style in a single paper, papers by more than one author were excluded from this study.
3. The three academic journals chosen were: Statistics – *Econometric Theory*; Linguistics (theoretical) – *Language*; and Philosophy (ethics) – *Philosophical Perspectives*.
4. To simplify the data analysis process, the so-called *unattended 'this'* was used as the only example for the second feature *broad reference*. In addition, since, according to the comments made by some journal editors interviewed in this study, *run-on sentences* hardly occurred in the manuscripts submitted to their journals, in this study, only *run-on expressions* were included in the analysis. Further, the inclusion of the imperative in the list of the features to be investigated was to facilitate the comparison between the present study and Swales *et al.* (1998).
5. The editor of the Philosophy journal stated in his e-mail interview: 'At *Philosophical Perspectives* I editorially control only split infinitives and sentences ending with prepositions. I deliberately try to be editorially flexible with respect to all of your other (grammatical) items' (Tomberlin, pc, 1997).

8

Researching the writer–reader relationship

ROZ IVANIČ AND SUE WELDON

Introduction

As the writers of chapters in Parts I and II have argued, writing consists of three interlocking dimensions: (1) the written text itself, (2) the social interaction which surrounds the production of the text and (3) the socio-cultural context within which this social interaction takes place. None of these operates independently, and in our view research which focuses on any one of them needs to take account of the other two. This is particularly true of research which focuses on the connecting layer – the social identities and social interaction involved in an act of writing, as ours does. Researching the fine detail of the minute-by-minute social and linguistic decisions which writers make involves also looking at the products of those decisions, and placing those decisions within the context of the socially available generic and discoursal possibilities.

One principle which guides our research is that understandings of these fine details of the social interaction surrounding writing are greatly enriched by collaborative research. We are writing this chapter on the basis of our experience of working as co-researchers on academic writing. In discussions, we have come to realise that, even though we both see ourselves as qualitative researchers, we have quite different takes on many research issues. We hope that what we write here retains some of the signs of struggle we have had in dovetailing our different perspectives.

In the main part of this chapter, we will discuss reasons for methodological decisions about different aspects of research: data collection, data analysis and presentation of findings. We call these 'aspects' of the research rather than 'stages' in order to emphasise the fact that they are not in any strict chronological order, but rather they are recursive processes, each leading to refinement of the others, and with no clear cut-off point between one and another. We will be also be discussing how methodology is inextricably intertwined with topic and theoretical perspective. I, Roz, will therefore first outline the research I have undertaken into academic writing, explaining its focus and showing how it connects to issues raised in earlier chapters in the book.

Over the past ten years I have been theorising, researching and publishing on the nature of 'writer identity'. My main claim has been that there are three aspects to a writer's identity, all three of which are shaped by the 'possibilities for self-hood' in the socio-cultural context in which a person lives and writes (Ivanič, 1994, 1995 [reprinted as Chapter 6 in Clark and Ivanič, 1997], 1998; Ivanič and Roach, 1990, Ivanič and Simpson, 1992a, 1992b). 'Possibilities for self-hood' are socially available subject positions, sustained by all forms of social practice. In my research, I have been particularly concerned with the way possibilities for self-hood are sustained by discourses and genres: the conventions for language use. I follow Kress (1988) and Fairclough (1992a) in distinguishing between genres and discourses. Discourses carry possibilities for self-hood in terms of the values and beliefs to which writers who deploy them become party; genres carry possibilities for self-hood in terms of the social relations and communicative purposes to which writers who deploy them become party. These cultural resources shape all three aspects of the identity of any particular writer.

1. The 'autobiographical self' is the 'self' which writers bring to an act of writing: their life-history, and sense of their roots. This 'self' is socially constrained and constructed by possibilities for self-hood which were available in the writer's life-history (see Ivanič, 1998: Chapters 7 and 8).
2. The 'discoursal self' is the 'self' which writers construct through linguistic and other resources in an act of writing. The possibilities for self-hood inscribed in the discourses and genres on which writers draw have the potential to be ascribed to them, once they draw on these discourses and genres (see Ivanič, 1998: Chapters 9 and 10).
3. I have also distinguished a third 'self' which overlaps with these two: the 'self as author'. This self manifests itself in the degree of authoritativeness with which a writer writes.

My main interest has been in the discoursal self, and the minute detail of how writers shape their self-presentation through the deployment of their discoursal resources. This has led me to treat writing as social interaction (cf. Myers, this volume) in which writers not only construct an ideational message, but also construct a message about themselves, and anticipate the response of their readers' values, beliefs and relative social power (cf. Chapters 1, 5, 7 and 9). All this is done, not simply between individuals, but in the context of a shifting constellation of possibilities for self-hood. Writers portray themselves, and reader(s) read these portrayals, only by reference to these socially available possibilities for self-hood. But the possibilities for self-hood which are available in any cultural context are themselves open to contestation. Acts of writing are processes of identification in which writers reinforce or challenge the patterns of privileging among possibilities for self-hood in their socio-cultural context. These processes of identification are the mechanisms which drive discursive and social change.

SUE: Roz?

ROZ: Yes Sue.

SUE: I wanted to know why you asked me to collaborate in writing this chapter. I see you as the expert. You have researched and written about writer–reader relationships, and about the ways in which writer identities are shaped by their social circumstances – both past and present. I understand that in the past you have asked me to collaborate in your research because you were interested in the factors which affected my development as a writer. At that stage I was struggling to reconcile and dovetail my eclectic life experiences with the disciplinary requirements of writing academically. Later on you helped me to resolve the interdisciplinary conflicts of writing a 'science studies' PhD thesis. But I was never a linguist and I have never researched the subject of academic writing. Can you explain how you see this collaborative venture developing?

ROZ: Firstly, I can see you explaining what it was like to be the person whose life, writing, experience of writing and perspectives on it were the data for research. Secondly, you are now yourself a researcher in a different field, and this experience is likely to enrich what we have to say about methodologies for studying writing. I'm hoping you will be able to look back at our research into academic writing and view its methodology through the lens of your own work, producing fresh insights from your somewhat different perspective.

SUE: Before I do that, perhaps you could tell me something about where you are coming from and how your research got started?

ROZ: I think my previous life as an Adult Literacy tutor is the driving force behind my interest in understanding the writing process and the reasons why people find it so difficult. This research started with my interest in the way in which people experience writing as an act of identity. I had heard many people say things like 'I don't feel this is me' when they were writing academic essays. This feeling seemed to play a powerful role in their writing, causing them either to dry up completely or to write in contorted ways as they attempted to take on discourses and genres – and, with them, identities – which seemed alien to them.

SUE: Well, we both know how I struggled with integrating the baggage of my past life and the conflicting discourses of an inter-disciplinary degree (as described in Weldon, 1994; and Ivanič, Aitchison and Weldon, 1996). I joined the science studies field in middle age after many years of doing other work, including scientific research for industry. Participation in your research into writer identity was a positive step in my development as an academic writer. But how did you acquire your own theoretical perspective on the development of writer identity?

ROZ: I read Goffman's work on self-representation (1969), and began to see writing as an act of self-representation. However, I recognised that Goffman did not pay sufficient attention to tensions and conflicts in the socio-cultural setting, and drew on Fairclough's account of discourse in relation to social change (1989, 1992a, 1995) in order to avoid the rather mono-cultural and static view of social context presented by Goffman. This led me to see each individual act of writing as identification with one or more subject positions from among socially available alternatives, and thereby contributing in some small way to reproduction or contestation of the social order.

SUE: This is very interesting. I would never have envisaged the possibility of making a contribution to maintenance, or otherwise, of a social order. However, in retrospect, I accept that 'discourse communities' might evolve through countless small acts of identification, although I think – to stretch the evolutionary metaphor even further – that maintenance or 'survival' must be linked with the relative power of a discourse. But, as a cultural theorist with an active research interest in the ways in which technoscientific theories are developed, I would like to know more about your research methodology.

ROZ: Goffman's research method was that of an anthropologist: to become very familiar with a social setting, in his case, the farming community of the Shetland Islands, to observe people's behaviour, to identify patterns in it and to deduce the principles which were guiding this behaviour. In order to apply this methodology to the social act of writing, I needed a way of observing the 'mental behaviour' which accompanies writing, including writers' thoughts about social context and social relations.

SUE: I can see that you would have some difficulty in observing those hidden aspects of writing and that you must have chosen your methodology with that in mind, but which research methods told you what?

Types of research and types of understanding

ROZ: I think that different types of research lead to different types of understanding. Stake (1978) advocates using case studies because

> Antipositivists . . . have claimed that Truth in the fields of human affairs is better approximated by statements that are rich with the sense of human encounter: To speak not of underlying attributes, objective observables, and universal forces, but of perceptions and understanding that come from immersion in and holistic regard for phenomena.   (p. 6)

These views of the nature of 'truth' and 'understanding' seem suited to my research aim, which is to understand better the nature of writer identity as it manifests itself in the writing of some actual writers, rather than testing an isolated hypothesis. Understandings are grounded in individual cases. What research of this sort loses in terms of the power of numbers, it gains and surpasses in other ways. Its power lies in revealing the richness and complexity of the phenomenon under investigation. As Stake says, it produces insights which have the psychological reality of being couched in terms of people's actual experiences and perceptions. Understandings drawn from this type of data are consistent with a subjective view of knowledge, and are also in harmony with the principles of integrating research and practice, which we'll discuss later.

My decision to investigate writer identity through case studies led me to use a variety of methods of data collection and analysis which are sometimes termed 'qualitative methods', or 'ethnographic methods'. The underlying principles for collecting and analysing qualitative and ethnographic data, derived from many research traditions, have been described in various places, for example, Spradley (1980), Goetz and LeCompte (1984), Lincoln and Guba (1985), Doheny-Farina and Odell (1985), Jacob (1988). Kantor *et al.* (1981) first mention such techniques as suited to studying the way writing classrooms work, and they have been popular in the study of writing classrooms during the 1980s. Ethnographic methodology has been used to study writing in non-academic settings (Heath, 1983; Doheny-Farina, 1984; Odell and Goswami, 1985; Barton and Padmore, 1991). Kaufer and Geisler (1989) describe using similar techniques for collecting data about the way four different writers approached a task they had set. These form the background for many of my principles for data collection and analysis in the study of writing.

SUE: Well, I thoroughly approve of your aim of understanding the richness and complexity of writer identity through individual case studies. My own research was based on an ethnographic study of an environmental impact assessment which, for me, involved a whole series of different types of data from participant observation of scientific fieldwork to examination of planning policy statements. What types of data did you collect?

Types of data

ROZ: It seemed to me that, in order to study writing as self-representation, I needed three types of data. First, I needed to understand as much as possible about the writer herself – you, in this case, Sue – where you were coming from in all its meanings: what values, beliefs, practices and previous experiences of written discourses and genres you were bringing to writing – the shaping of your identity a writer. These understandings developed from visiting you at home and from our more informal conversations – both when we met and over the telephone.

SUE: Yes, it's interesting to reflect back on the unravelling of my autobiography and to realise how much of one's life history is embedded in each written text. But as you know, the final print-out bore no resemblance to the first set of scribbled notes, and I considered an essay to be a finished artefact only if it kicked over the traces of 'cut and paste', or loose ends spliced together.

ROZ: That brings me to the second type of data. I needed to focus on one particular piece of writing you had done in order to find actual examples of linguistic decisions you had made which I could associate with particular views of knowledge and views of the world, and with particular social purposes, social roles and relations. In this respect I was drawing from the methodology associated with Critical Discourse Analysis: studying text in order to identify traces of discourses and genres (as described in Fairclough, 1992a). The difference from most applications of Critical Discourse Analysis was that I wanted to connect these observations with a thorough understanding of each writer's life, aspirations, motivations, intentions, previous encounters with discoursal resources, and her experience of institutional pressures to conform to certain norms. The reason for this was not to take a retrograde step into an individualistic view of writing as the outcome of the writer's intentions. Rather, it was to understand better the role of the social and ideological landscape in shaping a writer's 'discoursal self', and the role of the writer in perpetuating or transforming the social and ideological landscape through acts of identity.

SUE: Now I can see where you are coming from. I can see how you have adopted an anthropologist's approach to the social activity of academic writing using a theoretical perspective based on Critical Discourse Analysis. By foregrounding what you see as external pressures and internal conflicts of identity, decisions taken and others rejected, you have conducted an ethnographic account of the emergence of a particular text. The realisation of the sheer turgidity and valueladenness of the written word was, initially, a revelation to me. And for one who was trained as a scientist, whose aim was to tell the 'objective' Truth, this realisation made me feel like a fraud. The scientist in me had been looking for that 'view from nowhere' – the truly objective stance. But I have since begun to realise that those, like yourself, who research language and writing practices have much in common with those of us who study the activity of scientists. That is where my own research has taken me, so we could both be seen as trying to unravel the myths and meaning making practices within a social context.

ROZ: In my view it is a fallacy to assume that it is possible to reveal the 'truth' about anybody's identity. My research concerns perceptions: my co-researchers' perceptions of why they did things, and how they felt about the identities they seemed to be constructing for themselves; my perceptions of what they were doing and why; my interpretations of the way in which they were positioned by their discourse choices; and my speculative explanations for how this positioning occurred. It is important not to confuse this closeness to felt experience with 'ultimate truth'. With a subjective view of knowledge, I celebrate insights based on the experience and perceptions of real individuals, and am not seeking anything 'objective'.

SUE: Now that I see we have something in common, my next question emerges straight away, because this is a concern I have been grappling with myself. Given that you realise this inherent 'story-ladenness' of the written word, how do you justify the authority of your own research findings? I mean, how can you be sure that your own version of the writing process gives a better explanation of events than anyone else's version?

ROZ: I understand exactly what you mean. I did say I needed three types of data, and the third is an attempt to bridge the gap between purely anthropological or purely linguistic methods of research. You will remember when we worked together in the past that I needed to have a very far-reaching conversation with you about a particular piece of writing. The idea for this came from what Odell *et al.* (1983) called a 'discourse-based interview'.

I also had a similar sort of discussion with the tutors who had read and assessed your essays, trying to find out how they had reacted to your discourse choices. I asked them to explain why they had given the grade they did, to give any further responses they could to the essays, and particularly to comment on what the essay contributed to their impression of the writer. It was shocking to see how their 'reading' of your writing was often quite different from what you had intended it to convey – both about your subject-matter and about yourself.

SUE: Well I do remember in one instance, as an undergraduate, being uncomfortably aware of trying to address what I saw as the requirements of a good philosophy essay. This was less out of commitment to the discipline of philosophy and more to do with satisfying my tutor about my ability to use those particular disciplinary tools to address the wider theme of my inter-disciplinary degree.

ROZ: Interviewing the tutors made me realise that, in future research on the writer–reader relationship, it will be important to pay far more attention to the mismatch between the message and impression a writer intends to convey and the message and the impression which the reader receives. This mismatch has the potential to reveal cultural dissonances which will connect to the sort of research reported in Chapters 3, 6 and 9 of this book.

But returning to 'the discourse-based interview' as a data collection method, I think that the way we worked was less of an interview, more of a conversation in which we discussed how you actually saw yourself positioned by your writing, the problems you experienced with self-representation, the role of your tutor in affecting the way you presented yourself, and any ways in which you saw it as the product of your life-history. This was the part which I hoped would fulfil your aims as co-researcher: I hoped it would help you understand the processes you were involved in as you wrote, and the dilemmas you faced.

SUE: Indeed it did. By working *with me* rather than *on me* you gave me a new consciousness. Effectively you added another dimension to my writer identity – an awareness of my own learning. Also, I begin to see now how collaboration has shaped and enriched your own research. But perhaps you can explain what you were trying to achieve for yourself.

ROZ: My aim was to find examples of 'intertextuality'. Focusing on the essay itself, we attempted to identify the voices in the text: explicit quotation, scare quotes, words which seemed to be 'coming from somewhere', and what you felt was your 'own voice'. We discussed how you had approached this particular assignment, your practices and processes while engaged in it, and your feelings about it.

SUE: I presume that what you mean by intertextuality is that you were looking for instances where I was drawing on texts from various genres and discourse types. It was interesting and disconcerting to be made aware that you saw this as a subconscious process which, inevitably, involved a significant amount of ambivalence on my part. I have already mentioned that when I re-examined this process I felt exposed as a fraud because of my inability to dispel the impurity of my writing. Allied to this apparent deficit in my literacy practices, I was also made aware of not being part of a specific disciplinary community. The sense of being marginal, by virtue of being simultaneously a member of more than one community, has since been made real for me by a Science Studies paper by Susan Leigh Star (1991). She says:

> People inhabit many different domains at once . . . and the negotiation of identities, within and across groups, is an extraordinarily complex and difficult task . . . Marginality is a powerful experience. And we are all marginal in some regard, as members of more than one community of practice, and thus of many networks, at the moment of action we draw together repertoires mixed from different worlds. Among other things, we create metaphors – bridges between those different worlds.   (p. 16)

Star then goes on to add that we can trace power by observing 'whose metaphors bring worlds together, and hold them there' (1991: 16).

ROZ: Yes, it was exactly because you inhabited this borderland that it was so interesting to meet you and to work with you to explore your processes of negotiating an identity in such a heterogeneous discoursal environment.

Principles guiding collaborative research

The difference between tuition and collaborative research

SUE: I know you always say that we worked together as co-researchers, but I did often feel that I was the learner and you were there as my 'tutor'.

ROZ: The difference between 'tuition' and 'research' is a subtle, but crucial, one. In 'tuition', I, as tutor, would be suggesting how learners could improve their writing. In 'research', we were discussing why you wrote what you did, how it differed from other writing, and what you wanted to do about it. Instead of talking about how I thought the writing should be done, you often gave good reasons for keeping it the way it was. In 'tuition', I would be the knower, the tutor, the teacher. In 'research', we were joint investigators, each bringing different insights to the problem at hand. There were, inevitably, inequalities between us: my status as a member of university staff was a complicating factor. However, I believe that by the time we recorded the main interview, the effect of that was considerably reduced.

SUE: Yes, not only had you shared insights into your research practices but also, to a certain extent, you had invited me into your academic life. This, for me, was particularly important because I was able to see that you were often uncertain about analytical choices you had to make.

Relating research and practice

ROZ: Collaborative research with adult learners is part of the research-and-practice philosophy in several ways. Here are what I see as the main advantages of collaborative research of this sort. These advantages are set out in more detail in Hamilton *et al.* (1992), and discussed by Cameron *et al.* (1992), Entwistle and Marton (1984), Talk Workshop Group (1982) and Goswami and Stillman (1987).

(a) It avoids invasion of privacy.

(b) It brings different skills to the task.

(c) It respects and foregrounds informants' views and perspectives.

(d) It achieves richer insights, mainly as a result of (b) and (c).

(e) The 'researched' learn can as much as the researcher does, if that is their aim.

(f) Decisions about aims and methods are made jointly, ensuring that the aims of the research are interesting and relevant to everyone involved.

(g) It goes beyond just accountability and advocacy to empowerment (for discussion of the difference between these three types of responsibility in research, see Cameron *et al.*, 1992).

(h) Knowledge is not the researcher's property. It should serve the needs of both researcher and 'researched'. The 'researched' own the insights just as much as the researcher does.

(j) The 'researched' gain credit and status from publication.

(k) The 'researched' are in control of how they are presented in the publication.

(l) Publications are more accessible to other learners.

Working in this way is partly motivated by a desire to enrich the data (principle (d)), and partly by a commitment to the principles of responsible research (principles (a) and (e)–(l)). However, I recognise that ultimately I am still in charge and am bound to have compromised this principle under pressure of time and/or where it has suited me.

SUE: It was your ball-game, we were collaborating within your discipline and we played by your rules, but you explained the rules and you played fair.

Critical Language Awareness-raising as a research method

ROZ: Another important element in the way we worked together is what I call 'critical language awareness-raising', based on the concept of Critical Language Awareness (CLA), which colleagues and I have described elsewhere (see Clark *et al.*, 1990, 1991; Ivanič, 1990; Clark and Ivanič, 1991; Ivanič and Moss, 1991; Fairclough, 1992b; Clark and Ivanič, 1998).

CLA-raising as a pedagogical activity aims to help learners understand how language positions them: how their language choices are shaped by conventions and construct their identities. CLA is intended not only to raise learners' consciousness about language and social context, but also to help them gain control over their own roles in discourse, and find ways of challenging positions with which they may not wish to identify. CLA can simultaneously provide both learning opportunities and research data. (For a more detailed discussion of this dual function, see Clark and Ivanič, 1991; Ivanič, 1998: Chapter 5.)

SUE: The realisation that selective language use, in writing, can be empowering (or otherwise) has been a significant insight for me. Without these sorts of understandings, novice writers, such as myself, can find themselves positioned by discourse types without even being aware of it. I have also realised that different forms of writing can have different consequences and, as you say in *The Politics of Writing*: 'some types of writing have more status than others' (Clark and Ivanič, 1997). Similar insights, about the politics inherent in written representations, arise in my own inter-disciplinary area – particularly in feminist perspectives of scientific texts (see, for instance, Haraway, 1991).

The steering group

ROZ: Another way of ensuring collaboration on the project between all of us involved was to ask some of you to act as an informal steering group for the research. My intention was to discuss with you some of the issues which would be discussed on a regular research project by a steering group consisting of a panel of academic peers. In my view it is both more responsible and, in many ways, more informative to discuss such matters with the people who are going to be personally affected by the project, and who are also representative of the group of people who ought to benefit from the research in the long term. For example, in the final meeting of our steering group, we discussed the findings I was intending to present as a result of the analysis so far. I wanted to check whether they had 'psychological reality' for you: whether what I intended to write made sense to you. The discussion at this meeting enriched and made more coherent the understandings I was reaching. I also wanted to ensure that what I was planning to write about did not seem too theoretical and irrelevant to your aims and interests. I suppose I partly wanted to convince you, but I also wanted to bring myself down to earth: keep in touch with my driving purpose of writing something which would make sense to, and prove useful for, future generations of mature students struggling with academic writing.

One of the problems with this sort of research is that it is very time-consuming. I was only able to work in this way with eight people, and I guess the time you had to give to it was limited. Also I wonder whether actually too much navel-gazing could have become counterproductive for both of us. What do you think?

SUE: Not if both parties see it as a learning process – developing insights and understandings which they would not have had in isolation.

Principles guiding data collection

ROZ: In the course of conducting that research, I developed a set of principles for collecting data in the study of the writer–reader relationship. I'd be interested in your comments on them.

Study naturally occurring data

Recently several scholars have explicitly recommended more studies of student writers grappling with all the complex reading and writing activities as they occur in their own self-directed studies. For example, Stotsky (1991) lists nine methodological recommendations for future research, four of which refer specifically to the value of researching naturally occurring writing tasks. Both from the point of view of pedagogical relevance and from the point of view of research validity, a study of naturally occurring writing seemed to me preferable to one involving writing which was in any way directed by me as teacher or as researcher.

SUE: Yes. You were not, in that sense, 'an interested party'.

Collect participants' perspectives

ROZ: We've already talked about this as a principle of collaborative research. But it is worth adding that it would be naive to rely on participants' perspectives as data without recognizing the way that they themselves are socially constructed. Littlejohn (1988) questions 'the common assumption in social science research that there actually exist definable 'perceptions', 'views' or 'opinions', concluding that

> 'Perceptions', 'views' and 'opinions' . . . do not exist as 'thing-like entities'; they are fluid, changing, like a chameleon, according to the social location. Data, then, which actually permits generalizations about respondents' views, may simply not exist.   (p. 74)

By 'social location', Littlejohn means the conditions of data collection. He is drawing attention to the fact that what participants say may be greatly influenced by the nature of the interview, and their perceptions of my role and theirs within it. I think that Littlejohn's caution is important, especially when interpreting interviews, and adopting a collaborative approach to the research can help researchers to take it into account.

SUE: I agree. The collaborative process allows participants' perspectives to be tested against those of the researcher and for some mutual agreement to be reached about interpretation.

Recognise the subjective contribution of the researcher

ROZ: I am aware of my own role in shaping this research at every stage, as discussed by Steier (1991). In many ways I think this principle is more important in data analysis than in data collection. However, it affects data collection too in that I make no pretence that either my selection of data or my methods of interviewing were impersonal. The people with whom I made co-researcher relationships depended on my contacts, my social situation and my personality. My decision to collect and discuss specific texts rather than issues in general is the product of my linguistic orientation and training. The participants' perceptions I have on tape are to some extent influenced by my personality, choice of questions and ways of wording them.

SUE: I think this is a very important point. I'd like to point out that, in my own opinion, this principle applies as much to data collection as it does to analysis. My reason for saying this is because of my commitment to situated approach at every stage of the research process. I go along with the feminist philosopher of science, Sandra Harding (1991), who suggests that critical reflection and accountability are required in the context of data selection and in the context of data collection, as well as in the context of analysis.

Be a participant observer

ROZ: Being a participant observer means becoming a part of the situation you are researching. For example, ethnographers studying primary classrooms sometimes do all the class activities set by the teacher, use the primary school children's toilets, hang their coats in their cloakrooms, and play in the playground at break-time. Scholars disagree as to whether this is essential or not to qualitative methodology. Jacob (1988) illustrates this, pointing out that it is essential to the research tradition of anthropology as a discipline, but not others. I did not become a fully integrated member of a particular cultural group in the way I understand participant observation from the work of anthropologists. However, I did become an extremely close acquaintance of most of you. I met you all in your homes and most of you came to my home. I think that in most cases we internalised some of each others' culture. However, my case studies were individuals, not a group, so there was not a single location or activity in which I could become a participant observer.

SUE: I should hope not. That would be what anthropologists call 'going native'. The problem for me is how to be both 'in' (engaged) and 'outside' (disengaged) at the same time. I think that one of the most valuable aspects of collaborative research is to understand that differences can be maintained alongside mutual respect. As you have suggested, decisions and choices about writer identity are informed by differing situations and life histories.

Do not let predetermined theories constrain data collection

ROZ: This principle is commonly mentioned in the literature on qualitative research. However, this doesn't necessarily entail 'starting from a conscious attitude of almost complete ignorance' (Spradley, 1980: 4). I believe that researchers are deceiving themselves and their readers if they say that this is what they do. Certainly, you and I were open to discovering things that we couldn't anticipate. We also allowed ourselves to digress from tasks in hand, assuming that the discussion, whether tape-recorded or not, might lead us to insights which might be valuable. But this is not to say that our research activities were totally open and undirected. At the very least they were directed by my guiding intention to understand the nature and workings of writer identity. Beyond that, they were guided by plans I had made, advised by my steering group, as to the sorts of questions to ask in order to stimulate discussions which would enhance understanding. I think that, if we had not had some guiding themes to explore, the findings would have become 'everything about everything about mature student writing' (Simon Pardoe, in discussion), and the less interesting for that.

SUE: It seems to me that without some kind of framework for data collection, the result would be, as you say, total confusion. The important point is to be honest about the problem – and open to negotiation about the constraints of the 'framework'.

Take a holistic approach

ROZ: This principle involves looking at an object of enquiry from every possible point of view. It is connected both with having an open approach to data collection, as we have just discussed, and with using many types of data and methods of collecting it. Taking a holistic approach is motivated by the wish to produce a 'thick description' (Geertz, 1973). In order to do this, an ethnographer must not only collect a wide range of descriptive detail, but also be immersed in the context from which it is derived sufficiently to be able to recognise the meanings of this detail.

SUE: Again, I agree wholeheartedly. The idea of taking numerous situated points of view implies 'triangulation' and, in the absence of what we both agree is an unobtainable objective stance, or a 'view from nowhere', multiple perspectives must add depth to your understanding.

ROZ: In considering this principle, I had to identify what my
'object of enquiry' is. Was it (a) 'writer identity'? (b) the
eight writers who are my co-researchers? (c) the nature of
writer identity for these eight people? (d) the nature of
writer identity for those eight people writing this particular
essay? (e) the eight academic essays they wrote? The very
fact that it could be any of these convinces me that I am
taking a wholistic approach – I was studying all five in the
light of each other. However, I found it most useful to focus
my attention on (d). (a) is too abstract: it guided my data
analysis, but it was not the level at which I was making decisions about data collection. (b) and even (c) are too general: I wanted to be more specific than this. (e) was tempting:
as a linguist I felt most comfortable when devoting my attention to the texts. However, this would be too narrow a focus
for generating understandings about writer identity. I had
to think about what constituted holistic data for this object
of enquiry rather than any other.

SUE: When one realises how interconnected everything is, it's
difficult to isolate anything as the 'object of enquiry'. The
whole problem with method is knowing where to stand in
order to investigate the links, isn't it?

ROZ: Yes, and that leads us from data collection to data analysis.

Principles guiding data analysis

The problem of categories

ROZ: Doheny-Farina and Odell (1985) summarise what is involved
in analysing qualitative data under the headings 'developing categories' and 'linking categories and building a model'.
They see this process as 'intensive' and 'systematic', trying
'to identify specific phenomena as instances of a larger class
or pattern in the data' (p. 526), depending 'in part on intuition, serendipity, inspiration' (p. 527). Several researchers
using these methods of data analysis point to the danger of
'data analysis' becoming 'data reduction'. While searching
for categories, constructs and connections and while writing up, it is essential to keep as close as possible to the data
itself: to make generalisations 'without sacrificing flavor,

thick description, or a sense of the full context' (Kantor *et al.*, 1981: 304).

On the subject of 'linking categories and building a model', Doheny-Farina and Odell (1985) quote Shatzman and Strauss (1973: 111):

> For once the analyst gains a Key Linkage – that is, a meta-phor, model, general scheme, overriding pattern, or 'story line' – he [their generic pronoun] can become increasingly selective of the classes (categories) he needs to deal with: classes to look for, to refine further, or to link up with other classes. The principal operational advantage to the researcher of creating or finding a key linkage is that, for the first time, he has the means of determining the significance of classes. Without it, he . . . will never feel comfortable enough to im-plement closure. (p. 529)

This description of ethnographic research seems import-ant in three ways. Firstly, the categories are no use without the 'story line': it is essential to reach this final stage in the analysis. Secondly, Shatzman and Strauss admit that the researcher may 'create' this, rather than 'finding' it. Thirdly, it is clear from this account that searching for the key linkage must happen during the process of generating constructs and categories. It is not somehow cheating, but inevitable, to let the emergence of an overriding pattern guide the selec-tion of and relative attention to categories. This applied to our research in two ways. Firstly, I was imposing categories on linguistic data by labelling discourse types, as we dis-cussed earlier. But secondly, and perhaps more deserving of critical reflection, I was imposing categories on what you said about your experience of self-representation in your writing. I derived 'linking categories' to make sense of and organize the many diverse things you each said about your experience.

SUE: It seems to be essential to make sense of what would other-wise be 'a blooming buzzing confusion' (a metaphor I picked up from the philosophy of aesthetics). On the other hand, one does not want to constrain the data to the point of disengaging it from its social context – which made it what it was. I go along with the aims of Henry Moore, the sculp-tor, who always maintained a creative principle of 'truth to materials'. His goal was to establish a relationship between himself (the artist) and the material he worked with by letting that raw material speak through the interpretations he brought to bear on it. In my own research, I have always been aware of a commitment to this kind of integrity – of trying not to force my data to fit too snugly into a pattern of explanation.

ROZ: Qualitative/ethnographic research is sometimes dismissed as a subjective, private understanding (as Brumfit and Mitchell warn, 1989: 7). In order to increase the internal validity of my analysis, I did three things. Firstly, I described as exactly as possible the procedures I used to select and collect data, to generate categories, constructs and connections, and to match examples to them. Secondly, I involved you as my co-researchers in assessing the validity of my analysis of your writing and, to some extent, of what you said about your writing. At the second steering group meeting, I discussed with you the overall sense I was making of the data, and checked with you how far and in what ways this matched your own intuitions. Thirdly, I cross-checked ideas generated by one type of data with another type of data for the same individual, and cross-checked the eight case studies with each other.

Integrating linguistic analysis with analysis of the conversations

ROZ: As a linguist, my temptation was to fall back on my knowledge of ways of analysing texts and to sideline the understandings I had gained from our extensive conversations. I found it hard to decide what to do with the taped conversations, and even harder to avoid treating the two types of data in isolation.

A key role for the interviews was to identify parts of the texts which were worth focusing on for detailed linguistic analysis. I concentrated for my examples on parts of the text which you had identified as particularly interesting or troublesome for you, or as coming from some particular source. Often you identified discourse types which I may not have noticed alone. This provided an additional lens with which to look at the texts, helping me to know what else to turn my linguist's eyes on. So, for example, you had mentioned differences between ways of writing philosophy and science and had pointed out some instances; I then went on to look for others. I was then able to ensure that I had your commentary on many sections of text which I analysed, and that I had textual examples of many of the insights about the discoursal construction of identity which had arisen in the conversations.

Working in this way made it essential for me to develop cross-referencing systems. I listed all parts of the texts which were referred to in the conversations and cross-referenced them with the line numbers of the transcript of the interview in which we discussed it. I was then able to use these lists to trace the textual example of something which had been raised in a conversation, or a commentary on, or explanation of, something in a text.

Going beyond analysis to explanation

I drew on my insider knowledge of the institutions of higher education in Britain, and on my understandings of my co-researchers' experiences, interests, affiliations, values, beliefs and practices to take the crucial extra step of suggesting how the various discourse types in the essays positioned their users. Without this knowledge, linguistic analysis would be nothing but a series of descriptions of text which would mean little more in terms of writer identity than 's/he has become the sort of person who uses these words and structures'. With the benefit of cultural knowledge and in-depth conversations with writers, it is possible to suggest what sorts of values, beliefs and social relations these words construct for their users. This additional step can turn 'discourse analysis' into 'critical discourse analysis': making the connection between linguistic form and subject positioning. Language use can then be understood as an act of identification which can contribute to entrenchment or contestation of dominant values, practices and power relations.

Writing about research

ROZ: It is not common to find this issue addressed in a discussion of research methodology. However, this is just as much an area of decision-making as data collection and analysis are.

Qualitative research and the nature of academic writing

> The data, the analysis and the writing up are interrelated. I developed the terminology and categories which appear as subheadings in what I have written about this research by going back and forth between the data (texts and conversations), the theory and the writing. For me, the crucial issue was to hold on to the exact words of my co-researchers, and the exact examples of their discoursal choices, and not allow generalisations either to dominate my account or to eclipse the subtlety and complexity of the actual situations.

SUE: Had it ever occurred to you that your data could tell many stories? This means that the writing can be a patchwork of takes on the data from different perspectives. As you know, my writer identity is somewhat fragmented and my research has been inter-disciplinary. Being on the 'outside' and constantly struggling to write within the constraints of several discourse types has work-hardened me into what a cultural theorist might call 'postmodern eclecticism'!

The issue of confidentiality

ROZ: Confidentiality is not a straightforward issue in the context of a co-researcher relationship. On the one hand, I wanted to credit you with your insights in your own names. On the other hand, there are some issues which were raised in this research which were delicate and could be compromising for some co-researchers. These considerations led me to encourage co-researchers to agree to my adopting pseudonyms for them, at any rate in some situations, often when they themselves were less worried about confidentiality than I was. But in my view, even pseudonyms are not a carte blanche for unbridled revelations. However careful I am to preserve co-researchers' anonymity, anyone who actually knows them, and knows they were involved in this research, is bound to recognise them in what I have written. I know that I have been cautious on these grounds, sometimes sacrificing what might have been an interesting observation for fear that it might intrude on the privacy of one of my co-researchers.

SUE: As you say, it is a complex issue. On the one hand, when a writer has struggled to find her own 'voice' in a text, she may not want to be made anonymous, after all, in academia it is an unforgivable oversight not to acknowledge authorship of concepts and ideas. On the other hand, subjects of research are not always in complete control of how their interview responses will be interpreted and disseminated. I think there needs to be an element of trust on the part of the co-researcher and respect on the part of the principle researcher; it's not an easy balance to achieve.

Dissemination

ROZ: It is only because of established practice that we take it for granted that research will be written about and disseminated in particular language and formats. In line with research-and-practice philosophy, I am committed to producing a variety of outcomes from the research which are in different formats, and available and accessible to a wider readership: not just academic articles. Our joint articles with Mavis Aitchison are examples of this (Aitchison *et al.*, 1994; Ivanič, Aitchison and Weldon, 1996).

Conclusion

ROZ: The principles we've been discussing are things I feel strongly about, to do with the ethics of research and the subjective nature of knowledge. These principles dictate certain ways of working. It is part of my identity as a person and researcher that I choose to do research in particular ways. Some aspects of the methodology depend on the exact topic of the research and/or practical considerations, but the principles are a priority, I think. Sue, what are the consequences for *you* of having worked with me as co-researcher on this topic of writer identity, in terms of your development since then as a critically aware writer?

SUE: I think this should include your development too – I'm not the only one who's learning.

ROZ: You're right. I learnt a great deal from being involved in this research, and particularly from the opportunity to work closely with you all as co-researchers. I learnt not just about the nature of writer identity, but also about the research process – as we have been discussing here – and about myself as a writer. It is all too easy for writing researchers to leave themselves out of the picture: to forget that they, too, are learner-writers. I certainly learnt not to take linguistic terminology for granted, responding to your constantly questioning what I mean. This made me critically aware of the positioning effect of this terminology, locating me firmly in a disciplinary discourse community, and often making me sound exclusive: something I am trying to avoid now. Discussing your struggles with meaning made me more aware of my own, and I often learnt, directly or indirectly, from the solutions you found.

SUE: Well, let me tell you about how I have come to think about myself as critically aware of my writing. As you know, writing has never come 'naturally'. But I have become more and more fascinated by the process, by the experience of realising the massive number of translation layers between mind and written word. However, it was only after you helped me to see the ways in which my academic and cultural history had permeated my written words that I realised how much my writing was being shaped by my situation, and that realisation was a shock. It made me feel schizophrenic.

The awareness of one's own situatedness in writing has helped me to understand that, in any writing, we are writing our own stories. This is an insight which I have carried with me and which has enriched my own research. In my PhD, I have written about how scientific and professional experts, and others, frame their accounts of the environment for environmental impact assessments. The scientific accounts were supported by lots of empirical data, while local people with an interest in their environment often produced very different kinds of evidence. These were culturally rich stories, laden with references to individuals and personalities, but they were not very authoritative, in relation to scientific accounts. I became fascinated by how these different stories about the environment were produced, and how they succeeded (or not) in achieving their desired ends. For instance, how much did they influence a planning inspector to recommend permission to build an airport runway?

For me, issues about the essential qualities of these stories, and their authority or power, are very significant. I wanted all accounts to be influential by virtue of their quality, not just the powerful ones. As a researcher, I had no role to play in the process of writing an environmental impact assessment, or in selecting whose accounts would be influential. But, in re-telling how they were produced, I was able to write about how some of those accounts became universal and immutable whilst others had only local meaning and no staying power. This is one story which illustrates the way in which critical awareness has been seeping into my identity as a researcher, and also how the meaning-ladenness of other people's writings has now become my concern.

ROZ: It was your idea to write this chapter as a 'conversation'; do you think it has worked?

SUE: It has certainly been a dialogic shaping process and, in the course of conveying how we research collaboratively, we have been able to maintain our own writer identities. Our readers will be left in no doubt about who said what – but we cannot possibly know how they will interpret our text.

9

Engaging with the challenges of interdiscursivity in academic writing: researchers, students and tutors

CHRISTOPHER N. CANDLIN AND GUENTER A. PLUM

I Contexts and constructs in academic literacy

In characterising writing in terms of texts, processes and practices, this volume explicitly invokes the complexity which attends the study of the writing process in the academy and in the professional workplace. The title also acknowledges an interdependence among what might appear a set of dissimilar constructs, and implicitly suggests an interdisciplinary alliance among the specific research methodologies underlying the constructs themselves: linguistic and discursive description (for texts), hermeneutic and ethnomethodological interpretation (for processes) and sociologically and ethnographically grounded accounting and explanation (for practices). Such interdisciplinarity will present a range of challenges to researchers, particularly those directed at the degree of required researcher knowledge and skill, but also those which arise from having to accommodate the distinctive research perspectives of each of the methodologies in question.[1]

Constructing an integrated research programme in academic and professional writing amid such diversity will not be easy. Yet it may be necessary, as Cicourel in a paper dealing with hospital-based medical discourse (Cicourel, 1992) argues in a call for research into communication to be 'ecologically valid'. In their introduction, where they explicate Cicourel's position on research, the editors suggest:

193

> The ideal researcher in Cicourel's model of analysis is thus one
> who does not hide his or her sources of information and research
> choices but makes them into a common resource to be shared with
> readers in an attempt to unveil the hidden processes of the selec-
> tion of information which guides participants and analysts alike in
> the conduct of their daily lives.
>
> (Duranti and Goodwin, 1992: 292)

Accordingly, not only are the understanding of written and spoken
texts, the discursive processes in which they are embedded, and
the practices underlying the discourses concerned, addressed in
an integrative way by participants as part of their acquisition of
meaning as social actors, but also this same integrative perspective
could ideally be adopted by researchers. Cicourel makes this goal
a basic principle of analysis:

> Verbal interaction is related to the task at hand. Language and
> other social practices are interdependent. Knowing something about
> the ethnographic setting, the perception of and characteristics
> attributed to others, and broader and local social organisational
> conditions becomes imperative for an understanding of linguistic
> and non-linguistic aspects of communicative events.
>
> (Cicourel, 1992: 294)

Key to this integration is the construct of context. For Cicourel,
context is always seen from two perspectives: the broader perspective, which he terms 'the institutionalized framing of activities',
and the narrower, emergent in talk, which he terms 'context in
the sense of locally organized and negotiated interaction'. This
position is not in itself new. It is to be found, more or less explicitly, in the writings of a broad range of workers in social anthropology, social philosophy and, indeed, from a lexico-grammatical
perspective, in Halliday's reworking of Firth's concept of context
of situation (Halliday, 1978; J. R. Firth, 1957). This is what Gee
(1990) calls big 'D' discourse, to be seen not just, however, in
Gee's terms as a way of identifying self or membership in social
groups and networks, but from our perspective as an integration
of texts, interaction orders and the social processes and practices
which reference systems of power and knowledge in establishing
particular subject positions and objects of enquiry.

Such an expanded and integrated view of discourse is problematic to conceptualise. It also places demands on research
methodology. It is undeniably Cicourel who has called most clearly

for such a methodology to be canvassed. The key requirements for researchers to address in such a methodology can be summarised as having the following foci:

- the hidden processes of reasoning and information processing;
- how knowledge is stored and retrieved;
- the simultaneous access by participants to several layers of analysis;
- the situating of talk in larger institutional contexts;
- the slow uncovering of layers of information about participants' roles and mutual knowledge;
- the need to retain a 'critical' attitude.

Cicourel bundles these requirements in his 'ecologically valid', discourse-based research. The term is significant. It suggests a mutuality and interdependence of actions among actors and practices, but also implies that researchers should enhance their working environment by harmonising otherwise independent research paradigms in some more ecologically sound interdependence. His paper also indirectly enjoins researchers to cooperate with, and adopt a distinctively reflexive attitude to, those discourse participants they work with, collaborating with them to seek explanations of *why* and not merely to offer descriptions of *how*. This is not merely to describe discourse data as text, but to interpret it as a process of ongoing accomplishment among co-participants in knowledge creation and display, and, further, to set both description and interpretation in the context of a broader social and explanatory analysis of the structural and historical place of such discourses, their conditions of production and interpretation in relation to the social practices of the institution in question, and of its members (Candlin, 1987; Fairclough, 1989, 1992a).

Addressing the research challenge of this integrated model in the context of academic writing is the major purpose of this chapter, and explains its place in this third part of the present book, providing a bridge to the case studies that follow in Part IV.

The challenge is not one for researchers of writing alone. For students engaged in academic writing, each of the constructs – texts, processes and practices – presents a complexity arising in part from the epistemologically and ontologically distinctive disciplinary worlds of academic study in which they are engaged. The texts students encounter and have to produce within a single programme of study may now in the post-modern and fragmented world of the academy be extremely various in nature. A student of Business Studies, for example, may be expected to confront texts from the disciplines of Accountancy, Economics, Financial Management, Corporate Organisation, Marketing, Statistics *inter alia*, each of which gives rise to a plethora of different text-types. Examples in such a colony of texts (Bhatia, this volume) are not only regularly purposively differentiated, they may be more or less textually distinctive. They frequently draw intertextually on a range of text-types. Insofar as they also imbricate diverse interpersonal relationships between author(s) and reader(s), and different orders of discourse, they represent an hybridised interdiscursivity, unpacking which presents considerable challenges to readers, and also to student writers. This blurring of generic boundaries itself reflects restructurings in the academy, indicating how within a major area of study, sub-disciplines may arise and colonise each other, thus presenting reader/writers with a mixed landscape of both new and once distinctive areas of knowledge, carried within these hybrid text types (Bargiela-Chiappini and Nickerson, in press).

Such dynamic variation in a changing geography of knowledge not only produces textual consequences. Modes of processing such texts will also vary. This is in part a consequence of the varying textual structures and design characteristics of the products of these disciplines, partly a result of an increasingly mediated variation in the reception and delivery of such texts, and also partly a consequence of disciplinary differences in the social contexts of the locations and moments of writing. More of a challenge still, as Lea and Street point out in this volume, is that disciplines have various unstated and obscured objectives for writing which extend beyond the display of disciplinary knowledge in search of some qualitative absolutes. As Spinks (1996) indicates in a study of student writing at Australian universities, while first-year students across a range of disciplines are held to be very competent descriptive writers, they are said to have only vague ideas about how to write analytically. The issue is not so much whether they do or whether they do not. What matters is the unclarity about the meaning of these criteria to students in practice. The responsibility for this uncertainty does not lie only, or even principally, with students. Disciplines themselves are often unclear about what 'analytic writing' might consist of, or are content to leave it to be variously defined through some gradual, osmotic shaping of student writing performance in conformity to particular generic models whose conventions are imposed externally by certificating bodies and reproduced in the guise of handbooks, manuals and course guides. As we point out later, and as our student informants explicitly voice, this vagueness is of little assistance to them.

Finally, as Gollin (this volume) and Berkenkotter and Huckin (1995) argue, the social practices of writers in these distinctive disciplines also vary in terms of particular social relationships and interactions among writers and between writers and readers. These are constitutive of the social world of writing in different disciplines and are expressed in terms of variably distinctive discourses which sustain and advance the social practices and agendas of the disciplines themselves (Gee, 1990; Killingsworth and Gilbertson, 1992).

For tutors, as for students, the challenges also lie within the literacy practices of their home disciplines and in the newly hybridised practices stemming from the now regular interdisciplinarity of degree programmes. For tutors, there are additional complexities, ones which derive in part from their varied interpretations of the construct text, and in part from their difficulties in determining what the writing goals of their students should be. This complexity is made more intractable through the ineluctable integration of writing with the display of disciplinary knowledge. Lea and Street's chapter in this collection explores this issue in some detail.

Challenges to tutors arise also from often polar differences of attitude amongst them in how they construe their responsibilities towards students, especially in regard to writing. Seen from the perspective of a mentor, writing is a vehicle by which to lead apprentices through a process of continual improvement into membership of the disciplinary academy. From an often uncomfortably authoritarian perspective, it becomes a means by which to marshal students through a set of technical practices to ensure accuracy and conformity. Responsibility may be shelved, as in Gollin's (1998a) reference to a typical unwillingness among tutors in the Computing department studied to spend 'content time' developing the literacy of their students, preferring to 'leave the job to "outsiders" on the other side of the campus', whom tutors perceive as being more qualified in the area and thus likely to be able to improve students' 'clarity of thought and conciseness of argument'; see also here Elliot and Kilduff (1991). Although this recourse may be a chimera, Gollin making the point that there is 'a considerable body of opinion which disputes such a claim', citing Burnett (1996) and Perkins and Salomon (1989), this does not weaken our general point. These challenges may be sharpest for tutors, in that they confront literacy practices in the academy which are ontologically highly complex, embodying a range of discursive events that at one and the same time meld a range of texts, discursive practices and social practices (Fairclough, 1992a). It is also a world in which they need as educators to acknowledge the cognitive potential of the participating student-writers, and yet accept the limitations on explanation of these literacy practices posed by their own varied tutorial and didactic skills and strategies. Such explanations may be further constrained by their own personal commitments to particular ideologically conditioned interpretations of the nature and significance of each of the constructs we have listed.

The study of writing in the academy, from the stance of researchers, students and tutors, thus presents a complex picture of interdiscursivity (Fairclough, 1992a); a highly variegated and multi-dimensional world of overlapping communities of practice, where, within what may be more or less discipline-specific writing events within longer literacy cycles (Gollin, 1998), participants through their salient choice and accomplishment of texts, processes and practices, evidence their degree of membership of perhaps several fuzzy-edged orders of discourse, coping with whose often unclear norms, multiple purposes and variably explicit conventions constitutes a particular challenge.

The research project and its data drawn on in this chapter from the two academic disciplines of Psychology and Computing provide ample evidence of this interdiscursivity (Candlin and Plum, 1998; Candlin and Plum, in press). There are, however, considerable differences between these two disciplines in terms of their stance towards writing, and among the informing sources contributing to their stance. Psychology maintains a strong vocational orientation, conditioned by the demands of accrediting professional bodies. This external constraint is very largely interpreted within the university as requiring students to frame their written work in conformity to particular well-defined literacy practices, sanctioned by these external agencies and institutions. Law would be another criterial example (see Spinks, 1998; Plum, 1998; Candlin, 1998). In Computing, in contrast, at least in the particular department under study, although one might regard the post-university marketplace as an equally powerful incentive and an important modelling influence, literacy practices are marked by an absence of any such influence from professional associations or workplace groups. They also reflect considerable variation in staff views about the nature of literacy and how issues of literacy are to be addressed. Nonetheless, there are some commonalities. Tutors in both Computing and Psychology report favouring the demonstration of an ability to abstract and generalise (whatever in practice this may mean). However, while Psychology positively disfavours the introduction of the personal in student writing, and seeks conformity to established generic norms, it appears that tutors in Computing, in contrast, encourage originality and the expression of personal affect.

Concerning external pressures on academic writing in Computing, as Gollin points out in her Project Report, tellingly entitled 'Literacy in a Computing department: the invisible in search of the ill-defined' (Gollin, 1998a), while there may exist a strong desire on the part of academics to prepare students for workplace writing, with many of the tutors having first-hand experience of such workplaces, yet the variation in workplace conditions and settings and the lack of any explicit feedback from those workplaces into the academy on what literacy practices and standards these diverse workplaces require, means that any university-centred response can only be diffuse and heterogeneous. In practice, there exist distinctions, not at all clearly defined, between what Gollin describes as the different demands of 'writing for the academy and writing for industry', but this unclarity generates much of the interdiscursive tension we referred to earlier. Even if one attempts to focus on modes rather than on contexts and sites, as Murray (1988, 1991) shows, communication in computing employs a wide variety of computer-mediated modes, extending and challenging the traditional boundaries of reading and writing, and making commonly understood notions of literacy norms even more difficult to substantiate.

In the integrated research programme we describe, we attempt to address some of these challenges, seeking to address the call Fairclough (1992a), from his critical discourse analytical perspective, makes for a greater rationality:

> any development [in the study of discourse] must come to terms
> with what I would see as a major problem for non-critical discourse
> analysis, that is what I shall call the rationality of its research

programme. I take a 'rational' research programme to be one which makes possible a systematic development in knowledge and understanding of the relevant domain, in this case, discourse. Given the in principle infinite amount of possible data, a principled basis for sampling is necessary for such a programme. No such principled basis is possible so long as discourse analysts treat their samples as *objets trouvés*, i.e. as long as bits of discourse are analysed with little or no attention to their places in institutional matrices . . .

Having such a rational research programme in mind may go some way to meeting Cicourel's ecological validity requirement. As Bremer *et al.* (1996) acknowledge in their own attempt to position their research into immigrant second language acquisition against Cicourel's benchmarks, the issue is how to harmonise these distinctive methodologies into a workable programme of what we might call interdiscursive research. Inevitably, with this focus, we will need in our discourse world and our big 'C' context, to adduce experiences and perceptions not only from tutors but also from students, the other respondents to the challenges we have sketched so far.

As a way of meeting such a challenge, we select in the third section of this chapter two particular and currently contested issues in the study of academic literacy, and within these two address a third: the issue of *generic integrity* in the context of a descriptive orientation to research on text, the issue of *apprenticeship*, criterial for any explanatory orientation to research on practices and membership, and affecting both these, the issue of *participant relationships*, arising in any interpretative orientation to research on process.

II   Integrating research modes and methods in academic literacy

The multi-dimensional research design we propose integrated a systemic-functional text analysis (Halliday, 1994) using techniques drawn from Rhetorical Structure Theory (RST) (Mann and Thompson, 1986a, 1986b; Mann *et al.*, 1992) as a way of analysing a select corpus of student texts with a focus on their rhetorical structure (see Stuart-Smith, 1998; O'Brien, 1995), and linked this to accompanying discourse analytical studies of students' written texts, setting both against analyses of tutorial assessments of students' written work (Spinks, 1998; Gollin, 1998a).

Concurrently, ethnographic accounts (generated from interviews, open discussions and focus-groups) were elicited from a
selection of participating tutors and student-writers in the disciplines concerned, addressing their views on the nature and aims of
academic literacies, the conditions surrounding the writing process,
and their mutual understandings of, and reactions to, the literacy
demands posed by the institutional practices of their particular
disciplines (Plum, 1998). These aggregated data and these analyses were regularly interrogated by the research team and further
reference made to published in-house documents addressing preferred literacy practices in the disciplines concerned, together with
information on this topic provided by tutors in lecture sessions
devoted to the practices of writing, a number of which were transcribed and analysed (Plum, 1998). Further, less structured information was adduced from other out-of-house documents, some of
which derived from reports on pre-university school-based writing
practices, and reports from Examination Boards (Spinks, 1998), and
some from ephemera concerned with more or less substantiated
and usually negatively evaluated accounts of the supposed state of
literacy among university students.

We sought thus to effect that integration of the textual, pro-
cessual and practice-focused constructs we argue for above, with a
corresponding alliance of descriptive, interpretative and explanatory research orientations.

In terms of data, the research has constructed a sizeable
machine-readable database of some 450 optically scanned essays
and (lab and stats) reports in Psychology from first-, second- and
third-year undergraduate students in distinct course units. These,
together with some further 90 examples of diverse student writing
from Psychology and Computing, are also stored as hardcopy text,
covering a range of genres: laboratory (lab) reports, essays, statistics (stats) reports, critical analyses of the processes involved in
modifying a computer program, and reports on the preparation
of a business plan. These primary written data are further augmented by a tape-recorded archive of corresponding primary oral
data drawn from focus-group discussions with students in Psychology addressing four key issues of concern:

- student literacy: the functions of students' academic writing
- the practices of academic writing across disciplines
- the modelling of writing in Psychology
- student writing: the role of tutors in students' learning to write.

The student oral data were drawn from focus-group discussions with 28 groups of male and female students (with a bias towards female given the overall disciplinary bias) in five undergraduate courses in first-, second- and third-year Psychology programmes in the 1995–96 academic year. For fuller details of the participants and the data-gathering regime, see Candlin and Plum (1998). To these oral data from students were added tutorial talks given by individual tutors in Psychology in reaction to students' written assignments.

The data archive also contains additional secondary data drawn from discipline-specific writing manuals, assessment guidelines and marksheets, as well as tutors' notes extracted from student written texts. Discussion data between researchers and tutors in both Computing and Psychology on tertiary literacy issues is also included, associated with which are research-team discussions on the nature and quality of tutor feedback in Computing and Psychology, and on other relevant issues connected with the overall aims and conduct of the research project. In reviewing these data sets, it is important to recall Cicourel's point concerning ecological validity. The value of this interdiscursivity in research will only reveal itself in the context of addressing particular issues confronting the participants in the discourse worlds and communities of practice under study.

A brief example may be helpful at this point:

The RST analysis was only partly directed at demonstrating its viability as a tool for the analysis of academic texts. There were three other aims: firstly, to appraise the value of the methodology in assisting the exploration of relationships between writing performance, in particular the structure of written texts, and tutor assessment, 'to discover the types of structural features which were associated with essays graded A and C; in other words, which features were valued by markers' (Stuart-Smith, 1998). Secondly, on that basis, to formalise what tutors regarded as the features of 'analytical' or 'argumentative' writing, typically noted in markers' comments, and in university academic manuals, as characteristic of an 'A' grade, and explicitly set as a key disciplinary feature of valued writing performance in Psychology (see Spinks, 1998). Thirdly, to describe more precisely the rhetorical features of particular examples of student writing displaying the attainment of such desirable goals, noting any shortfalls, as well as exploring the extent students and tutors agreed on these characteristics, and their ascribed value. The analyses were then to be used for student academic writing training (as they have been, see Stuart-Smith, 1998), as a way of evidencing to students the rhetorical characteristics of preferred and dispreferred models. The option also exists (though we did not take it up in this research) of displaying any changes in students' writing, in respect of given rhetorical features, over the progress of an academic course, and to correlate these changes with any heightened student awareness of the literacy targets set for the discipline in question and its genres.

The data for the RST analyses consisted of 12 first-year Psychology essays, of which 6 were graded as A, 6 as C; within each set of 6, 3 were written by students who self-selected as having work-related writing experience and 3 by students without that experience. Results from the analyses provided a set of quantifiable rhetorical features that could be associated with A and C graded essays, and offered a means of comparing students' written performance within and across grades, and also suggesting detailed ways in which different student profiles, in relation to the rhetorical features isolated, could be set against grades received and the evidence of their rhetorical features. As Stuart-Smith (1998) concludes: 'identifiable patterns were found that could demonstrate differences between coherent, well-developed arguments and those that were less effective'.

Taking an integrated research perspective permits further objectives to be considered. Comparisons may be made between this descriptive textual evidence and how tutors in their written assessments comment on students' work, or how they assess writing goals in their manuals, guides and writing tutorials, or what students themselves perceive to be the requirements of different disciplines. Evidence from the project research suggests that there is by no means agreement among these various participants on this matter (see also the chapter by Lea and Street in this volume). Extending RST analyses across disciplines and across disciplinary genres would also facilitate closer linkage between the constructs of intertextuality and interdiscursivity, tying text to its institutional frame in Cicourel's and Fairclough's sense (see above), and offering a way of displaying more clearly differences in institutional norms and practices. It would provide clear textual and discursive evidence of what is inferable from other sources in our research data from Psychology and Computing, namely, how the former rigidly prescribes particular generic structures and the latter permits and encourages a much more *laissez-faire* hybridisation (Fairclough, 1992a; Bhatia, this volume; Gollin, 1998a).

III   Issues for research in academic literacy

Like the constructs of this chapter and their associated research orientations, the sample issues we have identified as a way of testing the viability and robustness of the research paradigm are also interdependent. The choice of *generic integrity*, *apprenticeship* and *participant relationships* is also relevant in that all three issues are current sites of debate (Bhatia, 1994 and this volume; Swales, 1990; Belcher, 1994; *inter alia*). The contested and inconsistent positions taken on the issues can only be identified and readied for explanation if the research programme is similarly integrated.

1   Generic integrity

As Bhatia (Bhatia, this volume, 1993, 1994) and other writers such as Berkenkotter and Huckin (1995), Swales (1990), Bazerman (1994a) and Freedman and Medway (1994) have indicated, genre identification is complex and contested, requiring a combination of indicators, only one of which relates to some specific selection and patterning of lexico-grammatical and rhetorical features. As Bhatia points out (this volume), genres may as well be indicated by 'the rhetorical context in which the genre is situated, the communicative purpose(s) it tends to serve, and the cognitive structure it is meant to represent'. Genres are also recognisable through their emblematic status as representatives of particular discourses and discourse worlds. Genres are constituted as such by virtue of their realisational value as evidential data of particular social and institutional practices and memberships, deriving their efficacy as genres, further underlining their integrity, from their instrumental value in achieving particular institutionalised purposes. Note that this integrity is a subtle mix of internal evidence and external attribution. Genres display textual characteristics, both lexico-grammatical and discursive, and are also identified as such by co-members of the institutions for whom they are both characteristic and useful, and quite possibly for a range of other reasons. Given the increasing intertextuality of genres (see Bargiela-Chiappini and

Nickerson [in press]), what we might call their status as recognis-able by members may well be increasingly unsure. This uncer-tainty may derive more from complex social-psychological factors not directly related to any obvious textual integrity, especially since the intertextuality is itself motivated by four powerful com-municative forces: those associated with personal intentions of the writer(s), those associated with the mediating vehicle, those with the expectations of recipient audiences, and those associated with some possibly aggressive discursive colonisation on the part of hegemonic institutions and authorities. Clearly, textual identity, the processes of participant relationships and the practices of in-stitutions all combine in helping to reveal the nature and extent of generic integrity, and do so across a wide range of genres. One good case in the business context is e-mail (Murray, 1995, Bargiela-Chiappini and Nickerson [in press]), as would be also the use of texts which have an explicitly textualised function as one genre but are transmuted into another; advertisements being a further classic case.

Accordingly, any exploration of *generic integrity*, whether in the academy or anywhere else, must draw on the integrated research paradigm we outline above if it is to accommodate and make sense of this diversity. *Generic integrity* is clearly a matter of text, of discursively mediated participant relationships and processes, and of institutional practices. These constructs will not necessarily be in harmony. It is likely that they will not corroborate each other. Textual features held to be generically indicative by some parti-cipants may not be seen so by others; considerable variation in textualisation, perhaps the product of some motivated and delib-erate intertextual admixture, for whatever reason, may or may not be admissible as generically appropriate by all. From an insti-tutional practice perspective, generic conventions governing the design of institutional texts may be more or less stable, well-policed and maintained or more or less unstable, and for a range of reasons: for example, lack of unanimity about audiences or purposes, or some flux in the present constitution and practices of the discipline or workplace. Here again, *participant relationships* are at the core of institutional practices, as they are of texts.

The academy is a promising community of practice (Lave and Wenger, 1991) for such an enquiry, and the disciplines of Psycho-logy and Computing identified in our research are equally useful critical sites (Candlin, 1997) for highlighting these issues.

Psychology

To begin with Psychology: here we have a small set of what the discipline regards as well-defined genres, essentially the Psychology essay and the Psychology report (subdivided into the lab report and the stats report). These genres encompass key attributes of writing in Psychology – the presence of a clear, cogent and concise argument and the presence of a tailored structure. The content, purpose and design of these genres are clearly announced via more or less hortatory instruments:

- guides and manuals on writing practices
- handbooks (internally produced)
- reference works on writing for psychology (externally published)
- tutorial lectures on writing
- assignment assessment proformas

or are conveyed indirectly through tutorial feedback in terms of grades and annotations on students' written work, and through face-to-face meetings with students. Psychology stands out among disciplines in providing students with models and with attendant advice on genre, subject content, style presentation (including spelling, correctness of grammar), rules to be observed (in terms of referencing and citing of sources, etc.), and sanctions regarding breaches of these rules (e.g. for plagiarism). Psychology genres would seem to meet at least some of Bhatia's criteria for *generic integrity*. They promise textual integrity, close participant relationships displaying adherence and conformity to authority, aided by a number of discipline-specific devices which underpin the discursive practices. Three examples from such instruments, drawn from Plum (1998), emphasise the point:

> . . . Psychology as a science involves the discovery of that knowledge through the special measures that researchers use to study behaviour and experience. Psychology as a profession involves, for example, the application of that knowledge to promote human welfare through the particular techniques that practitioners use to assist people. Thus, psychology involves a body of knowledge, research to obtain that knowledge, and the application of that knowledge.
>
> (PSY104 and PSY105: Introduction to Psychology I and II [Unit Study Guide])

Defining and understanding arguments:
In studying psychology, there are two broad goals to be met, firstly, to help you acquire knowledge about psychology and secondly, to help you learn to think in a critical way about this knowledge.
. . . Critical thinking is the key to understanding psychology. But what is critical thinking? It is an active and systematic process based on logical approaches. Critical thinking is based on arguments, and how these arguments are understood and evaluated. An introduction to critical thinking, the purpose of this tutorial is to introduce the concept of an argument and to resolve the argument into its component elements. That is, to give a detailed structural analysis of arguments.

> (PSY104: Introduction to Psychology I
> [Yr 1, Sem 1], Tutorial Guide)

psychology essays and reports are expected to show critical, rational analysis of data and methods and to be presented in a literary manner. In both forms of writing you need to read and present an argument, rather than just regurgitating existing information. (O'Shea 1993)

> (PSY104: Introduction to Psychology I
> [Yr 1, Sem 1], Tutorial Guide)

However, what our research shows (Spinks, 1998; Plum, 1998), in common with that of Lea and Street (this volume), is that while the teaching and discussion of structure and argument in guidelines, handbooks and tutorials present a view of shared, explicit, and thus teachable knowledge, the practice of feedback from tutors shows that in the specific instance of a student's piece of writing, these concepts are likely to be interpreted variably by markers. The many complaints concerning marker variability voiced in our focus-group data show that students also perceive matters this way. This is not to damn markers as inconsistent or hypocritical, simply to indicate that when a general concept meets particular instantiation in written work, markers' practices reflect the knowledge, assumptions and practices of the discipline, much of which is implicit, rather than reflecting the explicit guidelines set down in the manuals. Not that this discrepancy is only in relation to the manuals. From observation of tutorials on report writing to prepare students for the writing up of experiments in lab report form, tutors took considerably different approaches, less in terms of the assumed generic structure of the report, than in the actions students should take to meet the general disciplinary requirement, and what tutors saw as being the overall academic and professional purposes of practising report writing. The more these were couched in terms of 'training to be a psychologist' or 'being part of a scientific education', the less easy was it for students to follow the advice in their actual writing; yet the more tutors emphasised the mechanical conventions of producing a report, the less likely was it that students would avoid that 'regurgitation' proscribed in the external and internal handbooks and manuals. We infer that while the governing *participant relationship* between discipline and student is one of authority exercised in the service of disciplinary goals, students by no means necessarily accept this, or indeed even fully understand it. Such a relationship is in any case varyingly construed by the tutors themselves.

It appears then that such variation in tutorial instruction for writing in Psychology stems from the range of approaches taken to explaining and motivating its preferred generic structures in the context of its academic and professional purposes mediated by its preferred participant relationships. This variation introduces disjunction among textual structure, communicative purpose, interpersonal action and institutional rationality, undermining the tightly bound concept of *generic integrity* perhaps inferable from inspecting the modelling instruments alone. This disjunction arises among the practices of both tutors and students. Students appear to frame the writing of particular genres primarily in terms of the following of rules, models and procedures. There is little evidence in our data of students framing their own genre-specific writing in relation to their experience of other genres or more generally from their own cultural experience. Unmistakably, students frame their writing as something to be belittled (*bible, pedantic*) and dismissed as authoritarian imposition (*how to set out, follow, write*); a set of surface compositional rules imposed by authority. They make little link between technique and institutional membership and practice, in the way highlighted by Bazerman:

> With the article in psychology primarily presenting results, constrained and formatted prescription, authors become followers of rules to gain the reward of acceptance of their results and avoid the punishment of non-publication.   (Bazerman, 1987: 139)

In not making this connection, students undermine the concept of *generic integrity*, reducing it to a matter of text. This is not that students are unappreciative of the guidance given; the central issue is *why* students might appreciate the advice, whether as a means of helping them learn to write appropriately generically, thus recognising *generic integrity*, or simply because it helps them get good grades. Uncertain and contradictory student voices from the focus groups make this confusion plain:

> don't know what depth to go into, don't know how to analyse the data, or whether they want you to actually criticise or analyse or what.   (PSY104)

> Every subject has their own essay formula. Are we supposed to be describing or criticising?   (PSY104)

> The style of reporting and discussion is different in psychology from science subjects; it's non-conclusive.   (PSY105)

> In philosophy, you have to keep asking questions; you can't come to a conclusion.   (PSY104)

Computing

If there is such disjunction in the well-regulated discourse world of academic writing in Psychology, only revealed when texts, processes and practices are interwoven in the process of an integrated research methodology, *generic integrity* is tested to the full in the much more fluid world of Computing.

To begin with, the discipline diverges into two main sub-disciplines, Programming, where in a sense genres as such seem not to be clearly defined in literacy terms, and Business Systems (Technology Management). Although the colony of genres in Computing is complex and interdiscursive in consequence of some considerable interdisciplinarity in the formation of this relatively new area of academic study, there is a significant, if surface, homogenising effect to be noted, largely from the prevalent use of software programs such as Powerpoint, and Word, linked to the use of any one of a number of popular statistics packages. What is significant in our data is the complete absence of any of the discipline-specific guidelines or manuals characteristically present in Psychology, and the lack of any specific tutorial sessions directed at writing, though some indirect guidance is provided through tutorial assessment of assignments. Drawing on Gollin (1998), it appears that a wide range of genres is acceptable in Computing and no genre is especially privileged. As she points out:

> Students are neither rewarded nor penalised for writing in a particular genre or register. The examples range from personal journal to formal report, with many showing aspects of hybridisation . . .
>
> (Gollin, 1998: 319)

It is significant for the general argument about disjunction that Gollin does not see this deviance from disciplinary generic integrity as especially purposeful and motivated; rather, it is likely to derive from confusion over the nature of the communicative event itself, its purposes, and, especially, over the tenor of the *participant relationships* between students and the audience for which they are writing. Perhaps, also, the comparative newness of Computing as a discipline has not yet permitted the stabilising of its communicative practices. These uncertainties may also reflect some fundamental division concerning the discipline's literacy goals. Tutors appear to make sharp distinctions between the goal of becoming an IT professional (programmer, systems analyst, technology manager, etc) and the goal of becoming a competent writer of English. The general disciplinary view is that literacy consists of skill development, technical accuracy in composition, and, in part, the mastery of argument, with the latter probably being better taught elsewhere, usually in the Humanities, and imported.

Nonetheless, given the following tutorial comment, cited by Gollin:

> Students should not simply report what they did and when they did it. We spend quite a bit of time discussing the need for a 'story' or a 'line' (so in a sense this is like an essay, but the word 'essay' is never used to avoid bad associations that some of these students have!)   (e-mail from lecturer to researcher)
>
> (Gollin, 1998: 319)

it appears that notwithstanding rather generalised generic targets that tutors have in mind, however negatively defined, students at least were unclear about what their conventions were. This may be due to several reasons, and, as with Psychology, relatable to all three constructs under study. There may be a lack of clarity about *participant relationships*, especially about audience, resulting perhaps from a lack of experience by some students of workplace contexts or, if they have had workplace experience, from uncertainties surrounding their professional writing role(s) in a future workplace. It may stem from confusions between some abstract concept of academy requirements generally and what is disciplinarily specific about the literacy practices of Computing (in whichever sub-discipline). The diffuse range of remarks by tutors about text design and quality may be a further cause.

Where models were set, they varied among tutors, and on occasion tutorial assessment comments implied that writing as a technical skill might be disengaged from writing as the expression of subject-matter content. A further example from Gollin (1998) concerning what students conceived an 'abstract' to be, provokes more than a wry smile. Some, she notes, 'used it as a kind of personal message to their lecturer about their ability or inability to complete the assignment', another, whose abstract 'ran to a quarter of the whole assignment', received the comment '"This is not an abstract"'. Magritte lives . . .

In the light of the composite view of generic integrity set out by Bhatia (this volume), the assignments set further compound this uncertainty Two examples will make the point: one required students as part of a Technology Management course to observe the performance of a group in preparing a business plan, and to develop what might be best described as a social-psychological analysis and report of group behaviour measured against a set of qualitative indices; the other asked students in a Systems Software course to solve a computing problem and to provide a written critical analysis of their problem-solving process. The issue here is not one of expected differences in the two genres, it is more that the assignments vary in the degree they direct themselves to a pedagogic goal and to a post-university professional and workplace goal. The business-plan assignment, though reflecting the workplace, actually focuses on pedagogic practice, while the computing assignment partly does that but partly mirrors a workplace need to report on a project outcome and its constituent processes. For the research project, as for this chapter, the challenge to *generic integrity* lies in the tensions arising from the simultaneous framing of the students as professionals solving real-world problems and as students being assessed on their learning:

> pedagogical purposes don't always mesh with workplace purposes; student perceptions are seldom the same as professional perceptions; pedagogical success privileges process, whereas workplace success privileges productivity.
>
> (Burnett, 1996: 154, cited in Gollin, 1998: 308)

From this account, two matters are significant for the issue of *generic integrity*, and they are related. Firstly, all three constructs, textual structure, interpersonal relationships and institutional practices, need to be involved in its delineation and these may well not be corroborative of each other but in contestation. Secondly, only an integrated and interdiscursive research methodology can tease out their relationship and offer an explanation of their governing conditions.

2   Disciplinary apprenticeship

The ethnographic and social turn in the study of academic and professional literacies recognised by Swales (1990) in his call for the study of what he terms 'discourse communities', is not especially new, though it is now considerably debated. As Ann Johns points out (Johns, 1997), there is a long tradition of engagement of anthropological, sociological and ethnographic research in the study of literacies, for example the work of Geertz (1983); and with particular reference to the academy, Bazerman (1994a); Berkenkotter and Huckin (1995). To this we may add work in professional writing contexts, such as Latour and Woolgar (1979), as well as the much less referenced work on literacy in the academy by Bourdieu *et al.* (1994 [1965]), and the later study by Bourdieu and Passeron (1977). Not that 'discourse communities' has found universal favour as a term, indeed questioning the construct itself and exploring its presumed close relationship to the equally contested concept of 'genre' have produced a vigorous industry in the literature; see Rafoth (1990), Killingsworth (1992); and in the work of Swales himself (1990). The term has been matched by another powerful, if equally indeterminate, metaphor, that of 'communities of practice' (Lave and Wenger, 1991; Scollon, 1998) with its presumed correspondingly close association with members' shared systems of value and belief, allegiance to particular ideological positions, and its implication of shared activities and tasks. Both of these terms carry some baggage in relation to an implication of some gradually mentored pathway to membership, referred to explicitly by Berkenkotter and Huckin (1995) as a process of 'cognitive apprenticeship' similar to that envisaged by Lave and Wenger (1991) as a gradual *induction* from 'legitimate peripheral participation' to full exercise of membership privileges, marked by an awareness of institutional socio-rhetorical practices, referred to by Bazerman (1994a) as 'conversations of the discipline'.

Why is this concept of *apprenticeship*, and the associated notions of 'discourse community' and 'community of practice', of interest to this chapter? Chiefly, because our two research disciplines, Psychology and Computing, offer excellent sites from which to argue that, however appealing the general principle may be that underlies the terms, the understanding and acceptance of them by participants is by no means clear and self-evident. If this is so, then, as with the concept of *generic integrity*, an interdisciplinary and interdiscursive research methodology is needed to explore and explain such differences of understanding.

The metaphor that students in the academy are somehow akin to novitiates in a monastery or nunnery is well established and fits in with one interpretation at least of what education, as a process of leading towards some disciplinary, social and personal goals, may be said to be about (Spinks, 1998). The metaphor for this process becomes problematic metaphorically when termed *apprenticeship*, or when it is said to involve a process of 'induction' or, even more problematically, one of 'acculturation'. One interpretation of apprenticeship suggests a well-defined goal, achieving which confers membership privileges and responsibilities. The novice is set on some pathway, guided by some benevolent if eagle-eyed master, and in the process trades in or exchanges something of his or her original identity, or 'culture'. Some writers appear to take this view, such as Gee (1990), Latour and Woolgar (1979). If anything, apprenticeship to a 'discipline' is considerably more nebulous than apprenticeship to a trade. Gollin (1998a), sets out the traditional view of the apprenticeship process:

> The focus of an apprenticeship is on the development of the practical skills deemed necessary to perform the range of tasks an expert in the field can do. The apprentice observes and tries to emulate the example of the expert, and gradually assumes more responsibility for particular tasks or sub-tasks. These tend to be rehearsals of actual tasks in the field rather than merely pedagogic exercises.

Several interesting questions immediately arise: to what extent does the above correspond to literacy practices in the academy? How shared is such a view, or any other view, among the participants in the academic process? To what degree is such a view, or any other, shared across disciplines? Our contention is that responses to none of these deeply problematic questions can be taken as axiomatic, and that only an interdiscursive research methodology can offer any illumination of how they and their responses are formulated on the ground.

Several writers have addressed the issue of apprenticeship in the academy. Brown *et al.* (1989: 39) refer to a process of 'cognitive apprenticeship' where:

> the mentors (1) 'model' by making their tacit knowledge explicit and revealing their problem-solving activities; (2) 'coach' by supporting students' attempts to perform new tasks; and then (3) 'fade' after having empowered the students to work independently.

The test is whether such a process actually takes place, and if so, whether it does so across all sectors and in all circumstances. Belcher (1994), in a case study of three graduate students of non-English-speaking background in contact with their supervisors, shows the limitations of such a model, notably, that it depends crucially on some mutual bargain between the participants, is especially dependent on the ability or willingness of mentors to act in this way, and requires students to be willing to adopt what may be a continuing passive and recipient role. In Belcher's study, mentors did not necessarily provide the structuring support, nor the 'coaching' required, and did not make links between the pedagogic activities of the academy and real-world tasks. Even if one is sympathetic to Belcher's preference for Lave and Wenger's (1991) concept of 'situated learning', whereby learners are gradually to be drawn into this new community of practice through an active process of engaging with issues, tasks and problems of the 'lived-in world', there remain serious questions, at least from the perspective of our research. Students in Psychology may be being introduced to the cultural world of psychology through their writing assignments but this is a quite circumscribed pattern of contact, for the most part restricted to the performance of well-defined pedagogic tasks. There is little evidence from student feedback in focus groups that they perceive themselves as being 'apprenticed' as psychologists in any professional sense, even though some tutors take this perspective, and encourage students to take the risks Belcher associates with aspiring community participation. In general, however, at least at undergraduate level, there simply is not the close contact with experts on real-world field-derived problems that the term 'apprenticeship' conventionally implies. At best, we may say that some tutors seek in their comments on assignments to encourage students to identify with psychology as an intellectual community, particularly in our second-year student data, but that this goal is by no means understood as such by recipients. Even in a compulsory course unit designed to teach quite specific techniques about research methodology and psychological assessment protocols, the focus-group data suggest that students do not perceive tutors as adopting a professional trainer role. We conclude that undergraduate students in our sample lack opportunities, both qualitatively and quantitatively, for much 'peripheral participation' in the discourse community of psychology and do not enjoy enough of the 'conversations' with psychologists to acquaint them adequately with the current socio-rhetorical practices of their discipline.

Two other contexts in our data may provide a different perspective. The first is where students with prior work-related writing experience are involved and where another discipline, as here Computing, is the focus. There is evidence that Computing students with such experience do perceive themselves to varying degrees as apprentice professionals. This is largely due to the work-related nature of some of the assignments they undertake, and the links they can make to their own work experience. The connections between what Gollin (1998a) refers to as the 'writer-as-professional' and the 'writer-as-learner' are easier to establish in such contexts with such experienced learners. As she says, they may then identify more closely with the lecturer as an equal or as an insider who shares certain aspects of professional knowledge and practices. These connections are difficult to forge in undergraduate Psychology, though perhaps more possible in some specialised postgraduate training with clear vocational goals.

What advantages would our research model bring to the explanatory analysis of these questions concerning *apprenticeship*? Firstly, it is only by admitting participant accounts of the apprenticeship process that disjunction becomes evident, as in our student focus-group data. Secondly, it is only by a corroborative process of connecting those accounts with other process data, for example tutorial commentary on student assignments, that we can judge the degree to which tutors position themselves in this mentoring, apprentice-trainer role. An important addition, as in the case of *generic integrity*, is further data from manuals, guidelines and the like. Explaining the issues surrounding the apprenticeship goal(s) for student-writers requires the whole research enterprise to be so constructed as to set the local contexts of interaction against the broader Context of institutional practices, in the manner suggested by Cicourel at the outset of this chapter.

There is still a need, however, to incorporate the textual dimension. Fortunately, as several of the chapters in this book make clear (Hyland, Myers, Gollin), texts in the academy and the workplace always have participant relationships at their centre. Stance vis-à-vis current knowledge, other researchers and other practitioners, and stance vis-à-vis audience, lie at the heart of the processes of textualisation. Accordingly, in this case it will be textual evidence, in particular analyses of tenor and register choice in student writing, as much as process evidence from participant accounts and tutor appraisal, that will offer one basis for estimating the degree of 'mastery' achieved, or, perhaps, the degree of apprenticeship the writer wishes strategically to reveal. It is likely also that such evidence will offer insights into the nature of the multiple audiences that student-writers frequently are asked to address, and their *participant relationship* to them: peers, tutors potential employers (and in Computing there will be several), journal editors (to name just some), and into the varying discourse roles students are being asked to adopt in respect of each. Highlighting *participant relationships* further, and extending the textual analysis to tutor feedback, we may also appraise the degree to which the aspirant 'apprentice' enjoys that recognition by the master that membership of the community of practice guarantees. Our data from feedback on 'A' and 'C' grade assignments offers some confirmation of this (Spinks, 1998).

In sum, it will not be difficult at all to motivate this text-focused descriptive orientation as a stimulus for, and as a counterpoint to, the interpretative and the explanatory, thus further reinforcing the need for an interdiscursive research methodology in meeting the challenges posed by these issues.

Note

1. This chapter draws in part on data and analyses from a recently completed research project funded by the Australian Research Council (Grant #A79532392), with the title 'Framing student literacy: cross-cultural aspects of communication skills in Australian university settings', carried out in four tertiary institutions in Australia, namely, Curtin University, Perth (Professor Ian Reid – Chief Investigator), Edith

Cowan University, Perth (Professor Ian Malcolm), The University of Western Australia, Perth (Dr Susan Kaldor and Dr Michael Herriman) and Macquarie University, Sydney (Professor Christopher N. Candlin). The Macquarie research underpins this chapter, and was carried out with the support and resources of the Department of Linguistics, the National Centre for English Language Teaching and Research (NCELTR), and the Centre for Language in Social Life (CLSL). The authors wish to acknowledge the insights and experience of their Macquarie colleagues and that of the wider project teams. They are especially grateful to the staff and students of the two university departments which served as research sites for the Macquarie project.

PART IV

Realisation: focus on praxis

10

Lexical thickets and electronic gateways: making text accessible by novice writers

JOHN MILTON

This chapter first investigates problems that novice writers, especially learners of English, have in acquiring lexical features of
written discourse. It then describes features of an interactive writing kit (*WordPilot*) which assists them to access authentic text, and
then to transfer patterns they explore there to their own writing.
Relevant text corpora and specific lexical databases are made
available during the writing process through the mediation of this
integrated electronic reference, which incorporates several applications, including a concordancer, dictionary and thesaurus. This
learning and production device has been implemented for Cantonese-
speaking students in Hong Kong for whom English is a Foreign
Language, but the general principles have relevance to writers at
any point on the continuum of language proficiency.

1 Traditional constraints in access to text

Concern over the value of the explicit teaching of written discourse
has a long history. Issues debated in Plato's *Phaedrus* (Nehamas
and Woodruff, 1997) are still contested: the importance of written
discourse in the training of a citizen; what it is that makes discourse
effective; the discourse types (if any) that should be taught; and
even whether discourse can be explicitly taught or learned. These
questions are to be found at the heart of many current debates
among the diverse theories of Applied Linguistics and Second Language Acquisition. Beaugrande (1997), for example, reviews dialect-
ical contrasts between positions such as Pienemann's Teachability

Hypothesis (Pienemann, 1989) and Krashen's Natural Approach (Krashen and Terrell, 1983).

Much of this controversy is, I would argue, based on traditional, but primarily practical, limitations in accessing (and making accessible) appropriate text models and expert advice. Most novice writers need some combination of procedural and declarative support in understanding diverse rhetorical conventions, especially in extremes where students with limited L2 proficiency must write in the L2 in unfamiliar or poorly defined discourse roles and environments. Unfortunately, such support is often, at best, inadequate, and, at worst, counter-productive – sometimes even in the best-intentioned and best-resourced educational contexts.

2   Prefabricated text in novice writing

2.1   *The teaching of prefabs*

The emphasis on 'prefabricated patterns' or 'polywords' became an orthodox pedagogical technique about twenty-five years ago in the teaching of ESL/EFL, when Wilkins (1974) made the provision of prefabricated notional-functional lexical units of apparently high communicative value central to his approach. With the recent attention to findings from the computational analysis of lexis, many researchers (e.g. Sinclair, 1991; Altenberg, 1993) and syllabus designers (e.g. Willis, 1991; I. M. Lewis, 1993) advocate renewed pedagogical focus on collocational patterns of English. There is, however, no widely agreed definition of the term 'collocation', and therefore no standard way to measure performance – a continuing problem for both research and pedagogy. For the sake of simplicity, this chapter will conflate terms such as 'collocations' and 'fixed/prefabricated phrases', as does Kjellmer (1994: ix–xii), though, of course, collocational patterns occur in a very wide range of fixedness. Novice writers (L2 learners in particular) are often unaware of (or misinformed about) the precise combinatorial chemistry or pragmatic range of these expressions. Where social or pedagogical environments afford little access to sufficient and appropriate text models, novice writers need alternative ways to master these multitudinous patterns.

Certainly the mere provision of lists of lexis to the learner does nothing to promote the communicative principles which the proponents of lexical methodologies support. Nor does it necessarily lead to the production of accurate, fluent and situated discourse. For one thing, there are limits to how authoritative any lexical typology can be, since we are only beginning to understand the discoursal characteristics of grammatical and lexical structures. A great deal of research is still necessary to describe with any empirical rigour the lexis that is characteristic of particular purposes, genres and registers.

In circumstances where novice writers must compose formal text in an L2 that is not widely used in their immediate environment, they must usually depend on teachers and language textbooks to help them abstract effective language patterns for them. However, EFL novice writers are often provided only a fragmentary sense of the effect and purpose of the words and 'word chunks' of formal discourse. This limitation is not necessarily in the efforts made by teachers, but it is bound up with educational circumstances, as well as inherent restrictions in the nature of the print medium. Print may continue to be the best medium for extensive reading, and reading may be the best preparation for writing. But for advice on immediate production, students (and teachers) generally rely on printed pedagogical writing guides, which are inevitably restricted in how comprehensively and accurately they allow text to be represented, and in the timeliness and effectiveness by which the characteristic features of texts can be accessed. Such limitations often result in L2 novice writers having to rely on limited and unrepresentative lexical and grammatical patterns of the L2 (cf. Chang and Swales, this volume).

EFL teaching materials often do not provide adequate information about the precise meaning, pragmatic force, structural qualities, or appropriateness in various genres and registers of the lexical and grammatical formulae they present. At their worst, such materials present lists of words or phrases either out of context, or in artificial and misleading contexts, and encourage the rote learning of unexamined formulae. The purpose of such lists is often short term: to provide lexical first aid to students who need to satisfy immediate examination purposes. An example of such a list, distributed in a Hong Kong 'Tutorial School' (where students cram for examinations), is given in Figure 10.1, duplicated as it appeared (it had no accompanying explanations). It is difficult to see how such a list could assist novice writers learn to contextualize and manipulate linguistic formulae, or achieve rhetorical balance in their use.

Ways to express your own and other people's ideas:	Attitudes / Standpoints:

X (would) think/believe (that) . . .
 In my opinion . . .
 As far as I am concerned . . .
 From my point of view . . .
 It seems/appears (to me) that . . .
 X am/are of the opinion that . . .
 X am/are convinced that . . .
 Personally, I would tend to think/believe/argue
     that. . . .
 It is (generally) believed that . . .
 It has been argued/said/suggested that . . .
 Xs would argue/claim/consider that . . .
 A generally/widely accepted belief is that . . .
 (One of) the (main) arguments in favour
     of/against X is that . . .
 X has been (generally) regarded as/considered
     as . . .
 X is usually (being seen as . . .)
 Those who . . . + consider/are of the opinion . . .
	X are in favour of/for
	 X approve of . . .
	 X are against/critical
	     of . . .
	 X disapprove of . . .
	
	 Objective ideas:
	
	 It is true that . . .
	 It cannot be denied
	     that . . .
	 It is understood that . . .
	 There is no doubt
	     that . . .

Figure 10.1 Phrases recommended to L2 writers in teaching materials from a Hong Kong 'Tutorial School'

The essential problem with such a presentation is not the suspect (or at least misleading) grammaticality and collocability of several of the expressions. It is rather that novice writers limited in their exposure to written discourse are unlikely to hit upon the precise structural and pragmatic contexts in which these phrases are appropriate. Lexico-grammatical patterns are highly productive, offering more than just cookie-cutter templates for text production. However, besides being pragmatically undifferentiated, the true collocational range of the words and expressions is not conveyed by this list (e.g. how often are these words used in these and other structures?). There is no way for the novice writer (or novice teacher) to confirm whether these terms really are appropriate for, and characteristic of, expository text, and if they are, precisely how they function. If supportive opportunities are not provided for the flexible and creative manipulation of these devices, they can hinder rather than facilitate communication.

Novice writers who see the purpose of such supposedly fixed constructions as providing a way for them to avoid grammatical irregularities may be led to adopt a structurally repetitive style, regardless of the natural prosodies and argument structures of formal written discourse. One way the style of novice writers may be skewed is by the presentation of these expressions as if they occurred in only sentence-initial position, as in Figure 10.1. Such niceties may, of course, have little priority for the learners or their teachers in the face of the discourse for which they are preparing: the impending examination in the foreign language. The long-term danger is that, even should learners manage to achieve some approximation to what is 'grammatically tolerable' with the help of these formulae, they are given little advice, or are being misled, about what is 'textually tolerable' (Quirk *et al.*, 1985: 1460).

2.2   Prefabs in novice writers' texts

In order to arrive at a first approximation of the part that such formulaic phrases actually play in the formal school discourse of L2 student writers, especially in comparison with their use by accomplished L1 student writers, I counted the frequencies of all word strings in two representative corpora. I will not report here on the frequencies in L2 writers' texts of the 'Tutorial School' phrases from Figure 10.1, since there is no practical way to determine how many, or which, students were exposed to these lists. Table 10.1 lists the ten fixed (or nearly fixed) phrases (Nattinger and DeCarrico, 1992) which occur with the greatest disparity in these two corpora (for the purposes of this comparison, each corpus consists of 500,000 word-tokens). The corpus of L2 texts is composed of essays from the A Level school-leaving *Use of English* examination of Hong Kong students, with equal numbers of scripts graded in six bands (from A to F). The corpus of L1 texts consists of the writing of A Level school-leaving students in the UK who received grades of *A* or *B* on the *General Studies* written examination. The table also lists the frequencies of these expressions in textbooks used in Hong Kong secondary schools (described in Smallwood, forthcoming) and in a collection of published academic texts (articles from Linguistics and Social Science journals and collections).

2.3   Fronting and sign-posting

The phrases significantly overused by L2 students (see Table 10.1) appear almost exclusively in sentence-initial position. In the L1 student texts and the published articles examined for this study, the phrases are as likely to be embedded in subordinate positions.

Table 10.1 Frequencies of the ten most disparately occurring phrases in L1 texts compared with L2 student texts, with data from published texts

Lexical phrases occurring with the greatest disparity between L1 and L2 student texts:	Frequency of tokens in 500,000 words each of:			
	L2 student texts	L1 student texts	School texbooks	Published articles
Not used in L2 student texts				
In the/this case	0	9	11	16
It has also been	0	8	0	5
It can be seen that	0	8	0	4
An example of this is	0	8	0	3
This is not to say that	0	7	0	2
Overused in L2 student texts				
First of all	170	1	13	5
On the other hand	239	31	25	30
(As) we/you (all) know	118	2	22	3
In my opinion	110	12	8	0
All in all	59	2	1	0

Nor are sentence-initial discourse markers the most common fixed phrases in either the L1 student texts or the published academic articles. The most common fixed phrases in school textbooks used in Hong Kong, however, are biased toward sentence-initial positions. This conforms to the structure of the simple sentences favoured in these texts and may help emphasize the didactic and inquisitorial nature of the discourse (e.g. *This is a . . .*; *This is because . . .*; *What are the . . .*; *Do you think . . .*).

Sentence-initial discourse markers may thus be prominent in EFL student texts because these devices are implicitly (as above) or explicitly (as in Figure 10.1) made available to these L2 novice writers. Alternatively, L2 learners may, when they read, register fronted expressions more easily than non-fronted lexis, and possibly this list of head phrases may be more easily accessed from the mental phrasicon (a term gaining currency – see, for example, De Cock *et al.*, 1998). A less speculative reason why student writers might give sentence-initial discourse markers prominence is the importance attached in written school assignments and examinations to the communication of memorized content. Students may very well acquire, whether tacitly or expressly, the habit of emphasizing significant information in their texts by employing conspicuous lexical signposts as information markers.

The communication of content knowledge in educational contexts is especially endangered by infelicitous L2 sentence grammar and restricted or inappropriate vocabulary, which often makes the meaning of an EFL novice writer's text difficult (and, in the case of the weakest L2 writers, sometimes impossible) to understand. Because of this, readers who must grade such papers for content may consider themselves and their students best served by encouraging the use of 'strong' discourse markers which explicitly signify information structure. For proficient and experienced writers, discourse markers form part of a range of textual functions that distinguish between the marking of information and the marking of cohesion (Biber, 1988: 34). In contrast, EFL student discourse in formal assignments and examinations is probably affected by the need to compensate for syntactic irregularities by increasing the informational weight that sentence-initial discourse markers are made to bear. In this way, those grading the paper have clear signposts to significant content, and can thus save themselves the distraction or discomfort of interpreting any but the most relevant text. Students report that they are often advised to use 'logical connectors' for these purposes. This strategy, while it may help to make aspects of content prominent for some readers, manages to achieve this end by forcing the text to be untrue to any form outside the context of student–teacher reportage.

L2 writers often do not have the means to distinguish easily between the spoken and written conventions of the target language, and a constant across texts written by EFL learners of various L1s is that they tend to use features more characteristic of speech than written discourse (e.g. Petch-Tysen, 1998). It is difficult to measure what part social influences play in this: probably all students – both those who have the advantage of studying in their L1 as well as those who must master academic discourse in a foreign language – receive more exposure to spoken than to written English. However, the bias in much written school discourse toward information-focused lexis and structure may combine, in the case of L2 students, with communicative teaching methods to favour forms closer to speech than to formal written text.

Chafe (1982) and Chafe and Danielewicz (1987) describe the differences that spoken and written discourse demand of involvement on the part of the speaker and writer, and Lakoff (1982: 252) warns of the negative effect of confusing the features of registers (see also Malcolm, this volume). As Biber puts it (1988: 42), 'writing is typically for ideational purposes, to convey propositional information, while speaking is more often for personal, interpersonal and contextual purposes'. Much of the text written by students is expected to stress discrete units of memorized information, and rather than conveying propositions, it is routinely used to transmit what, for the purposes of school assignments, are held to be immutable facts. L2 students may also be less often expected to argue propositions effectively in a foreign language, and thus may feel less need to modify their text or acquire linguistic features so as to convey subtle arguments.

2.4   Limits in expression and cohesion

The discourse markers listed in Table 10.1 also suggest the reliance of the L2 student writers on a restricted set of grammatically simpler (and discoursally more explicit) expressions than are used by L1 students. The L1 student writers employ more complex language patterns (e.g. passives, auxiliaries, deixis) more often, and have a much wider variety of lexical and grammatical structures

Like other subjects, people study second languages may due to two reasons. First of all is they need to know them, for their jobs or for their further studies. Besides, they are interest in them, and they want to know more.

This is support indicated that second language cannot be learned fully if you don't participate in that language's culture. On the other hand, I want to talk about how the culture background affects the teaching styles and students' learning styles.

As we all know, in Hong Kong, our mother tongue is Cantonese and English is the second language we always use as an international communication way.

In my opinion, although the family background is an important factor to determine we can learn second language better or not, the positive attitude and the need to fully understand the foreign culture should not be forgotten.

All in all, getting too fat or too thin is an unhealthy phenomenon. People should have balance diet and take more exercise so as to avoid this.

Figure 10.2   Examples of the roles of overused discourse formulae in the writing of Hong Kong students

on which to call, as evidenced by the relatively infrequent use they make of any one phrase.

It is the proportionate frequencies of the expressions in Table 10.1, rather than their absolute frequencies, which are significant. The 170 occurrences of a phrase such as *First of all* in half a million words may not seem excessive, until we compare it with frequencies in a corpus of the same size and genre (i.e. 170: 1). The relative position of function words (or word chunks) on the logarithmic frequency curve of occurrences in a 'population' of words (i.e. corpus) is very stable and is often taken as an indicator of genre and register variation (e.g. Biber, 1988). The disproportionate occurrence of a limited set of functional expressions is an indication of the lack of variation in the L2 students' phrasicon.

On closer inspection of the L2 text, the expressions which are used significantly more often by the L2 writers, such as those in the bottom half of Table 10.1, often seem to act as 'fillers', employed without regard to their pragmatic force. Citations from the L2 corpus (Figure 10.2) suggest typical use of these phrases in the L2 texts (examples were randomly chosen).

The tendency of Hong Kong EFL student writing to rely on (but frequently misuse) a narrow range of additive and resultant conjuncts (e.g. *Besides, Moreover, Furthermore, So* and *Therefore* – almost exclusively in sentence-initial positions) has been much discussed (e.g. Crewe, 1990; Milton and Tsang, 1993). L2 novice writers frequently do not acquire (and likely are not always provided with) the information that will allow them to manipulate either these words or their longer 'prefab' cousins effectively. Rather than logically connecting processes and ideas, the operation of discourse markers in L2 text often works against the coherence that the writers attempt.

2.5   Emphasis vs. qualification

Entirely different textual effects and illocutionary values are created by the two disparate sets of discourse markers used by L1 and L2 writers. For one thing, the examples in Table 10.1 exemplify the contrasting effects of hedged expression conveyed by the L1 texts, compared with the over-zealous emphasis that the L2 texts communicate. Hyland and Milton (1997) discuss this phenomenon in L2 texts written by Chinese speakers as it relates to the use of modal verbs and other epistemic devices, and Lorenz (1998) describes the use of intensifying adjectives in English texts written by German speakers. English native speakers are more inclined to qualify their statements with phrases such as *This is not to say that* . . . , whereas at least these L2 writers tend to scaffold their text around expressions that (perhaps unintentionally) carry the weight of unequivocal generalization, such as *As we all know* . . . , *As we know* . . . , or *We all know* (the hedged variant *As far as we/I know* . . . appears to be unknown to the L2 writers).

Given the tendency toward unwarranted certainty in L2 text, it is ironic that it is also more likely to rely on expressions of personal subjectivity and involvement (e.g. *In my opinion*), which are more characteristic of speech than of written academic text. None of the instances of this expression in the L2 text explicitly acts to soften absolute statements in the text. Rather than suggesting careful speculation, it can be taken in every instance to indicate mere uncertainty.

This data does not justify concluding that pedagogical materials necessarily influence the L2 writers to abuse particular expressions (although, for example, variations of *As we all know* . . . / *As we know* . . . / *We all know* occur significantly more often in the corpus of school texts than in published journal articles). The narrowness of expression and imbalance in the functional use of language by L2 learners seems, however, to be at least partially a consequence of the educational environment, and even should EFL teachers recognize and warn of such problems, limitations in conditions and resources hamper effective advice or correction. In any event, school texts provide L2 students few opportunities for acquiring the referencing and qualifying expressions generally employed in text types that students are likely to have to produce if they enter professions or business. Other studies (e.g. Holmes, 1988) have also presented evidence for the general paucity of hedging expressions in school textbooks.

2.6   Attachment vs. development

Apart from a few interesting fluctuations, the patterns of discourse in this corpus of student L2 writing appear to be consistent across all ranges of English proficiency. Figure 10.3 charts the frequencies of the overused expressions listed in Table 10.1 at six proficiency levels in the school-leaving L2 examination scripts, in comparison with their frequency of use by L1 students. Even the most proficient of these L2 writers rely on a limited set of discourse markers to the exclusion of a wider range of more pragmatically effective devices (there are exceptions, such as *On the other hand,* which more proficient students make less use of). Since these writers tend not to reuse the same markers within any one script, their use may escape the comment or censure of readers. More importantly, neither examination markers nor even the students' own teachers are likely to have the time or resources to provide consistent guidance on the use of a wider range of more effective expressions in the face of such lexical aridity. The almost uniform reliance on restricted sets of 'lexical teddy bears' (Hasselgren, 1994) seems independent of grade, and thus possibly other aspects of L1 proficiency.

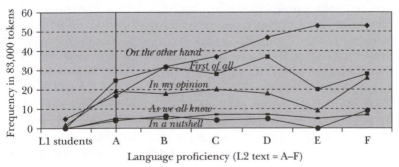

Figure 10.3   Frequencies of five phrases recurring in L2 text across proficiency levels, compared with L1 text

The point of this comparison is not to hold up L1 student texts (even those judged most proficient on an examination of written performance) *per se* as models for L2 production, nor to belittle the production of L2 writers, which in this case is from a range of proficiencies. L1 student examination writing is used as a benchmark for this study in order to compare L2 student writing with a control group, namely, a similar genre of L1 text. There is some indication from this limited evidence that even proficient L1 students may overuse certain formulae (e.g. *This is not to say that*) in comparison with academic published texts, although it may be that such discourse patterns are affected by the genre requirements of school assignments and examinations, as is the school discourse of L2 students.

What we can observe with some certainty is that proficient L1 writers make use of a very large number of lexical expressions (i.e. any one expression does not recur very often). Novice L2 writers, in comparison, understandably have access to a smaller lexicon and phrasicon. If this phrasicon is constructed and maintained out of a desire to avoid difficult syntactic and semantic features (e.g. passives, auxiliaries and aspectual structures), and without regard to the pragmatic consequence of words and word chunks, then the resulting text is, at best, stilted. It may remain so if these L2 writers do not have opportunities to move beyond parroting from inauthentic pedagogical materials, and so learn to adapt their style to various circumstances and audiences.

There is a variety of sources other than direct pedagogical influence to which such differences between L1 and L2 discourse have been credited. There may be developmental considerations, since orality and personal involvement (e.g. marked by predominance of first-person voice) appear to be standard features of novice writing (cf. Shimazumi and Berber-Sardinha, 1996). Immature habits in text production may be more readily retained in circumstances such as those of Hong Kong, where an incompletely acquired L2 must function as the main vehicle for formal discourse. Alternatively, Kaplan (1966), Kaplan and Connor (1987), Tannen (1982) and Besnier (1994) have argued that linguistic and cultural patterns from the L1 affect the patterns of L2 discourse. Given the lack of experience and training of these students in formal writing in their L1, it is just as likely that any such contrastive influences are an attempt to overcorrect for assumed differences between Chinese and English rhetorical patterns.

Whatever of these or other psycho-sociolinguistic factors may shape the lexical and grammatical choices of the L2 writers, L2 patterns of discourse are almost certainly reinforced by reliance on circumscribed subsets of lexical formulae. Since many of these L2 writers do not have much exposure to English outside school, they have little other direct evidence for constructing or refining hypotheses about the role of language in various genres or registers, or within any particular discourse community other than school. Under such circumstances, they have little choice but to rely on the sparse input they receive in the form of decontextualized lexical and syntactic structures of doubtful value. The unwritten understanding in the presentation of expressions of the type laid out in Figure 10.1 is that they are necessary for school, and especially examination, discourse. If indeed they are made to be so important, the institution may not be acting in the best long-term interests of its charges. The reliance on a limited and highly marked set of 'word chunks' inevitably has the effect of reinforcing the generally oversimplified, and, in the long run, inappropriate, discourse models novice writers often acquire.

One example is the repetitive pattern found in many school essays based on 'comparison and contrast' (marked in this corpus of L2 text by common key phrases such as *the advantages and disadvantages of,* which does not occur in any of the L1 corpora of this study). When this strategy is based on input that is sporadic and limited, as well as being generically, semantically and pragmatically poorly differentiated, it can easily give rise to banal and uninteresting texts. Such production may minimally satisfy the institutional demands that shape it, but it is unlikely to be sufficient for effective engagement with communities that value versatility in the production of written discourse.

These limitations in L2 production would not justify this concern if there were any indication that the usage described here is developmental, and leads to effective writing skills. However, L2 novice writers are rarely provided scope to advance beyond such usage, and it is likely that learners will remain attached to circumscribed language features when they are not afforded strategies and opportunities for acquiring more, and more pragmatically appropriate, patterns. Novice writers need to see the contexts in which proficient writers use language, and experiment with the language features they find there.

Much of the production of L1 novice writers can also be criticized as being inadequate, compared with professional text: the abundance of prefabs used by L1 novice writers does not necessarily translate into skilful writing. For example, much of the L1 student text relies rather too heavily on chained prefabs. The L1 student author of the following text seems well aware of her dependence on concatenated clichés:

> In trite terms, yes the best things in life are in financial terms free. A new dress will make you happy for hours or days but true love lasts years. However, everything you get you pay for in emotional and financial terms, in fact in any way possible. Everything is paid for in the most difficult way possible. It you care nothing for money you will pay for everything in deeply emotional terms, but of course it works the other way too.

However, many novice writers do pass through such stages, and learn to manipulate language features skilfully to become proficient writers. Woody Allen parodies the process of chaining clichés often practised by novice writers, but, as with much of his comedy, the caricature is probably semi-autobiographical:

> It is clear that the future holds great opportunities. It also holds pitfalls. The trick will be to avoid the pitfalls, seize the opportunities, and get back home by six o'clock.
>
> (My speech to the graduates, 1980)

3   Making text accessible

3.1   Current writing aids

This chapter has illustrated problems in the presentation of lexical patterns to novice writers of limited English proficiency. Currently, EFL learners are forced to rely on lists of questionable authenticity, often made up for short-term purposes, but which may have long-term negative consequences for the learners' expressive abilities. Despite the dangers for L2 novice writers associated with the rote learning of lexical formulae, the use of prefabs is a particularly economical, and probably essential, strategy for language acquisition. This section will describe a tool that makes a representative and contextualized range of the discoursal features of relevant written text available to novice writers. The availability of tools such as this should make it possible for novice writers to abandon short-term strategies and acquire styles appropriate to various discourse contexts.

Novice writers normally have few reliable or convenient resources at hand to assist them produce the particular characteristics of the type of text they need to create, and they often do not make very effective use of what guidance is available (either human or in print). According to recent studies (e.g. Harvey and Yuill, 1997), they do not, for example, make much use of dictionaries as writing aids. These researchers found that novice writers use dictionaries mainly to look up definitions rather than information on usage and collocation, which the best of the current learners' references attempt to provide. The information provided by printed dictionaries is necessarily limited and is not easily accessed by occasional users. More specifically, the medium cannot comprehensively illustrate how structures, words and 'word chunks' behave in different contexts, or provide adequate and appropriate information about the pragmatic effects of collocation, or afford opportunities for supported experimentation with these structures.

Nor do current electronic reference tools deal with these problems well. Writers who compose with wordprocessors have some electronic help during the writing process in the form of both procedural assistance (e.g. electronic dictionaries and thesauri) and declarative advice (such as spelling and grammar checkers), which operate interactively or pop up at the touch of a button or menu item. However, these tools do not help with the types of problems outlined in the first part of this chapter. A major conceptual and practical limitation of these programs is that they are generally unresponsive to the specific needs of individual writers, especially offering few concessions to novice writers of limited language proficiency. Not only do they not provide substantive and reliable information about discourse, neither do they help novice writers interact with language features so as to enable them to make hypotheses about the operation of language.

Perhaps the most potentially useful and liberating tool that has been made available to language learners is the concordancer. The potential of 'data-driven learning' (T. Johns, 1991) in making language accessible in a non-authoritarian (but nevertheless authentic) manner is well documented. Effective activities have been designed with the learner acting as researcher in control of an electronic concordancer (e.g. Tribble and Jones, 1990; Barlow, 1992; Murison-Bowie, 1993), and with the teacher using printed concordanced output in the classroom (e.g. Stevens, 1995). By displaying large numbers of keyword-in-context (KWIC) concordanced lines, these programs can provide information on both the paradigmatic and the syntagmatic behaviour of language (albeit often overwhelmingly so).

However, several limitations in conventional applications of concordancers prevent them from being popular with most novice writers. As Ball (in Ball and Taylor, 1995) complains, currently there are few features that make this tool any more useful for the novice writer than it is for someone studying language for more abstract purposes, such as linguistic or literary research, where professional researchers may have a clear idea of what they are looking for. Concordancers normally only display what users specify they want displayed. The use of 'wild cards' and other regular expressions widens the search, but only when all forms of the target expression are orthographically similar – and users have to be familiar with the morphological rules of the language and with the Boolean syntax of sometimes complex search patterns. To take the case of the misused and overused discourse markers discussed in this chapter, language learners with restricted knowledge of forms cannot search for what they don't already know (or suspect) they will or will not find (see Siemens, 1993).

Learners also often need more guidance in the operation of the language than a purely discovery-based approach to lexical acquisition provides. This need is analogous to the difficulty most people have with computer applications that require command-line instructions, as opposed to pull-down menus (Zimmerman, 1993), except that the lexis and syntax of human language is far more difficult to remember and use effectively than any computer language. Novice writers require a practical way to search for words and phrases in particular linguistic categories – i.e. a way to access a 'menu of words' from which to explore text. The following description will highlight the main features of a program that addresses these limitations for example, by providing learners lists of words or phrases, while still enabling the unfettered exploration of language.

3.2   Wordlist-driven learning

Figure 10.4 is a screenshot of such a menu-driven (i.e. wordlist-driven) concordancer, displaying a wordlist containing some of the expressions discussed earlier, which L2 writers are either not

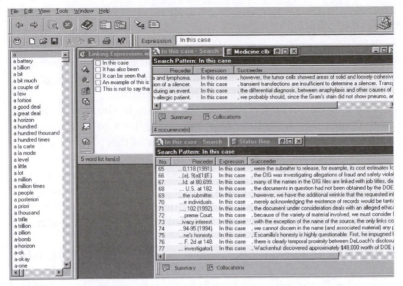

Figure 10.4   Collocation-driven concordancing

aware of, or which they avoid. This program (*WordPilot*) allows teachers and students to create and edit such wordlists, annotate expressions, and search for any expression (or multiple expressions) in specified text corpora (referred to as 'libraries' in this program). What sets this procedure apart from the phrasebook method of all-purpose language chunks often presented to learners is that the users have immediate information about the frequency and context of the expression(s) in various libraries (i.e. text types) that they themselves specify. The wordlist feature has also been designed so that numerical information such as relative frequency in spoken vs. written discourse, L1 vs. L2 use, etc. can be listed, and expressions sorted according to relative frequency of occurrence in various registers.

Of course, it is preferable that the expressions presented to the user be arrived at in some empirical way, but even if they are generated by intuition alone (the student's or the teacher's), users have the ability to check their actual occurrence and context in discourse. Learners are thus less likely to substitute one set of circumscribed expressions for another, and in any case, can explore the collocational properties of any expression they look up. Figure 10.4 displays a search in two libraries of the same size (each about

500,000 words) for *In this case,* selected from a short list of 'Under-used Linking Expressions' (i.e. underused by speakers of Chinese), which was generated as described in Section I of this chapter. One 'library' consists of a collection of medical articles and abstracts; another contains a collection of status reports from a US government agency responsible for settling complaints.

The expression *In this case* occurs 4 times in the first collection and 77 times in the other. Experienced writers of English might easily predict the disparity in the behaviour of this particular cohesive device between the two genres but, without this evidence, most novice writers could not. Flexible and user-friendly search strategies also allow the user to investigate the degree of 'fixedness' of expressions and discover what regularities there are in 'collocational clusters which can be freely adjusted as sentence constituents' (Beaugrande, 1998).

An index of words is displayed to the left in Figure 10.4. When an expression is chosen from a wordlist (or as it is typed in the 'search bar'), the program highlights its position in the index and completes the spelling of the expression. The expression *In this case* is not currently in the index (as it would not be in most dictionaries); however, an index of fixed phrases – empirically shown to be significant – can be easily added. Users can also annotate any expression by double clicking on it, which opens a box that allows them to store concordanced lines or other text and enter their own notes. The learner thus takes on the role of a lexicographer (Cobb and Horst, 1997), with the program providing guidelines on ways of creating, annotating and managing wordlists. Users can test themselves on any combination of expressions from any wordlist which the student or teacher considers to be problematic (e.g. a list of words or phrases that are frequently confused because of the morphological, semantic, syntactic or discoursal properties of the units).

3.3   Investigating the anatomy of text

The opportunity for teachers to collect appropriate electronic text corpora is becoming more feasible, as more text of various types is becoming available on the World Wide Web. It is now possible to collect large amounts of text from online sources representative of a very large range of genres, and reasonably free of copyright restrictions (at least insofar as they prevent educational use);

corpora of transcribed speech are also becoming available (Rundell [1996] lists a few).

However, a word of caution may be in order about the collection of corpora for pedagogical use. Although large amounts of text are becoming more available, the quality and appropriateness of the texts remains an issue. The adoption of concordancers that increase opportunities for learners to investigate the anatomy of texts directly does not remove the need to support learners in making decisions about text appropriateness. Corpus collection should be principled, and learners will profit by being informed of criteria that will allow them to judge whether a text is well written and representative. They also need guidance in the various ways of interpreting search results (e.g. What does it mean when few or no examples of a search expression are found?). Without such rigour, unprincipled applications of corpus evidence may come to have as prescriptive, but unjustified, an influence on teaching and language acquisition as less empirical and discovery-based methods have had (Beaugrande, 1998).

Even when the texts are 'well written', their appropriateness may be limited. For example, encyclopedia articles, written to be more 'user friendly', may be easier for EFL learners to understand (see Tribble, 1997), but it is arguable whether the style and argument structure of such texts provides more appropriate production models for apprentice writers than do school textbooks. *WordPilot* partly addresses such issues by allowing 'expert advice' in the form of hypertext annotation and guides to be attached to corpora and wordlists so that teachers and learners can gloss elements of style, vocabulary and schemata. This hypertext can also be made interactive and context-sensitive to the process of text analysis.

3.4 Consulting collocations

A feature of the program that makes it a particularly convenient writing tool is that it is directly available from the user's wordprocessor, through the use of 'object linking and embedding' (OLE) technology. After an expression is selected in the wordprocessor, one operation (i.e. mouse click) will open *WordPilot* and either perform a concordanced search on a specified library (or combination of libraries), or look up a definition or semantic word net (see 3.5 below). Figure 10.5 displays this chapter in the wordprocessor as it was being written. Overlapping this is a concordanced search

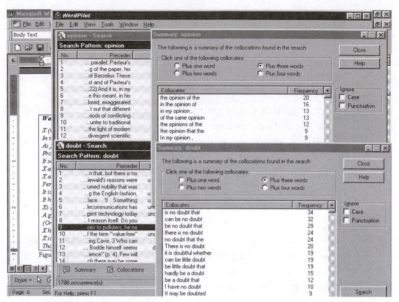

Figure 10.5   OLE concordancing – text on call during the writing process

and two summaries of collocations of targeted expressions. Simulating a novice writer (albeit one who has some motivation in reviewing lexical usage), I wanted to check whether the expressions that are recommended in Figure 10.1 (which may be the only 'relevant' expressions to which I have access) are appropriate for an academic text. Since I was preparing to write an article, I had previously set *WordPilot* to search by default in libraries containing only academic articles (several million words from published sources).

In my wordprocessor, I selected two words (*opinion* and *doubt*) from the list of phrases in Figure 10.1. The Tutorial School materials recommend three expressions as collocates of *opinion*: *In my opinion . . .* ; *X am/are of the opinion that . . .* and *Those who . . . + consider/are of the opinion. . . .* For *doubt*, they recommend *There is no doubt that. . . .* Without my having to leave my wordprocessor, *WordPilot* performed an 'approximate match' search for the selected words in about several million words of academic articles, and within a few seconds generated 1,044 concordances of all forms of the word *opinion* and 1,788 concordances of forms of *doubt*. I clicked on the 'Collocations' button in the concordance window of the program, chose 'Plus three words', and received the collocational summaries displayed in Figure 10.5. I could further explore these patterns, but already it is clear that, although the expression *in my opinion* does occur, the word *opinion* has a wider range of collocational patterns than those that were recommended in the Tutorial School materials. Again, this may be no surprise to the proficient writer of English.

It may be impossible ever to claim that any corpus is completely representative or that it is ever large enough; however, with reasonable care in the collection of texts, students who have little other support can be helped enormously by this information. In this case, some of the patterns recommended by the Tutorial School materials were found, although less often in sentence-initial position, and often with collocational neighbours not suggested by the materials. A few moments navigating around the text in this program will illustrate discoursal functions of the generated expressions not normally available to the learner. The word *opinion*, its forms and collocates, for example, does not always require the writer's involvement. The word *doubt* is more productive than I would have expected, and appears sometimes to take on a hedging role.

3.5   A reference for readers and writers

WordPilot also provides a dictionary and a thesaurus of semantic relationships (including synonyms, antonyms, attributive nouns, homonyms, hypernyms, hyponyms, meronyms and others) from the *WordNet* database (Miller *et al.*, 1993). It was decided to incorporate definitions because of the difficulty for L2 learners in dealing with the vocabulary of authentic text: words in the context of a search may be semantically more difficult than the target expression itself. Definitions are currently available for about 150,000 words, although the design of the program makes the collocational properties of the vocabulary as prominent as word meaning. Semantic relationships are included to prompt novice writers (especially L2 learners) to explore alternative vocabulary and break away from the circumscribed lexis to which they may otherwise be limited.

To continue our exploration of the word *opinion*: Figure 10.6 displays a definition of one of its senses, a list of synonyms of this

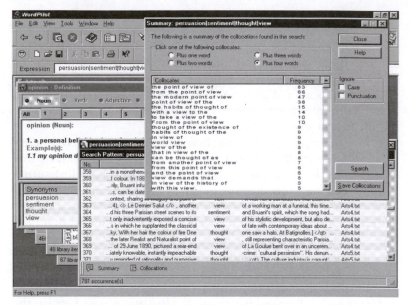

Figure 10.6   A display of the definition and synonyms of *opinion* and a multiple-search concordance of the synonyms in a corpus of academic articles

sense, and a multiple-search concordance of all these synonyms in a library of academic articles. The collocates of these synonyms in these texts are also summarized (the word *view* is particularly productive). The learner is thus provided access to a 'concept map' of possible alternative and semantically related phrases typical of academic articles. The instructor is also given a way to generate lists of phrases which have some empirical validity, and which can be made available from within the program (i.e. easily copied to a 'wordlist') for the learner to explore. Every encouragement is thus given to the learner to look up the expressions and understand their pragmatic effects from the contexts in which they appear.

This program logs what features are accessed and what look-up procedures are employed by users. A preliminary inspection of these logs shows that L2 novice writers use this program more often to consult texts for contextual and collocational information than they use it to simply look up word definitions. At least one study has found that EFL learners can more rapidly acquire the ability to use English in contextually appropriate ways through such electronic 'shortcuts', than they can through the normal process of extensive reading alone (Cobb and Horst, 1997).

In short, *WordPilot* makes readily available texts from a range of genres and supports the collocational and semantic look-up of words and phrases in authentic text. It encourages novice writers to experiment with grammatical and lexical patterns that they might otherwise be unaware of, or misuse, or avoid. It informs writers of patterns that account for the uniqueness and effectiveness of particular texts, and supports the exploitation of these features during the composing process (users can, of course, copy any text recovered by the program and paste it into their wordprocessor).

This tool offers writers the opportunity to get 'closer to the text' (Sinclair, 1991) by giving them access to authentic language of various text types as they write, and aids them in disambiguating the contextual and semantic features of the language they encounter in authentic texts. At the same time, it helps novice writers step back from the text and recognize the range of combinatorial patterns that is impossible to see from lists of decontextualized words and fixed patterns.

Conclusion

This chapter has illustrated how the problem of limited access to text adversely affects the acquisition of lexical aspects of discourse. It has also described features of a software program to help novice writers overcome limited access to text. *WordPilot* is an attempt to integrate lexical databases (e.g. various lexicons, as well as dictionary and thesaurus information), a procedural tool (i.e. a concordancer), hypertext guides, and libraries (corpora) of texts of various types so as to assist novice writers with their language production in ways that current print materials and electronic tools alone cannot. It allows novice writers to access and query the text of various discourse communities during the writing process and from the writing interface (i.e. wordprocessor). As a gateway to text, it provides novice writers opportunities to explore language features, and it assists academic gatekeepers in initiating learners into discourse.

11

The writing-talking cure: an ethnography of record-speech events in a psychiatric hospital

ROBERT J. BARRETT

The patient would proceed to describe in rapid succession and under brief headings the external events concerned and these I would jot down. During her subsequent evening hypnosis she would then, with the help of my notes, give me a fairly detailed account of these circumstances.

Joseph Breuer, *Studies on Hysteria*: Case 1: Fräulein Anna O. (Breuer and Freud, 1968: 36)

Introduction

Fräulein Anna O. called her treatment the 'talking cure' (Freud, 1981: 13). Had she recognized the importance of Dr Breuer's jottings, surely she would have dubbed psychoanalysis the 'writing-talking cure'. This chapter examines the day-to-day writing and talking practices of clinical staff in a psychiatric hospital, as they read case records, interviewed patients, discussed these patients among each other, and entered their clinical observations and opinions in the case records. The ethnographic analysis elucidates a cycle of interpretation that alternates between writing and talking, and proposes that psychiatric argot arises at the interface of written and spoken discourse.

Ethnography seeks to render familiar the strangeness of the exotic 'other', but when applied to institutions within one's own society, it transforms what was previously familiar into something very strange. In the 1980s, while a consultant psychiatrist at 'Ridgehaven Hospital', a modern psychiatric hospital in an Australian city,[1] I undertook a two-year ethnographic study of the culture of this hospital, the rituals that took place therein, the ideologies espoused by its clinical staff, and the minutiae of their day-to-day work practices (Barrett, 1996). I was interested in the way hospital clinicians (psychiatric nurses, psychologists, social workers, psychiatrists) communicated with each other, and with their patients. The study focused on a unit within the hospital dedicated to the treatment of schizophrenia; the irony of my own internal split – psychiatrist versus social anthropologist – was not lost on those who worked there.

Viewed through the ethnographic lens, each of my familiar clinical practices, and those of my colleagues, began to appear strange to me, none more so than the mundane routine of talking and writing – the most 'natural', taken-for-granted activity of all. At times I found the staff at Ridgehaven absorbed in the case records, reading them or making entries in them; at other times I observed them conversing with each other or interviewing patients; for the most part, however, this particular observer found them recording and conversing at the same time – these were writing-talking beings.

This chapter is about the intertwining and coalescence of clinical writing and clinical talk that occurs in a psychiatric setting. If there is a prevailing analytic influence, it is that of a phenomenologically grounded social anthropology, with its implicit claim that the analysis of speech and writing is impoverished unless informed by a fine-grained ethnographic understanding of cultural forms and social processes – in this instance, an ethnography of a psychiatric hospital. The discussion in this chapter edges out beyond the domain of psychiatry, for it explores a classic Weberian problem – the problem of the bureau (Weber, 1970) – which is to imply that the processes observed in this psychiatric setting have counterparts across a range of institutions within modern society. They may be found, I suggest, wherever the impulse to record becomes associated with, then integral to, and finally indistinguishable from, the impulse to communicate.

The analysis presented here seeks to offer a dynamic understanding of the processes whereby writing and speech penetrate each other. For me, the metaphor of the cycle (or the oscillation) is helpful in imagining how written language is dictated by oral discourse and infused with figures of speech, and conversely, how speech itself is captive to the writing process, and shot through with written idioms. But my chief purpose here is to collapse the two into a single process, by identifying the 'record-speech event' – an event in which the interpretation and production of a permanent record of proceedings, and the interpretation and production of speech, are mutually integral to the participants' interactions, and reciprocally influence each other (cf. Heath, 1982: 93; Hymes, 1972: 56). The concept of the 'record-speech event' implies its irreducible element, the 'record-speech act', and invokes a body of argument concerned with the performative aspect of language: when we write about a person whilst conversing with him or her, we are doing things with words and pens that may have a powerful transformative effect on that person.

Cycles of reading, talking, listening and writing

The daily routine of psychiatric treatment at Ridgehaven Hospital ran to a rhythm of face-to-face interaction and documentation, or 'seeing patients' and 'writing them up'. A common assumption among the clinical staff of that hospital was that seeing was primary, and that writing up was a secondary reflection of that primary reality: sometimes accurate, occasionally distorted, always incomplete, but usually adequate. It was less obvious that the record itself constituted a primary reality, and that face-to-face interaction was a reflection of that reality. 'It is not that records record things but that the very idea of recording determines in advance how things will have to appear' (Raffel, 1979: 48).

An entry in the case record served as an *aide-mémoire* for the writer and a communication to fellow cliniicians. But it was much more than this. It was data for statistical analysis and clinical research. It was a point of reference for professional supervision (Freidson, 1970: 101) or peer review. It could serve as a basis for administrative decisions, legal action, or judicial inquiry (Garfinkel, 1974: 120). If psychiatric case records lacked definition, it was because they were written with a strabismic gaze, one eye fixed firmly on the patient, but the other scanning an unknown future readership. As Ricoeur (1979: 86) demonstrates so well, the meaning of a text resides, at least in part, 'in the sense of its forthcoming interpretations'. This array of potential scrutineers resulted in a somewhat stiff, formalistic writing style (cf. Scott and Lyman, 1968: 57). It influenced the way patients were interviewed, affecting the questions asked and the answers provided. It shaped clinicians' perceptions of their patients; ultimately it shaped patients' perceptions of themselves. The dialogue between mental health professionals and their patients was punctuated by these documentary imperatives.

Clinical interaction was thus predicated on a cycle of reading, talking, listening and writing. It was an interpretative cycle, and the rules of interpretation differed, depending on whether one was in the written or the spoken phase. The cycle could be entered at any point, but commonly hospital clinicians read the case record before seeing the patient.

Patients, too, were involved in the cycle, and thereby contributed to the production of their case records, but they lacked the power of authorship and interpretation, for they were not permitted, except in extraordinary circumstances, to write in or read from their case record. From the patient's perspective, an interview was an encounter with a clinician who perused the case record, put questions in light of what was documented therein, and then made further notes in the record as the interview proceeded. By repeated exposure to this cycle of reading, talking, listening and writing, patients learned what it was about their illness that was germane to the record, and worthy of discussion. Thus, the written definition of the case influenced the way patients articulated an account of their illness, and influenced how they came to understand their inner experience.

Dyadic interaction: the interview as a record-speech event

The use of intermediate typifications to generate a recordable conversation

In an earlier publication (Barrett, 1988), I explored the writing-speaking interactions between clinicians and patients by following individuals through Ridgehaven Hospital, as they were first assessed and admitted to hospital by the medical officer, then passed on to be interviewed by one member of the psychiatric team after another, through to discharge. I recorded each interview on audio tape, and later made copies of clinical notes that were entered into the case records by the various hospital personnel as these interviews were being conducted. By fortune rather than design, I placed my sensitive recording equipment on the clinician's desk, and was subsequently able to identify when a clinician was actually writing, by the scratching noise of pen on paper. This allowed direct comparison between the official written account and the conversation taking place at the time. I was present throughout, keeping my own notes on the non-vocal communication and any other feature that appeared to contribute to the setting. My analysis derived from work on 20 cases, but was argued with reference to a single case study, that of Paul Lawrence, chosen as a mundane, work-a-day case of schizophrenia and drug abuse, who had a typical, uneventful period of inpatient treatment, and whose admission assessments illustrated the processes whereby patients were written into hospital.

I observed that the sheer speed of an interview dialogue necessitated that clinicians write in a telegraphic style. Such was the work load that cases were routinely documented as the interview proceeded – there was little time to write up afterward. The contrast between the rich, prolix interview dialogue, and the meagre, truncated entries in the record, was striking (cf. Cicourel, 1968: 318, 332; 1974: 64–65). Case records were punctuated with characteristic abbreviations and short-hand notations: 'crying +++' (crying a lot) '→' (lead to), '3–4/12' (three to four months), 'c' (with), or 'I-P problems' (interpersonal problems).

How was this reduction from rapid dialogue to concise document accomplished? Aside from the mysterious runes and glyphs, some so arcane that they were indecipherable even to the clinicians themselves, it was accomplished by means of intermediate typifications. Handelman (1978: 17) has described these as 'intermediate constructions of reality, often uncodified, which mediate between the "stock of knowledge" . . . of protagonists'. In psychiatry, they mediated between practical and theoretical knowledge, between lay and scientific terminology. They enabled a transaction between the particulars of a case and the abstract concepts of psychiatric illness.

The use of one such typification, 'conflict', was illustrated when Dr George, the admitting doctor, interviewed Paul's mother, Mrs James, prior to seeing Paul himself. Talking about her husband's relationship with Paul, Mrs James used such phrases as 'don't get on', 'can't live under the same roof' and 'thinks he's putting it over'.

[D = Dr George; M = Mrs James]

013   M: Unfortunately he doesn't, his stepfather and him don't get on.
014   D: Mm.
015   M: and, er, they can't live under the same roof.
016   D: I see.
017   M: because my husband's very impatient with this kind of illness. He thinks
018   he's putting it over all the time you know. He lives . . .
019   D: Mm hm.
020   M: he's been living on his own.
021   D: Mm. I see . . . What . . . how long has he been living on his own now?
022   M: Um . . . that's a good question. About three or four months I suppose.
023   D: Mm . . . And that's, is that because of conflict with his stepfather?
024   M: Mm. Yes.
025   [Dr George began writing.]

Whereas Mrs James used phrases dominated by verbs that described the interactional process between Paul and his stepfather, Dr George interpreted what she said with a noun, 'conflict' [023]. He put this to Mrs James, who concurred, and 'conflict' was entered in the record [025].

Son living on own 3–4/12 due to conflict c step-father.

The subtle nominalization of an interactional process went unnoticed. 'Conflict' was his word not hers, but it was close enough, and it made sense to Mrs James. At the same time, it connected with a psychiatric terminology that would not be out of place on the pages of the *British Journal of Psychiatry*. Case histories were replete with intermediate typifications: 'interpersonal problems', 'peer group', 'stress'. Writing in a purely lay idiom was discouraged – perpetrators were chastised in peer review meetings; writing in a conspicuously theoretical style was discouraged – offenders, usually novices, were chided by more experienced colleagues for having their 'heads in their books' (cf. Daniels, 1975: 322). It was through the use of intermediate typifications that clinicians accomplished a minor shift in the conversation toward a style that was easily rendered into note form.

In the process of documenting an interview in intermediate typifications, the common sense understandings which had underpinned them were not recorded. I observed that the dialogue between Dr George and Mrs James took place within a framework of lay meanings to do with madness or craziness, an uncodified ensemble of ideas to do with strangeness, illogical thinking, unpredictability, danger and loss of control. For example, Dr George asked three questions: whether Paul had been talking to himself, whether he had been different, and whether or not he had been making sense. At first Mrs James hesitated, as if she did not understand the point of the questions, but when she grasped that Dr George was asking about 'madness', or something like it, her replies flowed freely, canvassing evidence of Paul's 'strange' behaviour, his irrationality and irresponsibility, and the danger he posed, as well as her own fear of him. This tacit framework of shared meanings provided the basis on which they came to a negotiated understanding – it provided the underlying sense of Dr George's questions as well as her answers. But there was little trace of it in the corresponding case record entry (cf. Smith, 1974: 260). In other words, the taken-for-granted basis of the dialogue exerted a powerful, but silent, influence on the document.

The cardinal labour of case writing, to paraphrase Virginia Woolf, was excision. This 'editorial' work was a matter of omitting the common-sense meanings, recording the intermediate typifications, selecting out particular elements of the conversation that were relevant to the administrative purpose of the interview, and highlighting these in the record. Since Paul already had a documented history of schizophrenia and drug abuse, and since his admission to hospital had already been arranged between his mother and a senior psychiatrist at Ridgehaven, Dr George's immediate objective was to reconfirm the diagnosis, expedite the admission and move on to the next case awaiting assessment.

Record-speech acts and the articulation of power

Dr George was right-handed. He sat at the desk and offered Paul a chair on his right at the end of the desk. In this configuration, Dr George was well positioned to read the case record in front of him, look up at Paul as they conversed, then concentrate back on the record, glancing up and down with facility throughout the interview. Paul, on the other hand, could not read it, because from his angle it was nearly upside down. More importantly, Paul could see the doctor reading the record that he was not permitted to read; he could see the doctor writing in the record that he was not permitted to write in – and all of it about him.

This primal scene of institutional life displayed the asymmetry of power between doctor and patient. In such a context, every record-speech act was one of interrogator to respondent, recorder to recorded, reader to subject of written description (cf. Foucault, 1977: 189; Wheeler, 1969: 20). A clinical relationship came to an abrupt halt when any of these power differentials were reversed; as on one occasion when a patient began, during the interview, to take notes on his psychiatrist; or on another occasion, when a patient brazenly walked into the medical records department and, passing himself off as a member of staff, took possession of his own case records. Erikson and Gilbertson (1969: 411) have noted that in hospitals where patients are given direct access to their official case records, the staff experience a diminished control over patients, but they usually regain this control by developing a second, informal file which they withhold from the patients. At Ridgehaven, patients were not subject to the sinister power of a hidden dossier, but the more straightforward power of an open document which was tantalizingly visible, but not readable, a power that was at once candid and veiled. Faced with this coy power, most patients actively co-operated by disclosing highly personal information in order to produce an accurate, in-depth, written account of themselves (cf. Goffman, 1968: 32, 73–75, 143–148).

By means of record-speech acts, clinicians controlled the minutiae of the interview, determining, for example, the pace and content of the conversation. Experienced patients talked at a dictation tempo and might enquire, 'Am I going too fast for you?' Orchestrating a balance between writing and talking was the chief non-verbal means of directing patients when to talk and when not to talk. At times, frenetic note-writing encouraged a patient to expand on a particular topic; at other times, turning slightly in the swivel chair, adopting a more relaxed yet engaged posture, and laying the pen on the desk, encouraged the patient to open up, particularly if it were an intimate matter, or if the patient was visibly upset. Like the 'meta-actions' of speech identified by Labov and Fanshel (1977: 60), documentation regulated dialogue.

The primary cycle

To interview a patient, doctors would scan the record, formulate questions on the basis of what they had read, put them to the patient, then note their interpretation of the patient's response in the record. When Dr George interviewed Paul Lawrence, there were a few general opening enquiries, but most of the questions were derived from the history of drug use and schizophrenia that had been documented in the case record on previous admissions to hospital, and in the preliminary interview with Mrs James. When Paul said that he had been taking no other drugs, Dr George continued, 'LSD? Or?' [033], because there was a record of LSD use in the case record. The enquiry ceased only when Dr George had validated all the previously documented drug-taking.

[D = Dr George; P = Paul]

    012   D: You have been taking drugs? For how long now?
    013   P: I have been taking Serepax for about four weeks.
    014   D: Four weeks?
    015   P: Yeah.
    016   D: Uhuh . . . Can you . . .
    017   P: And Avils car sickness tablets, and Mogadon.
    018   D: Mm hm . . . (writing) that's er, what drugs have you been
    019   taking? Avil?
    020   P: Evil?
    021   D: Mm hm.
    022   P: Evil tablets? . . . Avil tablets.
    023   D: Avil tablets.
    024   P: Car sickness tablets.
    025   D: Yes I know that.
    026   P: Mogadon.
    027   D: Mogadon, yes.
    028   P: And Serepax.
    029   D: . . . (writing) And Serepax.
    030   P: And Serepax.
    031   D: Anything else?
    032   P: No.
    033   D: LSD? Or?
    034   P: Yeah. LSD.
    035   D: You have. Anything else Paul?
    036   P: No. Marijuana.
    037   D: Mm hm.
    038   P: That's all.

The archaeological cycle

Similarly, in reference to Paul's well-documented history of schizo-phrenia, Dr George focused his enquiry on symptoms recorded in Paul's previous hospital admissions. But his questions were additionally informed by a much deeper documentary source, namely the journals, monographs, volumes, books, papers, diagnostic manuals and other contributions that comprise the written corpus of clinical psychiatry. This body of knowledge is generated from the accumulated experience of psychiatrists and from clinical research. Ultimately, it is grounded in the processes of clinical recording analysed in this chapter, but it is also shaped by the process of scholarly citation, a vast extension of the documentary cycle in which elements of psychiatric knowledge are reproduced from text to text, from one generation of psychiatrists in training to the next.

I have argued elsewhere (Barrett, 1996: 186–188) that the rise of modern psychiatry itself was accompanied by (and enabled by) the emergence, in the early nineteenth century, of elaborate methods for the intensive recording of mental symptoms and life histories, and that it was the invention of the technologies of documentation, more than any other single factor, that gave shape to psychiatric knowledge as we now experience it. It is in this much broader sense of a world-wide, historically sedimented, psychiatric literature that the patient is questioned in the light of the record. Neither a sociology nor a genealogy of psychiatric knowledge will be attempted here, but I note, in passing, that there are a number of diagnostic issues pertaining to schizophrenia that have become inscribed in the psychiatric literature in this century. One has to do with auditory hallucinations or, to use the characteristic intermediate typification, 'hearing voices', and is concerned with the distinction between, on the one hand, voices with a real quality, heard as if coming from outside the head and, on the other, voices with an imaginary quality, heard from inside the head. The former are regarded as more typical of schizophrenia.

According to the literature, it is also important to distinguish between disturbances of perception (hallucinations) and disorders of thinking (e.g. so-called thought insertion or thought alienation). With respect to thought disorder, the literature focuses on the difference between thoughts experienced as one's own that seem to be located inside one's head, and thoughts experienced as belonging to someone else, as if they have been put into one's head from outside (Schneider, 1974). The following section of transcript suggests that these are the salient discriminations that inform Dr George's questions.

163   D: Mm. These voices. What can you tell me a bit more about them? Are

164   they actually, are they more thoughts in your head?

165   P: Well I don't know what . . .

166   D: Or is it coming from outside?

167   P: No I think it is thoughts in me head.

168   D: Mm hm. You don't hear the voices talking to you like I'm talking

169   to you at the moment, from outside you?

170   P: No. Sometimes I hear some of them say, 'Paul', and I look around and

171   there is no one there.

172   D: Mm hm. They just, you just hear a voice call your name?

173   P: Yeah.

174   D: And that's . . .

175   P: That's all. That's all. That's apart from the imaginary ones.

176   D: Mm hm. The ones in your head you mean?

177   P: Yeah. The ones I can talk to. Like me mate Bronco. He died a week

178   before I had me breakdown. I can talk to him spiritually when I'm lying

179   in bed. I can say, 'How are you going Bronco?' and I can say, I can

180   think he says, 'Really good, how are you?' You know?

181   D: Mm.

182   P: I can imagine him saying that.

183   D: But that's sort of more thought communication.

184   P: Yeah. Communication with the spiritually dead.

185   D: Yes. Right. But you don't actually hear the

186   voices talking?

187   P: No, only when the one says, 'Paul!'

188   D: Mm hm.

189   P: . . . [pauses while doctor writes] And I get paranoid when I'm straight,

190   about how, like when I'm walking down the street and I think there's a

191   car coming behind me or, I don't trust anybody.

192   D: Mm . . . Tell me more about these thoughts, in your head.

193   P: Well there's nothing. I've told you about as much as I can about that.

194   D: But . . . are those thoughts your own thoughts?

195	P:	They could be, I don't know. I can't understand 'em.
196	D:	Or are they thoughts that are put into your head but don't belong to you?
197	P:	I wouldn't say they don't belong to me. I'd say they're trying to contact
198		me. The dead people, the spiritually dead.
199	D:	Mm. Mm hm.
200	P:	They are trying to contact me and help me.
201	D:	Mm hm.
203	P:	Like Bronco says, 'Get help! Get help! Help yourself! Behave
204		yourself!' Because he died of an overdose of LSD.
205	D:	Did he?
206	P:	Yeah.

Paul's spiritual talk with Bronco did not fit with the questions that came from Dr George's training and his reading of the literature. For Paul, it was 'communication with the spiritually dead', and he became irritated with Dr George's repeated attempts to pin him down to the dichotomies of 'inside' versus 'outside', or 'your own thoughts' versus 'don't belong to you'. Paul was more concerned with Bronco's efforts to help him, and the special meaning of Bronco's death in relation to drug abuse. The corresponding entry written by Dr George was:

> Denied Schneiderian FRS [first rank symptoms] of thought disorder and perception. Occasional auditory hallucinations of a voice calling his name.

Thus the documentary imperative not only set the interview questions, but determined what ambiguities could be ignored (cf. Mishler, 1984: 128). Bronco, who could not be categorized as a hallucination, an abnormal thought, or a spiritual experience, did not appear in the case record.

Recycling

Further assessments carried out by different members of the mental health team focused the patient's attention on aspects of the illness which were already documented in his record, or anticipated from the psychiatric literature. Soon after Paul was admitted to Ridgehaven Hospital, Jean Potter carried out a nursing assessment, working from Dr George's entry in the case record. Paul's responses were smoother and more practised in this second assessment. By now he could efficiently list the drugs without much need of prompting.

[N = Nurse Jean Potter; P = Paul]

106   N: And what sort of things were happening?
107   P: Oh I was taking some downers, barbi . . . barbs . . . barbiturates.
108   N: Mmm.
109   P: Serepax, Avil car sickness tablets, Mogadon, marijuana, I don't drink.

And in contrast to the protracted negotiation with Dr George, Paul concisely summarized his hallucinations for the nurse, this time not bothering to mention Bronco at all. He had learned to abbreviate his account, focus it on the clinically relevant features of schizophrenia, and omit those elements that he suspected Nurse Potter would find extraneous or ambiguous. Subsequent encounters with other mental health professionals continued to narrow his version of his illness down to those elements that corresponded to standard textbook definitions of schizophrenia (cf. Strauss, 1969).

In a more extended treatment of this theme (Barrett, 1996: 136–142), I show how the documentary process separated patients from their subjective symptoms, so that they encountered their illness as a set of objective representations on the pages of the case record. Through repeated interactions with their record, mediated by clinician after clinician, they learned to resemble those representations of their illness more and more, so much so that many developed a close identification with their record. That is to say, the relationship between their illness and its documentation, between reality and representation, became problematic: as much as records represented patients, some patients became living representations of their records. This was poignant. On the schizophrenia unit, patients had come in the first place for help with problems pertaining to reality (hallucinations, delusions, thought disorder). In receiving this help, they were led into a documentary world in which a new reality (schizophrenia) formed itself in the resonance between their own oral version of their experience, and the written version in the record.

As interview followed interview, entries were layered one on the other in the case record. Each entry looked back to its predecessors, to encapsulate and validate them, or, alternatively, to add new information, to bring alternative perspective, to say something different. In the main, I observed that what was written in the record tended to reinforce, rather than refute, when fed through the cycle of documentation and dialogue.

Interaction between members of a psychiatric team

The case record as an index of professional autonomy and consensus

Taken as a whole, the case record was more than a linear accumulation of individual entries that took account of, then added to, the previous information. It was the production of an entire team. As such, it described the patient's illness in a way which reflected the play of power within the team, its overarching structures and underlying tensions (cf. Gollin, this volume).

The multi-disciplinary mental health team comprised psychiatrists, psychiatric nurses and social workers, as well as psychologists and occupational therapists, each with their distinctive training, specialized skills and different professional affiliations. At Ridgehaven, the trainee psychiatrist was a pivotal member of the team, whereas students of other disciplines were less central, reflecting the hegemony exercised by the psychiatric profession in this multi-disciplinary setting. Mental health professionals at Ridgehaven agreed that integration and conflict resolution were central to teamwork (see also Sands *et al.*, 1990: 70; Malone, 1991: 220). But the principle of professional autonomy, or 'legitimate control over work' (Freidson, 1970: 71–84), was more important. If threatened by the incursions of other professions, independence and autonomy were to be preserved at any price, even that of conflict. Thus, at the centre of the psychiatric team organization, lay a dynamic tension between integration and autonomy, conflict and consensus. This was the paradigm, with its structures and tensions, that provided the model for interactions between clinicians, and the template for their written and verbal communication.

The case record was a testament to professional autonomy, on the one hand, and team integration and consensus, on the other. Each entry was a discrete item, its author clearly identified by profession and name – 'Social Work Assessment, M. Sincock' – an affirmation, in miniature, of professional autonomy. Different writing styles and formats served to distinguish between professions, and signify the uniqueness of their respective contributions. During the period of the study, members of the Ridgehaven Hospital social work department developed new assessment forms, the better to reflect the distinctiveness of the social work perspective and the singular value of its clinical input.

Integration into a thematically coherent narrative was accomplished by the layering process I have described, wherein individual entries drew upon, then added to, previous entries. Another source of integration was the implicit temporal structure of the record; it was a chronicle that moved from the patient's developmental and background history, to current state, to progress, to prognosis; its diverse entries aligned themselves in single file, as it were, to this sense of movement through time.

Where consensus was threatened, a semblance of consensus was achieved by encoding differences of clinical opinion, personal piques, and outright animosities, in understatement. For example, the mental state of a patient, whom I have called Jill, deteriorated while she was in Ridgehaven, giving her and her husband cause for great concern. Jill's nurse, Carlo, asked the treating doctor urgently to review Jill's medication, and became exasperated when she did not oblige. Carlo then pencilled a note to John, his fellow nurse, in a nursing communication book (not intended for the record), asking John to prod yet again the reluctant doctor to review Jill's treatment.

> Much deteriorated. Requires <u>URGENT</u> review. Please push this John as these guys aren't very happy with the way things are going.

In the case record itself, Carlo wrote a more discreet version, its meaning obvious to the immediate staff concerned, but not to outsiders:

> Husband and Jill feel her condition is worse than when she was admitted. Jill appears to require some treatment review.

Thus the case record was a document of consensus (or pseudo-consensus), jointly written by a team of cooperative, but autonomy-championing, clinicians of differing species.

The case conference as a record-speech event

If a consensus view was possible, it was achieved through the case conference, the weekly meeting at which members of the team exchanged information about their patients, came to an agreed diagnosis, formulated common treatment plans, and made clinical management decisions.

Case conference discussions as a forum for the moral evaluation of patients

Treatment decisions made in case conferences were based on established clinical and scientific principles – experience, judgement, diagnostic logic, standard practice – established therapeutic protocols. But, more importantly, they were based on a moral evaluation of the patient. Numerous studies of the moral evaluation of patients have been carried out in general hospital settings (Glaser and Strauss, 1964; Duff and Hollingshead, 1968; Roth, 1972; Lorber, 1975; Jeffrey, 1979; Dingwall and Murray, 1983; Mizrahi, 1985; Liederman and Grisso, 1985) and in psychiatric hospitals (Stanton and Schwartz, 1954: 280–300; Belknap, 1956: 163–192; Strauss *et al.*, 1964: Chapters 5 and 12; Goffman, 1968: 117–155), yet most authors have adopted the view that value judgements are antithetical to humane care and effective treatment. At Ridgehaven Hospital, however, the moral evaluation of patients was central to the treatment process. While technical aspects of treatment were important (making the correct diagnosis and choosing the appropriate pharmacotherapy, psychotherapy and social rehabilitation), the central objective of treatment was to transform someone from a case of schizophrenia into a person who could be held responsible for his or her actions. Holding people to account in this way meant subjecting their actions, and them, to moral appraisal. It created the possibility of 'good' and 'bad' patients.

Yet assigning moral value to patients was awkward for the staff, especially when it involved devaluing people, because it was incompatible with the professional injunction to be 'non-judgemental'. The clinical discussion that took place in case conferences (and in a variety of other settings) was a suitable medium through which to negotiate these value judgements because, in contrast to writing, verbal communication lacked permanence and accountability.

Like the dyadic interaction between clinician and patient, the case conference cycled between document and dialogue. In the first instance, the discussion emerged from the written language of the case record. In fact, a 'case presentation', the initial exposition of clinical information designed to acquaint all team members with a patient's clinical details, was read verbatim from the record.

It had a formal quality, described by clinicians themselves as 'professional', 'objective', and 'non-judgemental'. Once the details of the case had been presented, however, there was a shift toward a more informal discussion. Clinicians remarked that, at times, they would speak about patients in a manner which they themselves regarded as 'unprofessional', 'subjective', or 'judgemental'. It was in this informal repertoire that it was possible to articulate a moral appraisal of the patient. While it would be mistaken to think that case-conference talk was solely preoccupied with making subjective, judgemental, unprofessional statements about patients, it is nonetheless important to recognize that such talk was the principal medium in which value could be ascribed to a patient.

Pseudo-technical idioms

Pseudo-technical idioms, a characteristic feature of case-conference talk, represented one means of accomplishing such value judgements. They were borrowed from the language of the case record. Of a patient who was exhibiting extremely disordered thinking, it might be said, 'He's thought disordered plus plus plus', as if the speaker were actually reading the notation '+++'. This apparently technical language of measurement was used in speech solely for the purpose of conveying extremes of dyscontrol, either in terms of psychosis or emotional expression. It would be inappropriate to say, 'She's angry, one plus'.

Diagnostic terminology, commonly taken from the so-called Axis II, or personality axis of the Diagnostic and Statistical Manual III (American Psychiatric Association, 1980), was taken up in speech and given an inflection which ascribed value to patients. These terms were carefully qualified in the Diagnostic and Statistical Manual by means of operationally defined diagnostic criteria. In speech, however, they could be used in a loose, unqualified and extravagant manner that capitalized on their pejorative potential: 'She's an out and out borderline', 'He's obsessional to the nth degree', 'Passive-aggressive plus plus plus', 'She's a grand hysteric', 'He's a real thorough-going little sociopath'.

The devaluation of patients could also be accomplished by making a humorous play on psychiatric illness categories proper, the so-called Axis I diagnostic categories. During the period of this study, the most difficult and objectionable patients of all were sometimes referred to as having MPD. A twist on MDP (Manic Depressive

Psychosis), MPD stood for Malignant Personality Disorder, and served to denote patients who, whatever illness they suffered from, caused trouble. They were the patients who were depicted as using 'stand-over tactics' to threaten the staff. They were said to undermine or 'sabotage' efforts to treat them. They were characterized as 'manipulators' or 'splitters', individuals who tried to turn one clinician against another. In a word, they were 'toxic'.

Each of these examples illustrate a characteristic element of clinical talk which took formal, technical terminology that might be found in a case record, twisted it, transformed it and appropriated it to the task of making evaluative, judgemental statements about patients.

Pseudo-lay language

The counterpart of pseudo-technical language was pseudo-lay language. It was frequently used by mental health professionals when they talked among themselves about their patients. While the former had its source in the record but operated within a moral space, pseudo-lay language was located, from the outset, in the moral domain, but pointed back to the record.

The quintessential examples of pseudo-lay language were not to be heard in the case conference itself, but in the most relaxed settings of all, the morning-tea room, where the staff were temporarily off duty and off guard – where what they said was off the record. In this setting, a patient might be described as 'not with it', 'out of it', 'out of his tree', 'away with the birds', 'away with the fairies', 'off in her own little world', or 'off the air', 'off', or 'right off', 'mad', 'crazy', or 'mad as a cut snake'.

It was very often in this domain of overtly 'unprofessional' talk that moral positions, attitudes and policies toward a patient were first mooted. It was here, outside the case conference, that ground-swell opinions among colleagues were first mobilized, later to be fed back into the case conference forum, and thence to the case record itself. What began off the record was ultimately translated back onto the record.

Epigrammatic appraisals

In the case conference itself, the corresponding pseudo-lay language was of a less colourful hue, and a more restrained note.

Epigrammatic appraisals were the distinctive elements of this language. These were brief elements within a swiftly flowing clinical conversation. Their hallmark was an abridged rather than discursive style. They assumed a detailed knowledge of the case, but summarized this knowledge in a compressed utterance with a compelling rhetorical force, sometimes just a phrase or a sentence, sometimes a short, illustrative vignette. In an epigrammatic appraisal, the speaker was not concerned so much with the illness and its effect on the patient as a passive object of suffering. Instead, the speaker articulated his or her moral evaluation of the patient as an active subject with volition and agency – canvassing the extent to which the patient was in control of the situation, encapsulating what the patient was doing to those around them, opining whether these actions were admirable or reprehensible. I coined the term 'epigrammatic appraisal', because the staff had no term for this type of clinical talk, although the notion of 'putting the patient in a nutshell' came close.

Epigrammatic appraisals are illustrated by a case conference discussion of Miss Treloar, a 59-year-old spinster, who had been admitted to Ridgehaven with a diagnosis of paranoid schizophrenia after she had openly expressed a number of delusions concerning her neighbours, in which she accused them of wanting to hypnotize her for their sexual benefit. For months, Miss Treloar had been causing trouble for the people in the block of apartments where she lived, loudly playing a selection of musical instruments late into the night, and performing noisy martial arts exercises down on the residents' grassy common area. She was brought to hospital by the police after a 'run-in' with some of these neighbours. In the first conference, a formal and detailed presentation of Miss Treloar's case took place, and by the second, one week later, each member of the team was ready to report on the additional investigations they had undertaken.

From there the discussion shifted to a less formal mode, in which members of the team came to a consensus opinion that Miss Treloar, notwithstanding her schizophrenic illness, was essentially an incorrigible old eccentric, and that the illness itself was only a problem in so far as it was a nuisance to those around her. The overall key, or mood, of the discussion became one of humorous resignation – an exasperated acceptance that whatever medical interventions they could devise, Miss Treloar would probably go on doing precisely what she wanted. The following three epigrammatic appraisals, extracted from different points in the case conference, encapsulate these sentiments:

Trainee psychiatrist: She functions reasonably well, it's just that she terrorizes the next door neighbours.

Social worker: She can cope with her illness, she can get on top of it, but she gets on top of everyone else as well.

Psychiatric nurse: She gets enjoyment out of annoying people.

These examples illustrate the power of epigrammatic appraisals to capture an opinion of Miss Treloar's personal qualities in a persuasive, pithy utterance.

They also illustrate the pseudo-lay quality of epigrammatic appraisals. Here was a group of sophisticated and experienced mental health workers, deftly using simple, common-sense words. The lay-like quality of these words served as a language bridge between members of diverse professions (with their potential for conflicting perspectives) because it was an egalitarian style of talk that touched on an area common to all members of the psychiatric team – the essentially 'human' aspect of the case. A social worker explained this to me: 'Sometimes I don't have the right language. I'm all at sea. I have to fall back on my common sense.' Paradoxically, the very 'layness' of the language also hinted at the speaker's specialized skills; its brevity belied the detailed command of the case that he or she was holding in reserve. It was a language form that conveyed the power of mental health professionals to summarize and encompass all that was known about a case, without having to say anything complicated at all. If teamwork was a matter of clinicians of different stamp achieving consensus while maintaining their own professional autonomy, then epigrammatic appraisals, with their pseudo-lay quality, were one of the primary linguistic means of achieving this exquisite balance.

By the third week, the team had decided to treat Miss Treloar's psychotic illness with a long-acting major tranquillizer (Modecate), to avoid a heavy-handed legal enforcement of this treatment, to pass her care back to her general practitioner in the community, to support the neighbours as much as was possible and, generally speaking, to hope that nothing would go too badly wrong. These decisions flowed directly from the epigrammatic appraisals of the previous case conferences. They were predicated on a consensus moral evaluation of Miss Treloar's character, her crankiness, her stubbornness, and her remarkable ability to control the people around her, including the clinicians themselves.

In turning back to the record, the skill of a sophisticated writer of discharge summaries was to capture the essence of the discussions, appraisals and decisions, yet render them in idioms tempered with professional care and concern. Thus, the final discharge summary on Miss Treloar was couched in a characteristic hybrid style of psychiatric writing that spoke to the technical issues of diagnosis and treatment, as well as hinted at the colourful discussions I had observed and tape recorded:

> *Discharge medication*: Modecate 25 mg IM weekly.
>
> *Prognosis*: Miss Treloar's well encapsulated paranoid delusions seem unlikely to change. Despite her schizophrenia she continues to function very well in the community, and hopefully will continue to do so. However her abnormal behaviour towards her neighbours is likely to continue, but we hope with close monitoring this can be kept to a minimum.

Some final observations

The record-speech event is a scenario intrinsic to institutional life; the record-speech act is a fundamental mode of doing things in the modern and post-modern world. They are predicated on a basic interpretative cycle which oscillates, *perpetuum mobile*, between written and oral discourse. Only by observing the revolutions of this cycle can one perceive the extent to which the production of speech is shaped by writing processes, and the production of writing is shaped by the spoken word. By following the course of this cycle through Ridgehaven Hospital, I elucidated some of the moments of translation: in an interview, the abbreviations and exclusions of common-sense meaning frameworks from the record; in a case conference, the precession away from the record along a discursive arc that ventured out into a moral domain and then back to the record again, where value judgements were finally encoded in attenuated form.

This approach casts light on the articulation of power in modern institutions. In this instance, it enabled me to demonstrate the indexical relationship between psychiatric discourse and the social relationships that gave structure and sense to its clinical setting: in an interview, the power differential between clinician and patient; in a case conference, the productive tension between members of a multi-disciplinary team bent on cooperating, but also on maintaining a wary independence. Each entry in the case record was an index to this power, as much as a description of the patient.

The study of psychiatric case records on a schizophrenia unit in a psychiatric hospital forces one to give up on the fruitless search for 'reality'. Classical distinctions between author, representation and object dissolve. This opens up a zone of reciprocal reference, in which speech becomes a way of representing writing in the same way that writing represents speech. In this zone of reflected and refracted images, the objects of discourse become the authors (the multi-disciplinary writing-speaking beings) as much as the patients do; case records reflect relationships between mental health professionals as much as they describe the mentally ill. Most importantly of all, the record represents the patient as object, but, through ceaseless repetition, the record itself becomes an object which the patient strives to represent.

This chapter looked at characteristic forms of expression which trade between writing and speaking: intermediate typifications, pseudo-technical language, pseudo-lay language, epigrammatic appraisals. I have pointed to the way such expressions address, on the one hand, the technical aspects of psychiatric science, and, on the other, the moral issues that are an inescapable part of psychiatric practice. My analysis has suggested that certain types of argot arise at the interface of writing and speech. It goes some way towards explaining why psychiatrists speak in the funny way they do – psycho-babble, according to those who do not delight in it, as I do. And it provides a method of approaching the various 'record-speech communities', whose membership comprises the mandarins of our society.

In identifying an archaeological cycle, I have established that there is a much deeper relationship between clinical literature and clinical interaction, one which enables a psychiatrist in Australia in the 1990s to put questions to a patient that are derived, via journals, books and the scholarly tradition, from what German patients told Schneider before the Second World War, from what Swiss patients told Bleuler early this century, and from what French patients told Esquirol a hundred years before that.

Here is a potential framework for an analysis of longer-term cycles of interchange between the arcane and the popular – between, say, sophisticated psychiatric models of psychic functioning and common-sense notions of how people think. Ideas expressed by patients, I suggest, are recorded by clinicians, nominalized, and thereby rendered abstract and theoretical, fed into the clinical literature, then dispersed through popular books, magazine articles, and films, back into the popular imagination again, each step transformative. The notion of the unconscious, for example, was already established as a broadly based theme within nineteenth-century thought (Ellenberger, 1970) by the time it was taken up by Freud and psychoanalysis, who gave it a particular theoretical inflection before handing it on to twentieth-century popular thought. Parallel histories might be proposed for the 'complex', 'repressed emotions', 'split personality' and 'schizophrenia', all of which have found their way from clinical literature into the vernacular. The work of Goody (1987) indicates some directions in which this theme may be pursued at a much broader cultural and historical level.

Already fundamental to the 'writing-talking' professions, to the 'recording-speaking' sciences, I anticipate that the record-speech act will become an increasingly pervasive way of acting in the world. The invention of devices that turn the spoken word directly into text will see to that.

Acknowledgements

For the privilege of entering their world, I am indebted to the patients and staff of Ridgehaven; for any insights into this world, I am indebted to Roy Fitzhenry.

Note

1. The identity of all those involved in this study, patients and staff, is protected by the use of pseudonyms, including the name 'Ridgehaven'.

12

'Why? I thought we'd talked about it before': collaborative writing in a professional workplace setting

SANDRA GOLLIN

Introduction

FIONA: I think we've really gotta think through it, I think . . .   [

MAX: [Why? I thought we'd talked about it before {inaud}.

FIONA: I think we might as well write it down now while we're thinking through it. So then we have something, then we just, we just you know, cut . . .

MAX: Yeah I don't agree with that. I think we've done most of the thinking through. Ahh . . . I've got it all up here (points to his head) so . . .

FIONA: [Ohh. I don't know, the more I write the more I think about it.

MAX: Oh yeah, you put, you keep on, you expand it, you write it but I think the thing we have to have on *paper* is the system . . .

FIONA: I haven't got that far . . .

MAX: You've gotta . . . Obviously the document we need at the moment is the *dot* point of what the system is.

FIONA: I don't think you can jump to that, I think you need this first.

MAX: Look, I think you're going to have to have the document for the client but I don't think, I thought we had been through in the last two days which had *got* us to that point.

FIONA: I don't think we *have*. I don't think we've thought about it *enough*.

(Vignette from case study: Gollin, unpublished)

267

In a workplace context, writing for or on behalf of an organisation is often done in groups or teams (Paradis *et al.*, 1985; Doheny-Farina, 1986; Winsor, 1989; Ede and Lunsford, 1992; Murray, 1992). In this chapter, it is argued that the processes in which such writing, often called 'collaborative', are embedded, differ significantly from the writing processes of individuals modelled in traditional pedagogy. The chapter also provides some suggestions on pedagogy for collaborative writing for professional contexts.

What is collaborative writing?

Although the practice of collaboration in workplace and educational contexts is widespread and well documented (Burnett, 1996: 123), there is no generally agreed notion of what constitutes collaborative writing (Ede and Lunsford, 1992). What is clear is that the practices which fall under the rubric of collaborative writing in these two contexts reveal very different purposes, scope and audiences. Burnett (1996: 153) identifies factors related to 'procedure, convention, affect, strategy' as well as 'sociopolitical concerns: exigence and expectations, situatedness and context, and impact' which set workplace and educational collaboration apart.

In educational contexts, collaborative writing is seen as valuable. It is found in collaborative learning environments (Bruffee, 1973), in English as a Second Language (ESL) classrooms (Nunan, 1992) and in primary schools where it is associated with process-writing (Graves, 1983). Flower *et al.* (1994) in a four-year project involving secondary and post-secondary classrooms have developed collaborative planning as a teaching tool and a heuristic for individuals to gain greater insight into their composing processes and those of others. In these pedagogical contexts, however, the primary purpose for using collaboration is as a means of developing the writing skills of individuals. For example, in process-writing, collaboration is largely restricted to peer response to the drafts of individuals, and responsibility for the final product rests with the individual writer. In some cooperative learning environments, forms of collaborative writing have been seen as beneficial in reducing dependence on teachers for learning and providing scaffolding (Bruner, 1983) for developing literacy skills. In theoretical terms these pedagogies draw heavily on the work of Vygotsky (1978, 1986) into the social and cognitive development of children.

Although there can be clear benefits to the individuals involved (Winsor, 1989), collaboration in workplace contexts occurs for pragmatic reasons centred on the goals of the organisation (Doheny-Farina, 1986; Paradis *et al.*, 1985; Odell and Goswami, 1982; Ede and Lunsford, 1992; Burnett, 1996). In the workplace, individuals are chosen for the already developed understanding and expertise they can contribute to a team, or for strategic reasons (Burnett, 1996). Some examples of contexts where collaboration is favoured are the preparation of internal company policy documents (Paradis *et al.*, 1985; Winsor, 1989) and public documents (Doheny-Farina, 1986; Murray, 1992). A typical example of the latter would be environmental impact statements (Killingsworth and Steffens, 1989). These documents are often too lengthy for one person to complete within the tight deadlines to which organisations typically adhere. The range of fields covered might be beyond the professional scope of an individual, or the audience for the document – whether internal to the organisation or external – could be diverse in background, and may need to be persuaded from different perspectives, which a single writer might not be able to adequately represent.

Witte (1992) distinguishes four modes of collaboration, *traditional, committee, incidental* and *covert*:

1. Traditional – involves 'two or more writers working jointly on the same text and assuming equal responsibility for the final product.'
2. Committee – involves 'two or more people working on the same text but having different levels of responsibility for the text produced, even to the extent that the person actually drafting the text has little actual responsibility for it and to the extent that the person ultimately responsible for the completed text may never have "put pen to paper" during its production.'
3. Incidental – involves 'brief, often highly focused interactions (which may be either planned or unplanned and writing-directed or not) between people (only one of which need be the "writer") through any medium.'
4. Covert – 'refers to writer's interactions (which need not be conscious and often are not) with other persons through both linguistic and non-linguistic texts.'   (Witte, 1992: 296)

Expanding on Witte's categorisations, this case study recognises that in addition to a core group of writers there might in fact be a number of other intersecting and overlapping groups of higher or lower status contributing to differing degrees and in different ways to the process and the product. This collaboration can be lengthy and recursive, with documents being cycled through different contributors and then being returned to the core writer(s) for further editing (Paradis *et al.*, 1985). Further, any or all of Witte's modes could be in play during particular stages in the process.

Impetus for research

In much of the research cited so far, the focus has been on the social processes in which the writing is embedded rather than on close analysis of the written and spoken texts thus generated. The impetus for the case study reported in this chapter arose from my interest in combining analyses from both perspectives. The case study aimed to explore, among a number of things, the following two questions:

1. In an institutional context, when texts are produced collaboratively, how does participation in the process by different categories of contributor affect the development of the written text that is the goal of the interaction?
2. How can the modelling of such a process inform the teaching of writing for professional purposes?

Choice of site

The Ecoplan project[1] reported in the case study exemplifies some of the kinds of collaborative writing activity with which professionals such as public servants, teachers and engineers regularly engage. In this case, the written product is a set of public documents. The project drew on the opinions of a wide range of stakeholders and the resulting documents had to satisfy the majority of those stakeholders if the proposed scheme was ever going to be workable. The rationale for using multiple writers, apart from completing the work within a limited time frame, was the need to draw on the expertise and breadth of background of a range of contributors. This would satisfy the need to consult widely and presumably pre-empt objections which could be raised against the scheme outlined in the documents.

The choice of research site is always subject to pragmatic constraints such as the availability of time and financial resources. This project was ideal in that it was not lengthy; the entire project was scheduled to take just over three months. A high degree of freedom of access for the researcher[2] also meant that this project had the potential to provide a rich store of ethnographic information.

The case study

Background

The case study followed the progress of a project undertaken by a team on behalf of Ecoplan, a small private consultancy firm. Ecoplan specialises in projects with an environmental focus such as environmental impact studies. Project teams are made up of staff with expertise in specialist areas and are augmented with consultants where further expertise is called for. In this instance, the task of the team was to investigate options for developing a national scheme for the accreditation of ecotourism on behalf of a federal government department. In the project brief, ecotourism was defined as:

> nature-based tourism that involves education and interpretation of the natural environment and is managed to be ecologically sustainable.   (Commonwealth of Australia, 1994: 3)

Aims of the project

The aims of the project were:

1. to encourage industry self-regulation through the development and implementation of appropriate industry standards and accreditation;
                    (Commonwealth of Australia. 1994: 31, Objective 4)
2. to facilitate the establishment of high-quality industry standards and a national accreditation system for ecotourism.
                    (Commonwealth of Australia. 1994: 41, Objective 8)

Published written products of the project were:

- an information paper for public consultation
- a questionnaire for ecotourism stakeholders to give input to the scheme
- a progress update for stakeholders
- the final report in three volumes.

Categories of contributor to the writing process

The project involved input and negotiation among a wide range of contributors. These are categorised as follows:

1 The inner circle

The inner circle consists of the employees of Ecoplan who were involved in the project. The designated writers who performed the core writing activity were *Fiona*, the project manager, and an independent consultant, *Max*, who had been contracted specifically to work on the project. These two were officially responsible for the production of written text drafts and the final documentation. Their colleagues had minor input to the writing, but contributed to editing and desktop publishing.

Fiona's official role was that of day-to-day project management, consultation and report preparation. In her mid-twenties, US born and educated, with a Bachelor of Economics, she had extensive experience as a planner in the tourist industry and had worked for government departments.

Max's official role was to provide strategic directions. In his late fifties, with an Australian Bachelor of Commerce and Diploma in Economics, he had over 23 years' experience in tourism strategic planning and strategic planning for state and local government in Australia and the Pacific. He had been closely involved in the preparation of other environmental accreditation mechanisms.

Workplace colleagues were consulted as necessary on a range of issues including content and style, and carried out the desktop publishing of the documents.

2 The outer circle

There were also other groups which by virtue of their input and ongoing dialogue with the designated writers were categorised as collaborators:[3]

Stakeholders in the tourism industry: Stakeholders in the project, apart from operators in the tourism industry itself, included professional tourism and environmental organisations, natural resource managers, tourism training bodies including tertiary institutions, conservation groups and local, state and federal government departments. Members of the grassroots level of stakeholder were invited to participate via public meetings (called workshops) at venues around the country. They were also invited to complete questionnaires handed out at the meetings and make written submissions. Responses from these three sources were collated and fed into the decision-making process.

A reference group: This group was drawn from national and international key players in the tourism industry, environmental interest groups, tertiary educational institutions and aboriginal groups involved in tourism. The reference group could also have been categorised as guides and mentors as their role involved being called upon as necessary for advice. However, Max and Fiona commented that time constraints prevented extensive consultation with members of this group, so for this project they are placed in the outer circle.

3   Guides and mediators

The steering committee, to which the inner circle had to report, performed an intermediary role between the inner and outer circles. The committee represented the Australian Tourism Industry Association, the Ecotourism Association of Australia, the Australian Conservation Foundation and the Commonwealth Department of Tourism. The steering committee's role was to ensure that the project brief was met. They would provide guidance to the designated writers, and would also seek to ensure that the interests of the three major categories of stakeholder in ecotourism – government, the tourism industry and conservationists or environmentalists – were catered to and would intersect for mutual benefit. They conducted a number of teleconferences with Max and Fiona and responded individually to drafts with faxed annotated copies.

4   The client

The Commonwealth Department of Tourism, headed by the Minister. The project brief was generated by this department, and it provided the funding for the project. During the project, all

Table 12.1 Categories of contributor

Category	Role
1. Inner circle	
Designated writers	
Fiona	■ produce the documents outlining the scheme
Max	■ provide specialised expertise
Fiona and Max together	■ plan, outline
	■ gather, analyse and synthesise data
	■ draft text
	■ edit text
	■ publish text
Workplace colleagues of designated writers	■ provide advice when asked
	■ word processing/desktop publishing
	■ surface editing (style, spelling, grammar)
2. Outer circle	
Industry stakeholders	■ attend workshops
	■ comment on elements of proposed scheme
	■ fill in questionnaires
	■ write submissions
Reference group	■ provide advice on specific areas of expertise when asked
3. Guides and mediators	
Steering committee	■ guide designated writers
	■ ensure interests of the stakeholders that they represent are met
	■ review and approve drafts and final documents
4. Client	
Government department (the Minister)	■ accept, modify or reject proposed scheme

communication with the client was mediated through the steering committee.

Table 12.1 summarises the roles of these groups.

Figure 12.1 attempts to capture the dynamic way in which these categories of contributor intersect and interact.

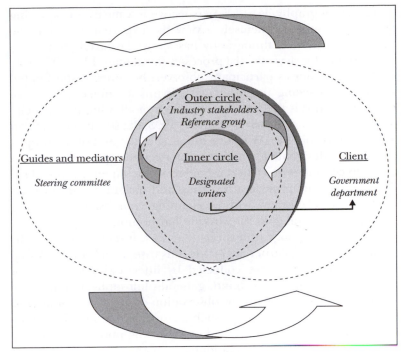

Figure 12.1   Dynamics of the collaborative process

Research methodology

In the interests of obtaining a *thick description* (Geertz, 1973) of the collaborative writing practices in this particular context an approach to research similar to that proposed by Candlin and Crichton (Candlin and Crichton, forthcoming) was taken. This approach is related to the work of Layder (1993), who proposes a multi-strategy combining micro and macro perspectives. In effect, this means drawing on research methods from a number of different traditions, a commitment to the principles of grounded theory and commitment to the explanation of local contexts as instantiations of macro social phenomena. Candlin and Crichton incorporate data from four different perspectives: ethnography/*Verstehen*, ethnomethodology, institutional / social organisational and textual in order to provide a thick account of the discursive practices of a particular social group.

The ethnography/*Verstehen* perspective is a means of capturing the way participants themselves view the experiences, 'from the inside', as it were. Ethnography has always favoured gaining an 'emic' or insider view of social processes (Silverman, 1993). The role of the researcher as participant observer, however, is still limited as she is still seeing the other participants as subjects. A way of overcoming this is the *Verstehen* approach of allowing the participants to speak for themselves (Layder, 1993: 38; see also Ivanič and Weldon, this volume). With this in mind, at the end of the project each of the designated writers was interviewed separately and also asked to comment on critical moments in the taped meeting data. Their comments provide a revealing and insightful view of their attitudes to collaborative writing, planning, composing and editing processes and strategies for working harmoniously as a team.

Ethnomethodology interprets data as instances of socially situated practice (Turner, 1974). In this case institutional / social organisational data were collected by interviewing directors of Ecoplan about the background, general philosophy and management style of the company, by observation of social behaviour and practices in different settings such as inner circle meetings, tele-conferences and workshops, and by collecting published information about the various stakeholders.

Textual samples formed the core of the research data. Eight collaborative planning and writing sessions of the inner circle were attended and tape-recorded. Access was also permitted to tape-recordings of two teleconferences between the designated writers and the steering committee. Numerous draft documents, which included annotated comments from reference group and steering committee members, were collected for analysis. I also attended one of the public meetings designed to promote the scheme and obtain feedback from the tourist industry and had access to completed questionnaires from these stakeholders. Textual data were analysed using Systemic Functional Linguistics (Halliday, 1985; Poynton, 1985; Martin, 1992) and Pragmatics (Levinson, 1983; Thomas, 1985) in the light of the findings from the three other social research perspectives.

Single-case naturalistic research such as this always raises questions as to the validity and reliability of the findings (Wiersma, 1991: 239–240). The multi-faceted approach described is a way of counteracting deficiencies in any particular research method as well as a way of cross-checking data. Whilst it would be impossible to generalise from one case, an in-depth study such as this serves to reconfirm or challenge existing information and provides a wealth of evidence which contributes to accumulated knowledge gathered by various researchers across sites and contexts. Whilst a naturalistic study such as this could never be exactly replicated, the researcher is satisfied that in its entirety it has internal consistency and provides sufficient information that others reading it could draw informed conclusions.

Assumptions

The research rests to a large extent on the assumption that language is constructed and only truly meaningful in the context of the social group or groups that use it and furthermore that language plays a significant role in constructing beliefs, thinking and social behaviour (Bakhtin,1981; Halliday, 1978; Hodge and Kress, 1979; Vygotsky, 1978, 1986; Fairclough, 1992a). Such social constructivist assumptions, labelled in some of their manifestations as post-modernist (Flynn, 1997: 551), have been criticised by some as being over-deterministic, placing slight importance on the idiosyncracies or actions of individuals. Flower (1994), for example, whilst acknowledging that all statements, social conventions and interpersonal events are collaboratively created over time, stresses that this process comes about through the efforts of individuals. She goes on to argue that meanings can only exist as the interpretations of individuals and suggests that it is impossible to isolate a social process from the minds that carry it out (p. 110). Although these objections have validity, the practical difficulties in getting an objective view of the composing processes of individuals as acts of cognition is well known. (For a critique of the use of talk-aloud protocols as used by Flower and Hayes, see Kowall and O'Connell, 1987.)

As can be seen from a number of other contributions to this volume, a social constructivist view does not necessarily deny the capacity of the individual to innovate within and at the boundaries of social practices. As Witte (1992) persuasively argues, a comprehensive theory of language would incorporate both psycholinguistic and sociolinguistic approaches. Indeed, the persuasiveness of social constructionist views has led even the cognitive theorists to reassess their models. Flower, in her more recent work (1994), explicitly acknowledges the social context in her work on collaborative planning as a heuristic in college writing courses. Nevertheless, her model is still based on the cognitive processes of the individual, and the goal of the pedagogy derived from it is to improve the writing of individuals rather than the collective writing of groups. In focusing on observable social interaction in the process of text production rather than entering into speculation on the workings of the individual mind, the study reported in this chapter aimed to make findings about language and social behaviour that could be translated into useful strategies for teaching people how to write more effectively as part of a team.

Why study the act of collaborative writing separately?

The Western idea of a writer as primarily an individual working in solitude has its roots in the rhetorical traditions of classical Greece (le Fevre, 1987: 15). This model has been reinforced by an educational tradition of assessment and other gatekeeping systems overwhelmingly valuing individual effort and competition over group work and collaboration. Influential models of writing, arguably the best known being Flower's and Hayes' (1981) Cognitive Process model, have tended to be based on experience in such educational contexts and have therefore focused on the composing processes of individuals.

In reality, outside the context of examination in educational institutions, most writers are not such free agents. The collaborative writer differs from the idealised solitary writer in a number of ways (Allen *et al.*, 1987), the most significant being restricted freedom of choice regarding all aspects of the writing process. There are innumerable constraints ranging from explicit publisher's guidelines to the tacit understandings of workplace culture (Winsor, 1989), which solitary writers contest at their own risk. A 'strong' interpretation of Bakhtin (1981) would declare that all writing is collaborative as writers always draw on other voices implicitly or explicitly. In overtly collaborative writing, voices from other sources can still be privileged, silenced or downplayed, or open to contestation. As a respondent in one study so aptly observed, in collaboration it is essential to 'check your ego at the door' (Allen *et al.*, 1987: 83). In the vignette at the beginning of this chapter, Max's exasperated outburst, 'Why? I thought we'd talked about it before' illustrates how failure to recognise potential interpersonal issues and come to an early agreement about fundamentals such as how to go about the writing process caused friction and time-wasting at a crucial later stage of the project.

Negotiation of meaning

Contestation, while complicating and often prolonging the writing process, is also seen as one of the major strengths of collaborative writing, and a reason why it is so often used in workplace contexts where it is crucial that certain documents be received favourably by their readers. However, the nature of this contestation has not been adequately studied. Models based on adversarial practices used in political or industrial negotiation fail to capture the subtlety of the negotiation which goes on in collaborative writing.

What is negotiation of meaning? Flower (1994: 36–84) distinguishes between the common-sense notion that all meaning is socially constructed and therefore negotiable, and a more precise definition of negotiation:

> Negotiation is a response to multiple voices or kinds of knowledge that would shape action.

> The meaning that is constructed out of such negotiation is a provisional resolution and a response to those voices.   (pp. 67–68)

Although Flower's focus is on how the cognitive processes of the individual writer operate within a social context, her definition is also extendable to group writing contexts, and in fact is easier to observe in those contexts. Individuals bring their own internal processes to bear on the group effort, but, in addition, many of the processes which are played out silently in the mind are also played out in spoken interaction within the group as members attempt to find 'a path that honours multiple goals and voices or arbitrates opposing demands' (Flower, 1994: 70). It is important to recognise too that this interaction is not always openly adversarial, as it is in dispute resolution (Fisher and Ury, 1983; A. Firth, 1995). Much of the negotiating process occurs subtly, politely and 'behind the scenes' as open conflict is neither conducive to the official goal of getting the writing task finished on time nor to the working relationships among the participants, which are usually expected to extend beyond the life of a single project. The vignette at the beginning of this chapter sees two writers of the inner circle of collaboration involved in negotiation on a number of levels. It is to the complexities of this process that we now turn our attention.

The model presented in this chapter sees negotiation of meaning in a collaborative writing situation as occurring on two planes: in the actual text being produced and among the players. The first and the second planes are intertwined and each may have sublevels. Paradis *et al.* (1985) concluded that the writing/editing cycle carried out on documentation between different levels of an organisation was not only an integral part of a larger social process which creates and maintains important professional relationships among co-workers; it also deeply influenced the success of the organisation. Latour and Woolgar (1979) theorised that the revisiting and rewriting (inscribing) of certain key concepts in documentation within scientific communities was an important way of building a common ethos. In this case study, we see various categories of participant not only contributing to the task at hand, producing written documents, but also reinforcing or renegotiating relationships involving power and affect at personal and organisational levels. These ideas are sketched out provisionally in Table 12.2.

Table 12.2   Planes of negotiation

Plane of negotiation	Kinds of negotiation
Plane 1 *Written text* Negotiating meanings in written text	1. Constructing written text genres in response to a brief 2. Arbitrating and integrating into the text multiple goals, voices and demands of stakeholders
Plane 2 *Relationships* Negotiating interpersonal relationships	1. Building and reinforcing interpersonal relationships 2. Protecting face and extending one's own power base
Negotiating organisational relationships	1. Building and reinforcing organisational relationships 2. Protecting face and reinforcing the organisation's power base

Table 12.3 Aspects of power (based on Martin, 1992)

Power relationship	Interpretation
Prominence	Construction of public figures by media
Authority	Positioning of individuals through job classification and/or expertise
Status	Reciprocity of choice (Poynton, 1985)
Control	Ability of participants to direct others

Influence (power) of contributors

Power is an important dimension of these negotiations but, like the notion of negotiation itself, the concept of power is a slippery one. The definition I am using here is taken from (Martin, 1992), who sees the ability to influence, *power*, as closely bound up with a number of intersecting and overlapping determinants which give differential access to *prominence, authority, status* and *control* (p. 527). Table 12.3 summarises these distinctions.

Allen *et al.* (1987) assumed that collaboration took place among participants who considered themselves peers with more or less equal influence over one another. Influence was characterised fairly simplistically as pertaining to level in a hierarchy external to the group. In the Ecoplan data, different categories of contributor were able to exert influence on others by virtue of belonging to different levels of the hierarchy, but contributors who were hierarchically differentiated in one collaborative circle acted as peers in another. For example, in their own meetings in the inner circle, Fiona and Max were of different status, and were seen to be negotiating power between themselves. But interacting with the steering committee meeting, they acted more like peers, and jointly protected their power as a group against the hierarchically more powerful steering committee. These distinctions mean that in different collaborative group contexts individuals may play different roles and may be able to exert more or less influence on the process of shaping the emerging text.

Prominence

Prominence refers to the way public figures are constructed by various media such as press releases or official documents. The

accreditation scheme being published and accepted by the ecotourism industry is an opportunity to provide the Minister with
media prominence. It is therefore advantageous for his name to
appear on the documents. For example, when the draft of the
Information Paper was submitted to the steering committee, the
chair re-wrote by hand the entire first paragraph of the draft she
had been sent, as follows (italics are new wordings, strikeouts are
wordings omitted from the final draft):

> In March 1994, *the Minister for Tourism, the Hon xx MP*, released the
> Commonwealth Department of Tourism's National Ecotourism
> Strategy. The Strategy recognise*s* the need for broad national
> directions to facilitate the ecologically sustainable development of
> tourism *and* the need for an integrated approach to the planning,
> development and future management of ecotourism. *In summary*,
> The strategy presents a vision for ecotourism in Australia ~~and broadly~~
> ~~describes issues and actions that need to be taken to achieve~~
> ~~agreed aims~~.

To this, on a separate fax, another member of the steering committee independently added a new theme (my italics) to a later
paragraph:

> *Under the Commonwealth Government Department of Tourism, four year*
> *$10 million National Ecotourism Program*, Ecoplan Consultants have
> been selected . . .

Halliday (1985: 38) defines 'theme' as 'the element which serves
as the point of departure of the message: it is that with which the
clause is concerned'. In formal written text, theme typically overlaps with information that is expected to be read as given or
understood by the reader. In both these examples, the changes
serve to foreground the Minister and his department as responsible for the initiatives in ecotourism. The Minister is named as
responsible for the release of the strategy, and, by implication,
for the recognition of the need for a scheme such as this and the
vision for ecotourism.

The steering committee in their role as mediators ensure that
the Minister and his department are accorded prominence in the
documentation. Ecoplan, as mere facilitators of the scheme, are
correspondingly downplayed, losing thematic status and being
passivised, as in the phrase, 'have been selected'.

This display of power was accepted by the writers in the
inner circle, who recognised not only the generic convention of

foregrounding the government department, but also the fact that, having lower status, they could not readily contest the wording even if they had wanted to.

Authority

Authority refers to the positioning of individuals through job classification and/or expertise. The Minister has authority and status because of his position. Invoking his name on a document sanctions the document by association. Fiona has authority by reason of her position as a full-time employee of Ecoplan and as project team leader. Max has authority by reason of his expertise as an outside consultant employed for this project.

The fact that the two writers both have legitimate claims to authority is a source of potential conflict when they are working together in the inner circle. This is seen, for example, in the vignette where Max becomes increasingly irritated by Fiona's approach to the writing. He draws on his greater experience as a consultant:

> MAX: Um I think that we put it *down* and *then* when we start to write we can start to *modify* it but until we have the framework . . . unless we have the scaffolding then we can't really er then start to justify.

However, he realises that he has to defer to Fiona's authority by reason of her position, so he begins to soften his objections with the modal *should.* He also stresses that this is his personal belief, not a universal rule.

> MAX: I, I believe that we *should* have a framework and then we *should* come round to look at the implications of that framework . . . ahhh and I, I think it's we *shouldn't have to* change any of the recommendations.

The data contain many critical moments (Candlin, 1987) where Fiona's authority is challenged by Max. The challenges are oblique and non-confrontational, but are still negotiated by the players.

Status

Status refers to reciprocity of choice (Poynton, 1985). In an unmarked case, Fiona as team leader would have the choice to command Max to carry out a task or indirectly persuade him to do it. However, age differences and gender roles complicate the workings of status. For Fiona to give a direct command to an older male would potentially put her at risk of, at worst, a face-threatening refusal or, at best, grudging consent. By reason of her higher status, she can choose to save face by expressing her command indirectly, 'Why don't you?' Max does not have the reciprocal choice of refusing outright. To refuse politely, Max chooses to use humour or plead insufficient expertise. For example, in another part of the case study the following exchange occurs:

FIONA: So, so what we'll have there is the objectives of the system . . . Why don't you be in charge of that, . . . yeah? do you wanna write, write that up?

MAX: Uh, do I? {laughs}

FIONA: Do, do you want me to write it up from that?

MAX: {laughing} I don't know, I haven't even thought of what we're going to do.

FIONA: You haven't thought. I'll write it up from this and then then you can review it. Do you wanna try and tackle the advantages and disadvantages of accreditation systems, for the information paper, or not really?

MAX: I don't know as much about accreditation systems for example as somebody like Julie does with the work they've been doing at Homebush.

In the inner circle, Max can make suggestions but Fiona does not have to take them up. For Max to contest the power relationship requires considerable subtlety and control on his part. After all, it is in his interests to maintain a harmonious working relationship since he wants to do more consultancy for the firm. Despite his best efforts, though, he can still be overridden, as in the following, where Fiona changes a previously agreed decision:

FIONA: Yeah, I changed . . . the grant . . . the granting of accreditation should be done by the small body, ok and then we had (reading from draft text) 'withdrawal of accreditation should be done by the large body'. *That* I thought is a real problem. The one small body doing granting and, and the big body doing withdrawal. So I put the granting with the big body, and what the smaller body does, it does the hard work, it reviews the applications.

Control

Control refers to the ability of participants to direct others. In the inner circle, Fiona can control through her job classification, but Max can control by reason of his seniority and gender and also through physical presence and force of personality. Max uses a number of strategies when he is alone with Fiona which, though not entirely gender-specific, tend to be under-used by females compared with males as females have traditionally tended to occupy positions of lesser social power (O'Barr and Atkins, 1980). His linguistic strategies include interrupting the other speaker and taking longer turns at talk. He also utilises paralinguistic strategies. For example, he takes up more physical space and expands this further by leaning back in his chair, hands behind head, while 'dictating' lengthy chunks of text which Fiona copies down. Occasionally he gets up and goes to a flip chart and sketches organisational plans on the butchers' paper. These behaviours position him in the role of instructor. As an older male, he is socially positioned such that for Fiona to contest these behaviours requires considerable effort. Nevertheless, she does fight back indirectly as seen in the vignette, through changing drafts without consulting him. She takes some pleasure in this, as an extract from her interview shows:

FIONA: Yeah, I did disagree with Max on that one.
RESEARCHER: And I can't remember now whether you won out in the end on that.
FIONA: I think I did, because basically it's a bit unfair, because I've got the whole document, so if I feel strongly about it I can change it and there's not all that much Max can do about it.

The foregoing examples demonstrate that power in collaborative writing is the result of a complex web of factors, unstable across contexts and subject to ongoing negotiation.

Contact

Contact refers to the frequency with which members of a group meet or communicate and their degree of familiarity. Contact and status are logically independent (Martin, 1992: 526). Asymmetrical status relationships of participants do not change through contact, but their degree of involvement can. High contact, for example, among work colleagues can reduce the levels of politeness. It can also produce more casual conversational forms. Compare the casual way Fiona speaks to Max when they are working together: 'yeah? do you wanna write, write that up?' with the formal, and formulaic, way she speaks when she is talking on the teleconference to the steering committee:

> FIONA: Ah, Max and I clearly recognise that continued consultation with these stakeholders is very important and I think Max and I are under the understanding that something like that needs to go out every couple of months to get people um aware of what's been going on and the problems that we are seeing.

Affect

Affect refers to the 'degree of emotional charge' (Halliday, 1978: 33) between participants. While affect is consciously avoided in the written texts in this case, it is manifest in the spoken inter-action which produces them. Affect works to increase solidarity among different categories of collaborator at different stages. For example, Fiona and Max talking together express positive or neg-ative appraisal of various ecotourism operators and the steering committee. This builds their sense of solidarity against other stake-holders. However, at another time, when in the company of the steering committee, whose role is to mediate, positive or negative appraisal is directed by the whole group outward to other bodies. Within the steering committee, any negative appraisal of the work of the designated writers is couched in modalised terms and heav-ily hedged:

> HEAD, STEERING COMMITTEE: Um, the newsletter. Um are you calling it a newsletter for some reason or is it you know information sheet two? A newsletter seems to me sort of um ring of something that, that's going to continue. Ah, that people are going to continue to be informed. Um, I'm not sure, hhh I mean how do other people feel about that?

We can clearly see here both the guiding and mediating roles of the steering committee in operation.

Pedagogical implications

The foregoing case study highlights the complexity and interactivity of collaborative writing. Current models of collaboration used in classroom pedagogy (Nunan, 1992; Murray, 1992; etc.) still have as their primary goal the development of individuals as writers. This is an important goal, yet there are difficulties in assuming that the interaction – including oral and written discourse – that accompanies the joint writing effort is in itself unproblematic. As we have seen, in 'real', that is, uncontrived, collaborative contexts, where the goals of an organisation rather than the pedagogical goals are uppermost, the negotiation of personal and organisational power is a significant factor which may undermine or derail the writing task if it is not sensitively managed. As Burnett (1996) has demonstrated in her study of university students attempting to carry out a workplace-based collaborative writing project, to teach learners to write collaboratively without attending to these and other contextual issues is to give them a false sense of what the process involves.

In a project at Macquarie University (Gollin, 1998; see also Candlin and Plum, this volume), researchers investigated one assignment for a subject which was part of a Technology Management course with a business focus. The aim was for students to collaboratively prepare a business plan for the promotion of an imaginary product. Groups of eight students made up from any or all of the disciplines in the school met six times over a number of weeks. They were given some introductory lectures and reading on group theory, but were not provided with any input on the discoursal aspects of group work. As part of the assignment they were required to observe their own group's behaviour and evaluate the success of their group in preparing a business plan. Each group considered the following attributes – stage of group development, group cohesiveness, roles, norms and conformities, status system, group size, cohesiveness, externally imposed conditions, group resources and processes (Robbins, 1994) – and ranked these according to significance for their particular group. One of the findings, unsurprisingly, was that most groups did not already know how to work collaboratively. In some groups, certain dominant individuals took over and virtually wrote the project. Students who were uneasy with this state of affairs didn't have the interpersonal or discourse skills to challenge the status quo. This situation was particularly marked for speakers of language backgrounds other than English in mixed background groups.

This particular case highlights many of the problems associated with teaching collaborative writing outside the contexts in which it will be used. Burnett (1996) questions whether it is possible to do so as so many of the factors which contribute to a successful collaborative writing effort are context-specific. She also expresses some doubt (p. 145) about how much transference of skills is possible across contexts. My own view is that many of the inter-personal skills needed for collaboration and collaborative writing can be taught, but that the context in which the writing takes place must be within a discourse community (Swales, 1990; Gee, 1990) that is familiar and accessible to the student. A number of chapters in this volume have drawn attention to both the import-ance of such community contexts to writing, and the problems students may have in participating in them. Expecting students to 'role-play' behaviours for which they have no experience or models is highly likely to result in failure. If, on the other hand, they can play 'themselves' and interact with others of greater or lesser power and status than themselves in a familiar environment, they may be able to rehearse some of the strategies for negotiating reported in this chapter.

As we have seen in the group dynamics assignment reported above, setting up the task and letting students loose on it does not guarantee they will learn many useful collaborative skills. There is a need to identify reasons for collaboration and model alternative ways of going about the process. The learners need explicit input and scaffolded activities which will enable them to collaborate effectively. An important part of the learning process would involve sensitising students to aspects of negotiation on two planes de-scribed in this chapter: around the written text and around rela-tionships. This would involve understanding the need to negotiate different ideological standpoints and approaches to writing as well as shifting roles and responsibilities. There should be ongoing monitoring of the negotiation taking place in the collaborative project, discussion of progress and issues arising, and a debriefing at the conclusion of the work.

For example, an authentic collaborative project might involve learners in researching the needs of particular groups of students in a tertiary institution (for example, those with physical or learning disabilities) on campus, and writing a report with recommendations for improved conditions or services. Legutke and Thomas (1991: 182–187) provide useful guidelines for project work along these lines trialled in the field of ESL. Prior to the beginning of the project, learners would be introduced to fundamental issues in collaboration, such as participant roles and group dynamics. Collaborative tasks might involve preliminary research, designing the study, dividing up the tasks, designing a questionnaire, interviewing students and university or college staff, collecting plans and other printed information, photography and sketching, further research, planning, drafting and editing the report, publishing the report and possibly oral or multimedia presentation of the results. Such a project could be a real-world task with positive outcomes for the subjects. Working with one another as well as dealing with the various stakeholders – students, medical and other support personnel, lecturers and members of the administration to name a few – would provide valuable insights for the collaborators in terms of the processes involved in negotiating power relationships as well as meanings in written and spoken discourse.

Conclusion

Collaborative writing is complex and needs to be actively taught. Firstly, it needs to be recognised that there is a difference between having students collaborate as a heuristic towards the goal of improving their own composing processes and having them collaborate in order to fulfil a goal on behalf of a third party. Both kinds of collaborative effort should be encouraged. The first should be encouraged because 'making thinking visible' (Flower *et al.*, 1994) provides students with insights into their own composing processes and those of others. The second should be encouraged because in the world outside the classroom, collaborative writing is increasingly taking place. The widespread use of networked computers and the internet, and software which enables easy development and annotation of joint texts by writers who are remote from one another, will facilitate this kind of activity. The study reported on here is a small contribution to the need for better understanding of what goes on when people produce texts as groups. More research is needed into different contexts and ways of working in order to build a comprehensive picture of the collaborative process.

Notes

1. The name of the company and persons mentioned in connection with it in this chapter are all pseudonyms.
2. The researcher gratefully acknowledges the generosity of management and staff of 'Ecoplan' in providing open access to information, documents and meetings associated with this project.
3. This expanded concept of agency in writing draws on the work of Bakhtin (1981) and others and is explored later in the chapter.

Bibliography

AITCHISON, M., IVANIČ, R. and WELDON, S. (1994) Writing and re-writing writer identity. In *Life Histories and Learning: Language, the Self and Education*. Papers from the conference held at the University of Sussex, Brighton, pp. 5–8.

ALBERT, T. and CHADWICK, S. (1992) How readable are practice leaflets? *British Medical Journal* 1305: 1266–1268.

ALLEN, N., ATKINSON, D., MORGAN, M., MOORE, T. and SNOW, C. (1987) What experienced collaborators say about collaborative writing. *Iowa State Journal of Business and Technical Communication*, September, pp. 70–90.

ALTENBERG, B. (1993) Recurrent verb–complement combinations in the London-Lund corpus. In J. Aarts, P. de Haan, and N. Oostdijk (eds.), *English Language Corpora: Design, Analysis and Exploitation*. Amsterdam: Rodopi, pp. 227–245.

AMERICAN PSYCHIATRIC ASSOCIATION (1980) *Diagnostic and Statistical Manual III*. Washington: American Psychiatric Association.

ANDERSON, A. B., TEALE, W. B. and ESTRADA, E. (1980) Low income children's preschool literacy experience: some naturalistic observations. *The Quarterly Newsletter of the Laboratory of Comparative Human Cognition* 2 (3): 59–65.

ARISS, R. (1988) Writing black: the construction of an Aboriginal discourse. In J. R. Beckett (ed.), *Past Present: The Construction of Aboriginality*. Canberra: Aboriginal Studies Press, pp. 131–145.

ATKINSON, D. (1992) The evolution of medical research writing from 1735 to 1985. *Applied Linguistics* 11: 337–374.

ATKINSON, D. (1996) The Philosophical Transactions of the Royal Society of London 1675–1975: A Sociohistorical Discourse Analysis. *Language in Society* 25: 333–371.

BAKER, P. (1997) Developing ways of writing vernaculars: problems and solutions in a historical perspective. In A. Tabouret-Keller, R. B. Le Page, P. Gardner-Chloros and G. Varro (eds.), *Vernacular Literacy: A Re-evaluation*. Oxford: Clarendon Press, pp. 93–141.

BAKHTIN, M. M. (1981) Discourse and the novel. *The Dialogic Imagination: Four Essays by M. M. Bakhtin*, trans. C. Emerson and M. Holquist. Austin: University of Texas, pp. 259–422. (First published 1934–35.)

BALL, C. N. and TAYLOR, K. B. (1995) MicroConcord and corpus collections. *Computers and the Humanities* 29/1.

BARGIELA-CHIAPPINI, F. and NICKERSON, G. (eds.) (1999) *Writing Business: Genres, Media and Discourses.* London: Longman.

BARGIELA-CHIAPPINI, F. and HARRIS, S. (1996) Requests and status in business correspondence. *Journal of Pragmatics* 26: 635–662.

BARLOW, M. (1992) Using concordance software in language teaching and research. In W. Shinjo *et al.* (eds.), *Proceedings of the Second International Conference on Foreign Language Education and Technology.* Kasugai, Japan: LLAJ and IALL.

BARRETT, R. J. (1988) Clinical writing and the documentary construction of schizophrenia. *Culture, Medicine and Psychiatry* 12 (3) 265–301.

BARRETT, R. J. (1996) *The Psychiatric Team and the Social Definition of Schizophrenia: An Anthropological Study of Person and Illness.* Cambridge: Cambridge University Press.

BARTON, D. and HAMILTON, M. (1998) *Local Literacies: Reading and Writing in One Community.* London: Routledge.

BARTON, D. and PADMORE, S. (1991) Roles, networks and values in everyday writing. In D. Barton and R. Ivanič (eds.), Writing in the community, *Written Communication Annual: An International Survey of Research and Theory. Volume 6.* Sage Publications, pp. 193–223.

BAUDRILLARD, J. (1994) *Simulacra and Simulation.* Ann Arbor: University of Michigan Press.

BAULEZ, M. J. (1904) *Méthode de tamoul vulgaire.* Pondicherry: Imprimerie de la Mission. Reprinted (1990): New Delhi: Asian Educational Services.

BAZERMAN, C. (1987) Codifying the social scientific style: the APA publication manual as a behaviouristic rhetoric. In J. S. Nelson, A. Megill and D. N. McCloskey (eds.), *The Rhetoric of the Human Sciences.* Madison: University of Wisconsin Press, pp. 125–144.

BAZERMAN, C. (1988) *Shaping Written Knowledge: The Genre and Activity of the Experimental Article in Science.* Madison: University of Wisconsin Press.

BAZERMAN, C. (1993) Intertextual Self-Fashioning: Gould and Lewontin's Representations of the Literature. In J. Selzer (ed.), *Understanding Scientific Prose.* Madison: University of Wisconsin Press, pp. 20–41.

BAZERMAN, C. (1994a) Systems of genres and the enactment of social intentions. In A. Freedman and P. Medway (eds.), *Genre and the New Rhetoric.* London: Taylor and Francis.

BAZERMAN, C. (1994b) *Constructing Experience.* Carbondale: Southern Illinois University Press.

BAZERMAN, C. (1998) *The Languages of Edison's Light.* Chicago: University of Chicago Press.

BAZERMAN, C. and PARADIS, J. (eds.) (1991) *Textual Dynamics of the Professions*. Madison: University of Wisconsin Press.

BEAUGRANDE, R. DE (1997) Theory and practice in applied linguistics: disconnection, conflict or dialect? *Applied Linguistics* 18 (3): 279–313.

BEAUGRANDE, R. DE (1998) Large corpus linguistics and applied linguistics: dedicating new bridges. *Applied Linguistics*. In press.

BEAUVAIS, P. (1989) A speech-act theory of metadiscourse. *Written Communication* 6 (1): 11–30.

BECHER, T. (1989) *Academic Tribes and Territories: Intellectual Inquiry and the Cultures of Disciplines*. Milton Keynes: SRHE/Open University Press.

BELCHER, D. (1994) The apprenticeship approach to advanced academic literacy: graduate students and their mentors. *English for Specific Purposes Journal* 13 (1): 23–34.

BELKNAP, I. (1956) *The Human Problems of a State Hospital*. New York: McGraw Hill.

BEREITER, C. and SCARDAMALIA, M. (1987) *The Psychology of Written Composition*. Hillsdale, NJ: Lawrence Erlbaum.

BERKENKOTTER, C. and HUCKIN, T. (1995) *Genre Knowledge in Disciplinary Communication*. Hillsdale, NJ: Lawrence Erlbaum.

BERNSTEIN, B. (1990) *Class, Codes and Control, 4: The Structuring of Pedagogic Discourse*. London: Routledge.

BERNSTEIN, D. (1997) *Advertising Outdoors: Watch This Space*. London: Phaidon.

BERRY, D. C., MICHAS, I. C., GILLIE, T. and FOSTER, M. (1997) Evaluating explanations about drug prescriptions: effects of varying the nature of the information about side effects and its relative position within leaflets. *Psychology and Health*.

BESNIER, N. (1994) Involvement in linguistic practice: an ethnographic appraisal. *Journal of Pragmatics* 22: 279–329.

BHATIA, V. K. (1993) *Analysing Genre: Language Use in Professional Settings*. London: Longman.

BHATIA, V. K. (1994) Generic integrity in professional discourse. In B.-L. Gunnarsson, P. Linell and B. Nordberg (eds.), *Text and Talk in Professional Contexts*. ASLA: Skriftserie 6, Uppsala, Sweden.

BHATIA, V. K. (1995) Genre-mixing in professional communication: the case of 'private intentions' v. 'socially recognized purposes'. In P. Bruthiaux, T. Boswood and B. Du-Babcock (eds.), *Explorations in English for Professional Communication*. Department of English, City University of Hong Kong, Hong Kong.

BHATIA, V. K. (1997) The power and politics of genre. *World Englishes* 16 (3): 359–371.

BHATIA, V. K. (1998) Genres in conflict, Paper presented at the 1998 AAAL Conference, Seattle, USA. To be published in A. Trosborg (ed.), *Analysing Professional Genres*. Amsterdam: John Benjamins.

BIBER, D. (1988) *Variation across Speech and Writing.* Cambridge: Cambridge University Press.

BIBER, D. and FINEGAN, E. (1989) Styles of stance in English: lexical and grammatical marking of evidentiality and affect. *Text* 9 (1): 93–124.

BIGLAN, A. (1973) The characteristics of subject matter in different scientific areas. *Journal of Applied Psychology* 57 (3): 204–213.

BIZZELL, P. (1992) *Academic Discourse and Critical Consciousness.* Pittsburgh: University of Pittsburgh Press.

BLICQ, R. (1997) Centres for excellence in technical communication: where are they? *TC Forum: Technical Communicators Forum* 4/97, p. 17.

BLOOME, D. and GREEN, J. (1997) Ethnography and ethnographers of and in education: a situated perspective. In J. Flood *et al.* (eds.), *Handbook of Research on Teaching Literacy through the Communicative and Visual Arts.* New York: Macmillan, pp. 181–203.

BLOOR, T. (1996) Three hypothetical strategies in philosophical writing. In E. Ventola and A. Mauranen (eds.), *Academic Writing: Intercultural and Textual Issues.* Amsterdam: John Benjamins, pp. 19–43.

BOLTER, J. (1991) *Writing Space: The Computer, Hypertext, and the History of Writing.* Hillsdale, NJ: Lawrence Erlbaum.

BOURDIEU, P. (1977) *Outline of a Theory of Practice,* trans. R. Nice. Cambridge. Cambridge University Press. (First published 1972.)

BOURDIEU, P. (1993) *The Field of Cultural Production.* R. Johnson (ed.). Cambridge: Polity Press.

BOURDIEU, P. and PASSERON, J.-C. (1977) *Reproduction in Education, Society and Culture.* London: Sage Publications.

BOURDIEU, P., PASSERON, J.-C. and DE SAINT MARTIN, M. (1994) *Academic Discourse: Linguistic Misunderstanding and Professorial Power,* trans. R. Teese. Cambridge: Polity Press. (First published 1965.)

BRANDT, D. (1989) The message is the massage: orality and literacy once more. *Written Communication* 6 (1): 31–44.

BREMER, K., ROBERTS, C., VASSEUR, M.-T., SIMONOT, M. and BROEDER, P. (1996) *Achieving Understanding: Discourse in Intercultural Encounters.* London: Longman.

BREUER, J. and FREUD, S. (1968) Studies on hysteria. In J. Strachey and A. Freud (eds.), *The Standard Edition of the Complete Psychological Works of Sigmund Freud. Volume II.* London: Hogarth Press and the Institute of Psychoanalysis.

BRICK, J. and CANDLIN, C. N. (1995) *Mastering Academic English: The Language of Economics and Accounting. Report and Learning Modules.* CAUT Grant. Sydney: NCELTR, Macquarie University.

BROWN, J., COLLINS, A. and DUGUID, P. (1989) Situated cognition and the culture of learning. *Educational Researcher* 18: 32–42.

BROWN, P. and LEVINSON, S. (1987) *Politeness: Some Universals in Language Usage.* Cambridge: Cambridge University Press.

BRUFFEE, K. A. (1973) Collaborative learning: some practical models. *College English* 34: 634–643.

BRUFFEE, K. A. (1986) Social construction: language and the authority of knowledge. A bibliographical essay. *College English* 48: 773–779.

BRUMFIT, C. and MITCHELL, R. (1989) The language classroom as a focus for research. In C. Brumfit and R. Mitchell (eds.), *ELT Documents 133: Research in the Language Classroom.* London: Modern English Publications.

BRUNER, J. (1983) *Child's Talk: Learning to Use Language.* London: Oxford University Press.

BURNETT, R. E. (1996) Some people were notable to contribute anything but their technical knowledge: the anatomy of a dysfunctional team. In A. H. Duin and C. J. Hansen (eds.), *Non-academic Writing: Social Theory and Technology.* Mahwah, NJ: Lawrence Erlbaum.

CADMAN, K. (1997) Thesis writing for international students: a question of identity? *English for Specific Purposes* 16: 3–14.

CAMERON, D., FRAZER, E., HARVEY, P., RAMPTON, M. B. H. and RICHARDSON, K. (1992) *Researching Language: Issues of Power and Method.* London: Routledge.

CAMPBELL, P. (1975) The *personae* of scientific discourse. *Quarterly Journal of Speech* 61: 391–405.

CANAGARAJAH, A. S. (1996a) From critical research practice to critical research reporting. *TESOL Quarterly* 30: 321–330.

CANAGARAJAH, A. S. (1996b) 'Nondiscursive' requirements in academic publishing, material resources of periphery scholars, and the politics of knowledge production. *Written Communication* 14 (4): 435–472.

CANDLIN, C. N. (1987) Explaining moments of conflict in discourse. In R. Steele and T. Threadgold (eds.), *Essays in Honour of Michael Halliday.* Amsterdam: John Benjamins.

CANDLIN, C. N. (1997) General Editor's preface. In B.-L. Gunnarsson, P. Linell and B. Nordberg (eds.), *The Construction of Professional Discourse.* London: Longman, pp. vii–xiv.

CANDLIN, C. N. (1998) Researching writing in the academy: participants, texts, processes and practices. In C. N. Candlin and G. Plum (eds.), *Researching Academic Literacies: Framing Student Literacy: Cross-cultural Aspects of Communication Skills in Australian University Settings.* Sydney: NCELTR, Macquarie University.

CANDLIN, C. N. and CRICHTON, J. (forthcoming) Cicourel, interdiscursive methodology and questions of accountability. In N. Coupland, S. Sarangi and C. N. Candlin (eds.), *Sociolinguistics and Social Theory.* London: Longman.

CANDLIN, C. N., MALEY, Y., KOSTER, P. and CRICHTON, J. (1995) Orientations in lawyer–client interviews. *Forensic Linguistics* 2 (1).

CANDLIN, C. N. and PLUM, G. (eds.) (1998) *Researching Academic Liter-acies: Framing Student Literacy: Cross-cultural Aspects of Communication Skills in Australian University Settings.* Sydney: NCELTR, Macquarie University.

CANDLIN, C. N. and PLUM, G. (in press) Becoming a psychologist: con-testing orders of discourse in academic writing. In C. Barron, N. Bruce and D. Nunan (eds.), *Discourse Practices and Social Change.* London: Longman.

CARRINGTON, L. D. (1997) Social contexts conducive to the vernacular-ization of literacy. In A. Tabouret-Keller, R. B. Le Page, P. Gardner-Chloros and G. Varro (eds.), *Vernacular Literacy: A Re-evaluation.* Oxford: Clarendon Press, pp. 81–141.

CATALDI, LEE (1994) Review of M. Duwell and R. M. W. Dixon (eds.), Little Eva at Moonlight Creek and other Aboriginal song poems. *Aus-tralian Aboriginal Studies* 1: 58–60.

CHAFE, W. (1982) Integration and involvement in speaking, writing and oral literature. In D. Tannen (ed.), *Spoken and Written Language: Exploring Orality and Literacy.* Norwood, NJ: Ablex, pp. 35–53.

CHAFE, W. (1986a) Writing in the perspective of speaking. In C. Cooper and S. Greenbaum (eds.), *Studying Writing: Linguistic Approaches.* Lon-don: Sage Publications.

CHAFE, W. (1986b) Evidentiality in English conversation and academic writing. In W. Chafe and J. Nichols (eds.), *Evidentiality: The Linguistic Coding of Epistemology.* Norwood, NJ: Ablex.

CHAFE, W. (1994) *Discourse, Consciousness and Time.* Chicago: University of Chicago Press.

CHAFE, W. and DANIELEWICZ, J. (1987) Properties of written and spoken language. In R. Horowitz and S. Samuels (eds.), *Comprehend-ing Oral and Written Language.* San Diego, CA: Academic Press, pp. 83–113.

CHANG, Y. Y. (1997) *Elements of Informality in English Scholarly Writing: Prescriptivism vs. Practices.* Qualifying Research Paper. Ann Arbor: Uni-versity of Michigan.

CHANNELL, J. (1990) Precise and vague expressions in writing on eco-nomics. In W. Nash (ed.), *The Writing Scholar: Studies in Academic Dis-course.* Newbury Park, CA: Sage, pp. 95–117.

CHERRY, R. (1988) Politeness in written persuasion. *Journal of Pragmatics* 12: 63–81.

CHRISTIE, M. J. (1994) Yolngu linguistics. In G. Steff (ed.), *TESOL: Making Connections. Proceedings of the 1994 ACTA-WATESOL National Conference.* Perth: Westralian Association of Teachers of English to Other Languages, pp. 25–35.

CICOUREL, A. V. (1968) *The Social Organization of Juvenile Justice.* New York: John Wiley.

CICOUREL, A. V. (1974) Interviewing and memory. In C. Cherry (ed.), *Pragmatic Aspects of Human Communication*. Dordrecht: Reidel, pp. 51–82.

CICOUREL, A. V. (1992) The interpenetration of communicative contexts: examples from medical encounters. In A. Duranti and C. Goodwin (eds.), *Rethinking Context: Language as an Interactive Phenomenon*. Cambridge: Cambridge University Press, pp. 291–310.

CLARK, R., FAIRCLOUGH, N., IVANIČ, R. and MARTIN-JONES, M. (eds.) (1990) Critical language awareness part I: a critical review of three current approaches to language awareness. *Language and Education* 4 (4): 249–260.

CLARK, R., FAIRCLOUGH, N., IVANIČ, R. and MARTIN-JONES, M. (eds.) (1991) Critical language awareness part II: towards critical alternatives. *Language and Education* 5 (1): 41–54.

CLARK, R. and IVANIČ, R. (1991) Consciousness-raising about the writing process. In P. Garrett and C. James (eds.), *Language Awareness in the Classroom*. London: Longman.

CLARK, R. and IVANIČ, R. (1997) *The Politics of Writing*. London: Routledge.

CLARK, R. and IVANIČ, R. (1998) Critical discourse analysis and educational change. In L. van Lier and D. Corson (eds.), *The Encyclopaedia of Language and Education. Volume 6: Knowledge about Language*. Dordrecht: Kluwer.

COATES, J. (1983) *The Semantics of the Modal Auxiliaries*. Beckenham: Croom Helm.

COATES, J. (1987) Epistemic modality and spoken discourse. *Transactions of the Philological Society* 85: 100–131.

COBB, T. and HORST, M. (1997) *The Learner as Lexicographer: User-Friendly Concordancing*. Talk delivered at FLEAT III, Japan.

COE, R. M. (1994) 'An arousing and fulfilment of desires': The rhetoric of genre in the process era – and beyond. In A. Freedman and P. Medway (eds.), *Genre and New Rhetoric*. London: Taylor & Francis, pp. 181–190.

COLEMAN, H. (1989) *Working with Language: A Multidisciplinary Consideration of Language Use in Work Contexts*. Berlin: Mouton de Gruyter.

COMMONWEALTH OF AUSTRALIA (1994) *National Ecotourism Strategy*. Canberra: AGPS.

CONNOR, U. (1996) *Contrastive Rhetoric: Cross-cultural Aspects of Second-language Writing*. Cambridge: Cambridge University Press.

COULMAS, F. (1992) On the relationship between writing system, written language and text processing. In D. Stein (ed.), *Cooperating with Written Texts: The Pragmatics and Comprehension of Written Texts*. Berlin: Mouton de Gruyter, pp. 15–29.

COULTHARD, M. (1994) *Advances in Written Text Analysis*. London: Routledge.

COUTURE, B. (ed.) (1989) *Functional Approaches to Writing: Research Perspectives.* Norwood, NJ: Ablex.

CREWE, W. (1990) The illogic of logical connectives. *ELT Journal* 44 (4): 316–325.

CRICHTON, J. (1996) Researching discourse: a quartile model. Paper presented at the 1996 ALAA Conference, Sydney, October.

CRISMORE, A. and FARNSWORTH, R. (1990) Metadiscourse in popular and professional science discourse. In W. Nash (ed.), *The Writing Scholar: Studies in Academic Discourse.* Newbury Park, CA: Sage.

CRISMORE, A. and KOPPLE, W. J. V. (1988) Readers' learning from prose: the effects of hedges. *Written Communication* 5: 184–202.

CRISMORE, A., MARKKANEN, R. and STEFFENSEN, M. (1993) Metadiscourse in persuasive writing: a study of texts written by American and Finnish university students. *Written Communication* 10 (1): 39–71.

CROSS, G. (1990) A Bakhtinian exploration of factors affecting the collaborative writing of an executive letter of an annual report. *Research in the Teaching of English* 24 (2): 173–203.

CRYSTAL, D. (1997) *English as a Global Language.* Cambridge: Cambridge University Press.

DANIELS, A. K. (1975) Professionalism in formal organizations. In J. B. McKinley (ed.), *Processing People: Cases in Organizational Behaviour.* Holt, Rinehart and Winston, pp. 303–338.

DAVIES, T. (1997) State of education. *Communicator,* New Series 5: 14–16.

DAY, R. A. (1988) *How to Write and Publish a Scientific Paper* (3rd edition). Phoenix, AZ: Orxy Press.

DE BEAUGRANDE, R. (1984) *Text Production: Toward a Science of Composition.* Norwood, NJ: Ablex.

DE COCK, S., GRANGER, S., LEECH, G. and MCENERY, T. (1998) An automated approach to the phrasicon of EFL learners. In S. Granger (ed.), *Learner English on Computer.* London: Longman.

DE JONG, M. D. T. and SCHELLENS, P. J. (1998) Focus groups or individual interviews: a comparison of text evaluation approaches. *Technical Communication* 45: 77–88.

DENNY, J. P. (1991) Rational thought in oral culture and literate decontextualization. In D. R. Olson and N. Torrance (eds.), *Literacy and Orality.* Cambridge: Cambridge University Press, pp. 66–89.

DEYA (DEPARTMENT OF EDUCATION AND YOUTH AFFAIRS) (1983) *Cultural Background Papers: Yugoslavia.* Canberra: Australian Government Publishing Service.

DILLON, G. (1991) *Contending Rhetorics: Writing in Academic Disciplines.* Bloomington: Indiana University Press.

DINGWALL, R. and MURRAY, T. (1983) Categorization in accident departments: 'good' patients, 'bad' patients and 'children'. *Sociology of Health and Illness* 5 (2): 127–148.

DODD, J. S. (ed.) (1986) *The ACE Style Guide: A Manual for Authors and Editors.* Washington, DC: American Chemical Society.

DOHENY-FARINA, S. (1984) Writing in an emergent business organization: an ethnographic study. Unpublished PhD dissertation, Rensselaer Polytechnic Institute.

DOHENY-FARINA, S. (1986) Writing in an emerging organisation: an ethnographic study. *Written Communication* 3 (2): 158–185.

DOHENY-FARINA, S. and ODELL, L. (1985) Ethnographic research on writing: assumptions and methodology. In L. Odell and D. Goswami (eds.), *Writing in Non-academic Settings.* New York: Guildford Press, pp. 281–307.

DUFF, R. S. and HOLLINGSHEAD, A. B. (1968) *Sickness and Society.* New York: Harper and Row.

DUFFY, T. M., CURRAN, T. E. and SASS, D. (1983) Document design for technical tasks: an evaluation. *Human Factors* 25: 143–160.

DUMAS, J. S. and REDISH, J. C. (1993) *A Practical Guide to Usability Testing.* Norwood, NJ: Ablex.

DURANTI, A. and GOODWIN, C. (eds.) (1992) *Rethinking Context: Language as an Interactive Phenomenon.* Cambridge: Cambridge University Press.

ECKERT, A. (1982) Analysis of written style: an imperative for readable translations. In G. R. McKay and B. A. Sommer (eds.), *Application of Linguistics to Australian Aboriginal Contexts.* Occasional Papers No. 5. Parkville, Victoria: Applied Linguistics Association of Australia, pp. 18–25.

EDE, L. and LUNSFORD, A. (1992) *Singular Texts / Plural Authors: Perspectives on Collaborative Writing.* Carbondale and Edwardsville: Southern Illinois University Press.

EDWARDS, T. (1992) Whose culture? Whose literacy? In *Literacies: Reading the Culture: Selected Papers.* Carlton, Victoria: Australian Reading Association, pp. 155–160.

EDWARDS, V. and SIENKEWICZ, T. J. (1990) *Oral Cultures Past and Present: Rappin' and Homer.* Oxford: Basil Blackwell.

EEMEREN, F. and GROOTENDORST, R. (1984) *Speech Acts in Argumentative Discussions.* Dordrecht, Netherlands: Foris.

EGGINGTON, W. (1992) From oral to literate culture: an Australian Aboriginal experience. In Fraida Dubin and Natalie A. Kuhlman (eds.), *Cross-cultural Literacy: Global Perspectives on Reading and Writing.* Englewood Cliffs, NJ: Regents / Prentice Hall, pp. 81–98.

EGGINS, S. and MARTIN, J. R. (1997) Genres and registers of discourse. In T. A. Van Dijk (ed.), *Discourse as Structure and Process (1).* London: Sage, pp. 230–256.

ELLENBERGER, H. F. (1970) *The Discovery of the Unconscious: The History and Evolution of Dynamic Psychiatry.* London: Allen Lane / Penguin.

ELLIOTT, N. and KILDUFF, M. (1991) Technical writing in a techno-
logical university: attitudes of department chairs. *Journal of Technical
Writing and Communication* 21: 411–424.

ENKVIST, N. (1985) Coherence, composition and text linguistics. In
E. Enkvist (ed.), *Coherence and Composition: A Symposium.* Åbo, Finland:
Åbo Akademi Foundation, pp. 11–26.

ENTWISTLE, N. and MARTON, F. (1984) Changing conceptions of learning and research. In F. Marton, D. Hounsell and N. Entwistle (eds.),
The Experience of Learning. Edinburgh: Scottish Academic Press.

ERIKSON, K. T. and GILBERTSON, D. E. (1969) Case records in the
mental hospital. In S. Wheeler (ed.), *On Record: Files and Dossiers in
American Life.* New York: Russel Sage Foundation, pp. 389–412.

FAIGLEY, L. (1997) The literacy of image, colour, and movement.
Paper delivered at the Penn State Conference on Composition,
July. URL: http://www.dla.utexas.edu/depts/drc/faigley/after.essay/
after.essay.html

FAIRCLOUGH, N. (1989) *Language and Power.* London: Longman.

FAIRCLOUGH, N. (1992a) *Discourse and Social Change.* Cambridge: Polity
Press.

FAIRCLOUGH, N. (ed.) (1992b) *Critical Language Awareness.* London:
Longman.

FAIRCLOUGH, N. (1993) Critical discourse analysis and the marketization
of public discourse: the universities. *Discourse and Society* 4 (2): 133–
168.

FAIRCLOUGH, N. (1995) *Critical Discourse Analysis: The Critical Study of
Language.* London: Longman.

FAIRCLOUGH, N. (1996) Technologisation of discourse. In C. R. Caldas-
Coulthard and M. Coulthard (eds.), *Texts and Practices.* London:
Routledge.

FERGUSON, C. A. (1996) Diglossia. In D. Hymes (ed.), *Language in Culture
and Society.* New York: Harper and Row, pp. 429–439.

FIRTH, A. (ed.) (1995) *The Discourse of Negotiation: Studies of Language in
the Workplace.* Oxford: Pergamon.

FIRTH, J. R. (1957) *Papers in Linguistics (1934–1951).* London: Oxford
University Press.

FISH, S. (1980) *Is There a Text in This Class?* Cambridge, MA: Harvard
University Press.

FISHER, R. and URY, W. (1983) *Getting to Yes: Negotiating Agreement Without Giving In.* New York: Penguin Books.

FLESCH, R. (1948) A new readability yardstick. *Journal of Applied Psychology*
32: 221–233.

FLOWER, L. (1994) *The Construction of Negotiated Meaning: A Social Cognitive
Theory of Writing.* Carbondale: Southern Illinois University Press.

FLOWER, L. S. and HAYES, J. R. (1980) The dynamics of composing:
making plans and juggling constraints. In L. W. Gregg and E. R.

Steinberg (eds.), *Cognitive Processes in Writing.* Hillsdale, NJ: Lawrence Erlbaum, pp. 31–50.

FLOWER, L. S. and HAYES, J. R. (1981) A cognitive process theory of writing. *College Composition and Communication* 32: 365–387.

FLOWER, L. S. and HAYES, J. R. (1984) Images, plans and prose: the representation of meaning in writing. *Written Communication* 1: 120–160.

FLOWER, L., WALLACE, D., NORRIS, L., BURNETT, R. (eds.) (1994) *Making Thinking Visible: Writing, Collaborative Planning, and Classroom Inquiry.* Illinois: NCTE.

FLYNN, E. A. (1997) Rescuing postmodernism. *College Composition and Communication* 48 (4): 540–555.

FOLDS, R. (1989) A socio-cultural approach to the bilingual curriculum in Central Australian schools. *Curriculum Inquiry* 19 (1): 33–50.

FORCEVILLE, C. (1996) *Pictorial Metaphor in Advertising.* London: Routledge.

FOUCAULT, M. (1972) *The Archaeology of Knowledge.* London: Tavistock.

FOUCAULT, M. (1977) *Discipline and Punish: The Birth of the Prison.* Harmondsworth: Penguin Books.

FOUCAULT, M. (1981) The order of discourse. In R. Young (ed.), *Untying The Text: A Post-Structuralist Reader.* Boston: Routledge, Kegan, Paul, pp. 48–78.

FOWLER, A. (1982) *Kinds of Literature.* Oxford: Oxford University Press.

FREEDMAN, A., ADAM, C. and SMART, G. (1994) Wearing suits to class: simulating genres and simulations as genre. *Written Communication* 11: 193–226.

FREEDMAN, A. and MEDWAY, P. (eds.) (1994) *Genre and the New Rhetoric.* London: Taylor and Francis.

FREIDSON, E. (1970) *Profession of Medicine: A Study in the Sociology of Applied Knowledge.* New York: Harper and Row.

FREUD, S. (1981) Five lectures on psycho-analysis: first lecture (1910 [1909]). In J. Strachey and A. Freud (eds.), *The Standard Edition of the Complete Psychological Works of Sigmund Freud. Volume XI.* London: Hogarth Press and the Institute of Psychoanalysis, pp. 9–22.

GALE, M. A. (1992) Publish or perish?: observations on the reasons for writing in Aboriginal languages. *Australian Aboriginal Studies* 2: 42–48.

GARFINKEL, H. (1974) 'Good' organizational reasons for 'bad' clinic records. In R. Turner (ed.), *Ethnomethodology: Selected Readings.* Harmondsworth: Penguin Books, pp. 109–127.

GAZDAR, G. (1981) Unbounded dependencies and coordinate structure. *Linguistic Inquiry* 12 (2): 155–184.

GEE, J. P. (1990) *Social Linguistics and Literacies: Ideology in Discourses.* London: Falmer Press.

GEERTZ, C. (1973) *The Interpretation of Cultures.* New York: Basic Books.

GEERTZ, C. (1983) *Local Knowledge: Further Essays in Interpretive Anthropology.* New York: Basic Books.

GEISLER, C. (1994) *Academic Literacy and the Nature of Expertise.* Hillsdale, NJ: Lawrence Erlbaum.

GEISLER, C., KAUFER, D. S. and STEINBERG, E. R. (1985) The unattended anaphoric 'This': when should writers use it? *Written Communication* 2: 129–155.

GILBERT, G. and MULKAY, M. (1984) *Opening Pandora's Box: A Sociological Analysis of Scientific Discourse.* Cambridge: Cambridge University Press.

GLASER, B. and STRAUSS, A. (1964) The social loss of dying patients. *American Journal of Nursing* 64: 119–21.

GODDARD, C. (1990) Emergent genres of reportage and advocacy in the Pitjantjatjara print media. *Australian Aboriginal Studies* 2: 27–47.

GOETZ, J. P. and LeCOMPTE, M. D. (1984). *Ethnography and qualitative design in educational research.* New York: Aldine.

GOFFMAN, E. (1967) *Interaction Ritual.* Garden City. NY: Anchor Books.

GOFFMAN, E. (1968) *Asylums: Essays on the Social Situation of Mental Patients and Other Inmates.* Harmondsworth: Penguin Books.

GOFFMAN, E. (1969) *The Presentation of Self in Everyday Life* (2nd edition). London: Allen Lane, The Penguin Press. (First published 1959.)

GOLLIN, S. (1998) Literacy in a Computing department: the invisible in search of the ill-defined. In C. N. Candlin and G. Plum (eds.), *Researching Academic Literacies: Framing Student Literacy: Cross-cultural Aspects of Communication Skills in Australian University Settings.* Sydney: NCELTR, Macquarie University.

GOODY, J. (1987) *The Interface between the Written and the Oral.* Cambridge: Cambridge University Press.

GOSDEN, H. (1993) Discourse functions of subject in scientific research articles. *Applied Linguistics* 14 (1): 56–75.

GOSWAMI, D. and STILLMAN, P. (1987) *Reclaiming the Classroom: Teacher Research as an Agency for Change.* Upper Montclair, NJ: Boynton / Cook.

GRABE, W. and KAPLAN, R. (1996) *Theory and Practice of Writing.* London: Longman.

GRAVES, D. (1983) *Writing: Teachers and Children at Work.* London: Heinemann.

GREEN, J. and BLOOME, D. (1997) Ethnography and ethnographers of and in education: a situated perspective. In J. Flood *et al.* (eds.), *Hardbook of Research on Teaching Literacy through the Communicative and Visual Arts.* New York: Macmillan, pp. 181–203.

GRICE, P. (1975) Logic and conversation. In P. Cole and J. Morgan (eds.), *Syntax and Semantics,* New York: Academic Press.

GRICE, P. (1989) *Studies in the Way of Words.* Cambridge, MA: Harvard University Press.

GUNNARSSON, B.-L. (1997) On the sociohistorical construction of scientific discourse. In B.-L. Gunnarsson, P. Linell and B. Nordberg (eds.), *The Construction of Professional Discourse*. London: Longman, pp. 99–126.

HAAS, C. (1994) Learning to read biology: one student's rhetorical development in college. *Written Communication* 11 (1): 43–84.

HALLIDAY, M. A. K. (1978) *Language as Social Semiotic: The Social Interpretation of Language and Meaning*. London: Edward Arnold.

HALLIDAY, M. A. K. (1985) *An Introduction to Functional Grammar*. London: Edward Arnold.

HALLIDAY, M. (1988) On the language of physical science. In M. Ghadessey (ed.), *Registers of Written English*. London: Pinter, pp. 162–178.

HALLIDAY, M. A. K. (1994) *An Introduction to Functional Grammar* (2nd edition). London: Edward Arnold.

HALLIDAY, M. A. K. and HASAN, R. (1985) *Language, Context and Text: Aspects of Language in a Social-semiotic Perspective*. Oxford: Oxford University Press.

HALLIDAY, M. A. K. and MARTIN, J. R. (1993) *Writing Science: Literacy and Discursive Power*. Pittsburgh, PA: University of Pittsburgh Press.

HAMILTON, M., IVANIČ, R. and BARTON, D. (1992) Knowing where we are: participatory research in adult literacy. In J. P. Hautecoeur (ed.), *ALPHA 92: Current Research in Literacy: Literacy Strategies in the Community Movement*. Hamburg: Unesco Institute of Education, pp. 105–118.

HAMMOND, S. L. and LAMBERT, B. L. (1994) Communicating about medications: directions for research. *Health Communication* 6: 247–251.

HANDELMAN, D. (1978) Bureaucratic interpretation: the perception of child abuse in urban Newfoundland. In D. Handelman and E. Leyton (eds.), *Bureaucracy and World View: Studies in the Logic of Official Interpretation*. Social and Economic Studies No. 22. Institute of Social and Economic Research, Memorial University of Newfoundland. Toronto: University of Toronto Press, pp. 15–68.

HARAWAY, D. (1991) *Simians, Cyborgs and Women: The Reinvention of Nature*. London: Free Association Books.

HARDING, S. (1991) *Whose science? Whose knowledge?* New York: Cornell University Press.

HARMON, J. E. and GROSS, A. G. (1996) The scientific style manual: a reliable guide to practice? *Technical Communication* 1: 61–72.

HARVEY, K. and YUILL, D. (1997) A study of the use of a monolingual pedagogical dictionary by learners of English engaged in writing. *Applied Linguistics* 18 (3): 253–278.

HASAN, R. (1985) The structure of a text. In M. A. K. Halliday and R. Hasan, *Language, Context and Text: Aspects of Language in a Social-semiotic Perspective*. Victoria: Deakin University Press, pp. 52–69.

HASSELGREN, A. (1994) Lexical teddy-bears and advanced learners: a study into the ways Norwegian students cope with English vocabulary. *International Journal of Applied Linguistics* 4 (2): 237–260.

HAUGEN, E. (1972) *The Ecology of Language.* Stanford, CA: Stanford University Press.

HAYES, J. R. (1986) Is this text clear? How knowledge makes it difficult to judge. Paper presented to the American Educational Research Association, San Francisco, CA.

HAYES, J. R. (1996) A new framework for understanding cognition and affect in writing. In C. M. Levy and S. Ransdell (eds.), *The Science of Writing: Theories, Methods, Individual Differences and Applications.* Mahwah, NJ: Lawrence Erlbaum, pp. 1–27.

HAYES, J. R. and FLOWER, L. S. (1980) Identifying the organisation of writing processes. In L. W. Gregg and E. R. Steinberg (eds.), *Cognitive Processes in Writing.* Hillsdale, NJ: Lawrence Erlbaum, pp. 3–30.

HAYES, J. R., HATCH, J. and HILL, C. (1992) Reading the writer's personality: the functional impact in communication. In M. Steehouder, C. Jansen, P. van der Poort and R. Verheijen (eds.), *Quality of Technical Documentation.* Amsterdam: Rodopi, pp. 33–44.

HEATH, S. B. (1982) Protean shapes in literacy events: ever-shifting oral and literate traditions. In D. Tannen (ed.), *Spoken and Written Language: Exploring Orality and Literacy.* Norwood, NJ: Ablex, pp. 91–118.

HEATH, S. B. (1983) *Ways with Words.* Cambridge: Cambridge University Press.

HINDS, J. (1987) Reader versus writer responsibility: a new typology. In U. Connor and R. B. Kaplan (eds.), *Writing across Languages: Analysis of L2 Text.* Reading, MA: Addison Wesley.

HINKEL, E. (1997) Indirectness in L1 and L2 academic writing. *Journal of Pragmatics* 27: 361–386.

HODGE, R. and KRESS, G. (1979) *Language as Ideology.* London: Routledge and Kegan Paul.

HOEY, M. (1991) *Patterns of Lexis in Text.* Oxford: Oxford University Press.

HOLMES, J. (1984) Modifying illocutionary force. *Journal of Pragmatics* 8: 345–365.

HOLMES, J. (1988) Doubt and certainty in ESL textbooks. *Applied Linguistics* 9: 20–44.

HOLMES, J. (1995) *Women, Men and Politeness.* London: Longman.

HUCKIN, T. N. (1993) Stylistic prescriptivism vs. expert practice. *Technostyle* 11: 1–17.

HUCKIN, T. N., CURTIN, E. H. and GRAHAM, D. (1986) Prescriptive linguistics and plain English: the case of 'Whiz-deletion'. *Visible Language* 2: 174–187.

HUCKIN, T. N. and PESANTE, L. H. (1988) Existential there. *Written Communication* 5 (3): 368–391.

HYLAND, K. (1996a) Writing without conviction? Hedging in science research articles. *Applied Linguistics* 17 (4): 433–454.

HYLAND, K. (1996b) Talking to the academy: forms of hedging in science research articles. *Written Communication* 13 (2): 251–281.

HYLAND, K. (1997) Scientific claims and community values: articulating an academic culture. *Language and Communication* 16 (1): 19–32.

HYLAND, K. (1998a) *Hedging in Scientific Research Articles.* Amsterdam: John Benjamins.

HYLAND, K. (1998b) Exploring corporate rhetoric: metadiscourse in the Chairman's letter. *Journal of Business Communication* 35 (2): 224–245.

HYLAND, K. (1998c) Persuasion and context: the pragmatics of academic metadiscourse. *Journal of Pragmatics* 30: 437–455.

HYLAND, K. (1999) Talking to students: Metadiscourse in introductory coursebooks. *English for Specific Purposes* 18 (1).

HYLAND, K. (in press) Academic attribution: citation and the construction of disciplinary knowledge. *Applied Linguistics.*

HYLAND, K. and MILTON, J. (1997) Qualification and certainty in L1 and L2 students' writing. *Journal of Second Language Writing* 6 (2): 183–205.

HYMES, D. (1972) Models of the interaction of language and social life. In J. J. Gumperz and D. Hymes (eds.), *Directions in Social Linguistics: The Ethnography of Communication.* New York: Holt, Rinehart & Winston, pp. 35–71.

IVANIČ, R. (1990) Critical language awareness in action. In R. Carter (ed.), *Knowledge about Language and the Curriculum: The LINC Reader.* London: Hodder and Stoughton, pp. 122–132.

IVANIČ, R. (1994) I is for interpersonal: discoursal construction of writer identities and the teaching of writing. *Linguistics and Education* 6 (1): 3–15.

IVANIČ, R. (1995) Writer identity. *Prospect: The Australian Journal of TESOL* 10 (1): 8–31.

IVANIČ, R. (1998) *Writing and Identity: The Discoursal Construction of Identity in Academic Writing.* Amsterdam: John Benjamins.

IVANIČ, R., AITCHISON, M. and WELDON, S. (1996) Bringing ourselves into our writing. Research and Practice in *Adult Literacy Bulletin* 28 (29): 2–8.

IVANIČ, R., McENERY, T., ORMEROD, F. and SMITH, N. (1997) Visuality, materiality, and action in children's topic writing: the interface between texts and practices. In S. Hunstan and M. Bloor (eds.), *Language at Work.* Papers from the British Association for Applied Linguistics Annual Meeting, Birmingham. Clevedon: Multilingual Matters.

IVANIČ, R. and MOSS, W. (1991) Bringing community writing practices into education. In D. Barton and R. Ivanič (eds.), Writing in the community, *Written Communication Annual: An International Survey of Research and Theory Volume 6.* Sage, pp. 193–223.

IVANIČ, R. and ROACH, D. (1990) Academic writing, power and disguise. In R. Clark, N. Fairclough, R. Ivanič and M. Martin-Jones (eds.), Critical language awareness part I: a critical review of three current approaches to language awareness. *Language and Education* 4 (4): 249–260.

IVANIČ, R. and SIMPSON, J. (1992a) Who's who in academic writing? In N. Fairclough (ed.) (1992b), *Critical Language Awareness*. London: Longman.

IVANIČ, R. and SIMPSON, J. (1992b) Putting the people back into academic writing. In H. Dombey and M. Robinson (eds.), *Literacy for the Twenty-first Century*. Brighton Polytechnic, Falmer: The Literacy Centre, pp. 203–216.

JACKSON, R. A. and HUFFMAN, D. C. (1990) Patient compliance: the financial impact on your practice. *The NARD Journal*, July, pp. 67–71.

JACOB, E. (1988) Clarifying qualitative research: a focus on traditions. *Educational Researcher*, Jan./Feb., pp. 16–24.

JACOBY, S. (1987) References to other researchers in literary research articles. *ELR Journal* 1: 33–78.

JEFFREY, R. (1979) 'Normal rubbish': deviant patients in casualty departments. *Sociology of Health and Illness* 1 (1): 90–107.

JOHNS, A. M. (1997) *Text, Role and Context: Developing Academic Literacies*. Cambridge. Cambridge University Press.

JOHNS, T. (1991) Should you be persuaded – two examples of data-driven learning materials. *English Language Research Journal* 4: 1–16.

KANTOR, K. J., KIRBY, D. R. and GOETZ, J. P. (1981) Research in context: ethnographic studies in English education. *Research in the Teaching of English* 15 (4): 293–309.

KAPLAN, R. B. (1966) Cultural thought patterns in intercultural education. *Language Learning* 16: 1–20.

KAPLAN, R. (1987) Cultural thought patterns revisited. In U. Connor and R. Kaplan (eds.), *Writing across Languages*. Reading, MA: Addison-Wesley.

KAPLAN, R. B. and CONNOR, U. (1987) *Writing across Languages: Analysis of L2 Text*. Reading: MA: Addison Wesley Publishing Company.

KAUFER, D. and GEISLER, C. (1989) Novelty in academic writing. *Written Communication* 6 (3): 286–311.

KILLINGSWORTH, M. J. (1992) Discourse communities local and global. *Rhetoric Review* 11: 110–122.

KILLINGSWORTH, M. J. and GILBERTSON, M. K. (1992) *Signs, Genres and Communities in Technical Communication*. Amityville, NY: Baywood Publishing.

KILLINGSWORTH, M. J. and STEFFENS, D. (1989) Effectiveness in the environmental impact statement. *Written Communication* 6 (2).

KJELLMER, G. (1994) *A Dictionary of English Collocations*. Oxford: Clarendon Press.

KNORR-CETINA, K. (1981) *The Manufacture of Knowledge*. Oxford: Pergamon Press.

KOLB, D. A. (1981) Learning styles and disciplinary differences. In A. Chickering (ed.), *The Modern American College*. San Francisco: Jossey Bass, pp. 232–255.

KOWALL, S. and O'CONNELL, D. C. (1987) Writing as language behavior: myths, models, methods. In A. Matsuhashi (ed.), *Writing in Real Time: Modelling Production Processes.* Norwood, NJ: Ablex.

KRASHEN, S. D. and TERRELL, T. D. (1983) *The Natural Approach.* Hayward, CA: Alemany Press.

KRESS, G. (1987) Genre in a social theory of language: a reply to John Dixon. In I. Reid (ed.), *The Place of Genre in Learning: Current Debates.* Geelong, Australia: Deakin University Press.

KRESS, G. (1988) *Linguistic Processes in Sociocultural Practice.* Oxford: Oxford University Press.

KRESS, G. (1997) *Before Writing: Rethinking the Paths to Literacy.* London: Routledge.

KRESS, G. (1998) Visual and verbal modes of representation in electronically mediated communication: the potentials of new forms of text. In I. Snyder (ed.), *Page to Screen: Taking Literacy into the Electronic Era.* London: Routledge, pp. 53–79.

KRESS, G. and OGBURN, J. (1998) Modes of Representation and Local Epistemologies: The Presentation of Science in Education. SISC Paper No. 2 (ISBN 0906784 174) London: Institute of Education.

KRESS, G. and VAN LEEUWEN, T. (1996). *Reading Images: The Grammar of Visual Design.* London: Routledge.

KUHN, T. (1970) *The Structure of Scientific Revolutions* (2nd edition). Chicago: University of Chicago Press.

LABOV, W. and FANSHEL, D. (1977) *Therapeutic Discourse: Psychotherapy as Conversation.* New York: Academic Press.

LAKOFF, R. T. (1982) Some of my favourite writers are literate: the mingling of oral and literate strategies in written communication. In D. Tannen (ed.), *Spoken and Written Language: Exploring Orality and Literacy.* Norwood, NJ: Ablex, pp. 239–260.

LAMBERT, B. L. (1995) Directness and deference in pharmacy students' messages to physicians. *Social Science and Medicine* 40: 545–555.

LAMBERT, B. L. (1996) Face and politeness in pharmacist–physician interaction. *Social Science and Medicine* 43: 1189–1198.

LATOUR, B. and WOOLGAR, S. (1979) *Laboratory Life: The Social Construction of Scientific Facts. Volume 80.* Sage Library of Social Research. Beverly Hills, CA: Sage.

LAVE, J. and WENGER, E. (1991) *Situated Learning: Legitimate Peripheral Participation.* Cambridge: Cambridge University Press.

LAYDER, D. (1993) *New Strategies in Social Research.* Cambridge: Polity Press.

LEA, M. (1998) Academic literacies and learning in higher education: constructing knowledge through texts and experience. In *Studies in the Education of Adults,* 30 (2).

LEA, M. and STREET, B. (1997) *Perspectives on Academic Literacies: An Institutional Approach.* Economic and Social Research Council: Swindon.

LEA, M. and STREET, B. (1998). Student writing in higher education: an academic literacies approach. In *Studies in Higher Education* 23 (2): 157–72.

LEECH, G. (1983) *Principles of Pragmatics.* London: Longman.

LE FEVRE, K. B. (1987) Invention as social act. Published for the Conference on College Composition and Communication. Carbondale: Southern Illinois University Press.

LEGUTKE, M. and THOMAS, H. (1991) *Process and Experience in the Language Classroom.* London: Longman.

LEMKE, J. (1998) Multiplying meaning: verbal and visual semiotics in scientific text. In J. R. Martin and R. Veel (eds.), *Reading Science: Critical and Functional Perspectives on Discourses of Science.* London: Routledge, pp. 87–113.

LEVINSON, S. (1983) *Principles of Pragmatics.* Cambridge: Cambridge University Press.

LEWIS, I. M. (1993) Literacy and cultural identity in the Horn of Africa: the Somali case. In B. V. Street (ed.), *Cross-cultural Approaches to Literacy.* Cambridge: Cambridge University Press, pp. 143–155.

LEWIS, M. (1993) *The Lexical Approach.* London: Language Teaching Publications.

LEY, P. (1988) *Communicating with Patients: Improving Communication, Satisfaction and Compliance.* London: Chapman Hall.

LIEDERMAN, D. B. and GRISSO, J.-A. (1985) The Gomer phenomenon. *Journal of Health and Social Behaviour* 26: 222–232.

LINCOLN, Y. and GUBA, E. (1985). *Naturalistic Inquiry,* Beverly Hills, CA: Sage Publications.

LINTON, M. and TRAFTON, B. F. (1972) *A Simplified Style Manual: For the Preparation of Journal Articles in Psychology, Social Sciences, Education, and Literature.* New York: Meredith Corporation.

LITTLEJOHN, A. (1988) How to fail interviews. In A. Littlejohn and M. Melouk (eds.), *Research Methods and Processes.* Lancaster University: Department of Linguistics and Modern English Language.

LIVINGSTONE, J., AXTON, R. A., MENNIE, M., GILFILLAN, A. and BROCK, D. J. H. (1993) A preliminary trial of couple screening for cystic fibrosis: designing an appropriate information leaflet. *Clinical Genetics* 43: 57–62.

LONGINO, H. (1990) *Science as Social Knowledge: Values and Objectivity in Scientific Inquiry.* Princeton, NJ: Princeton University Press.

LORBER, J. (1975) Good patients and problem patients: conformity and deviance in a general hospital. *Journal of Health and Social Behaviour* 16 (2): 213–225.

LORENZ, G. (1998) Overstatement in advanced learner English: stylistic aspects of adjunctive intensification. In S. Granger (ed.), *Learner English on Computer.* London: Longman.

LOWE, R. (1993) *Successful Instructional Diagrams.* London: Kogan Page.

LUKE, A. (1998) *Literacy Textbooks and Ideology.* London: Falmer Press.

LUUKKA, M. R. (n.d.) *Scientific Text as Social Practice.* Mimeo: University of Jyvaskyla.

LYONS, J. (1977) *Semantics: Volumes 1 and 2.* Cambridge: Cambridge University Press.

MACDONALD, S. P. (1994) *Professional Academic Writing in the Humanities and Social Sciences.* Carbondale: Southern Illinois University Press.

MACLACHLAN, G. and REID, I. (1994) *Framing and Interpretation.* Melbourne: Melbourne University Press.

MALCOLM, I. G. and ROCHECOUSTE, J. (1997) *Framing Student Literacy: Cross-Cultural Aspects of Communication Skills in Australian University Settings. Edith Cowan University Report No. 2: Aboriginal Student Literacy.* Report to the Australian Research Council. Sydney: NCELTR, Macquarie University.

MALONE, J. (1991) The DSM-III-R versus nursing diagnosis: a dilemma in interdisciplinary practice. *Issues in Mental Health Nursing* 12 (3): 219–228.

MANDL, H. and LEVIN, J. R. (eds.) (1989) *Knowledge Acquisition from Text and Pictures.* Amsterdam: North Holland.

MANN, W. C., MATTHIESSEN, C. and THOMPSON, S. A. (1992) Rhetorical structure theory and text analysis. In W. C. Mann and S. A. Thompson (eds.), *Discourse Description: Diverse Linguistic Analyses of a Fund-raising Text.* Amsterdam: John Benjamins, pp. 39–78.

MANN, W. C. and THOMPSON, S. A. (1986a) Relational propositions in discourse. *Discourse Processes* 9: 57–90.

MANN, W. C. and THOMPSON, S. A. (1986b) *Rhetorical Structure Theory: Description and Construction of Text Structures.* ISI Reprint Series, ISI/RS-86–174 October 1986, USC/Information Sciences Institute, Marina del Rey, CA. Also in G. Kempen (1987) (ed.), *Natural Language Generation: New Results in Artificial Intelligence, Psychology and Linguistics.* Dordrecht: Martinus Nijhoff, pp. 85–95.

MANN, W. C. and THOMPSON, S. A. (1988) Rhetorical structure theory: toward a functional theory of text organization. *Text* 8 (3): 243–281.

MARTIN, J. R. (1985) Process and text: two aspects of human semiosis. In J. D. Benson and W. S. Greaves (eds.), *Systemic Perspectives on Discourse. Volume 1.* Norwood, NJ: Ablex, pp. 248–274.

MARTIN, J. R. (1987) *Factual Writing: Exploring and Challenging Social Reality.* Melbourne: Deakin University Press.

MARTIN, J. R. (1992) *English Text.* Philadelphia: John Benjamins.

MARTIN, J. R. (1993) A contextual theory of language. In *The Powers of Literacy – A Genre Approach to Teaching Writing.* Pittsburgh, PA: University of Pittsburgh Press, pp. 116–136.

MARTIN, J. R., CHRISTIE, F. and ROTHERY, J. (1987) Social processes in education: a reply to Sawyer and Watson (and others). In I. Reid (ed.), *The Place of Genre in Learning: Current Debates.* Geelong, Australia: Deakin University Press.

MARTIN, J. and HALLIDAY, M. (1993) *Writing Science.* London: Falmer Press.

McGILL, G. (1982) The implementation of bilingual education in the Northern Territory. *Wikaru* 10: 56–69.

McGREGOR, W. (1988) A survey of the languages of the Kimberley region. Report from the Kimberley Language Resource Centre. *Australian Aboriginal Studies* 2: 90–101.

McKAY, G. R. (1982) Attitudes of Kunibidji speakers to literacy. *International Journal of the Sociology of Language* 36: 105–114.

McKAY, G. R. (1996) *The Land Still Speaks: Review of Aboriginal and Torres Strait Islander Language Maintenance and Development Needs and Activities.* Commissioned Report No. 44. Canberra: National Board of Employment, Education and Training.

McKAY, S. L. and WEINSTEIN-SHR, G. (1993) English literacy in the US: national policies, personal consequences. *TESOL Quarterly* 27 (3): 399–419.

MEYER, B. (1985) Prose analysis: purposes, procedures, and problems. In B. Britton and J. Black (eds.), *Understanding Expository Text: A Theoretical and Practical Handbook for Analyzing Explanatory Text.* Hillsdale, NJ: Lawrence Erlbaum.

MEYERS, M. (1990) Current generic pronoun usage: an empirical study. *American Speech* 65: 228–237.

MILLER, C. R. (1984) Genre as social action. *Quarterly Journal of Speech* 70: 157–178.

MILLER, C. R. (1994) Rhetorical Community: The Cultural Basis of Genre. In A. Freedman and P. Medway (eds.), *Genre and the New Rhetoric.* London: Taylor and Francis, pp. 67–78.

MILLER, G., BECKWITH, R., FELLBAUM, C., GROSS, D. and MILLER, K. (1993) Introduction to WordNet: an on-line lexical database. URL: http://www.cogsci.princeton.edu/~wn

MILTON, J. and TSANG, E. (1993) A corpus-based study of logical connectors in EFL students' writing. In R. Pemberton and E. Tsang (eds.), *Studies in Lexis.* Hong Kong: HKUST, pp. 215–246.

MISHLER, E. G. (1984) *The Discourse of Medicine: Dialectics of Medical Interviews.* Norwood, NJ: Ablex.

MITCHELL, S. (1994) *The Teaching and Learning of Argument in Sixth Forms and Higher Education.* School of Education: University of Hull.

MITCHELL, S. (1996) *Improving the Quality of Argument in Higher Education.* Interim Report for the Leverhulme Trust. Middlesex University, UK.

MIZRAHI, T. (1985) Getting rid of patients: contradictions in the socialization of internists to the doctor–patient relationship. *Sociology of Health and Illness* 7 (2): 214–235.

MORGAN, W. (1993) Aboriginal texts for Australian classrooms. *English in Australia* 104: 3–10.

MORRELL, R. W., PARK, D. C. and POON, L. W. (1989) Quality of instructions on prescription drug labels: effects of memory and comprehension in young and old adults. *The Gerontologist* 29: 345–354.

MUECKE, S. (1983) Discourse, history, fiction: language and Aboriginal history. *Australian Journal of Cultural Studies* 1: 71–79.

MÜHLHÄUSLER, P. (1996) *Linguistic Ecology: Language Change and Linguistic Imperialism in the Pacific Region.* London: Routledge.

MURISON-BOWIE, S. (1993) *Microconcord Manual: An Introduction to the Practices and Principles of Concordancing in Language Teaching.* Oxford: Oxford University Press.

MURRAY, D. E. (1988) The context of oral and written language: a framework for mode and medium switching. *Language in Society* 17: 351–373.

MURRAY, D. E. (1991) The composing process for computer conversation. *Written Communication* 8 (1): 35–55.

MURRAY, D. E. (1992) Collaborative writing as a literacy event. In D. Nunan (ed.), *Collaborative Language Learning and Teaching.* Cambridge, MA: Cambridge University Press.

MURRAY, D. E. (1995) *Knowledge Machines.* London: Longman.

MYERS, G. (1989) The pragmatics of politeness in scientific articles. *Applied Linguistics* 10: 1–35.

MYERS, G. (1990a) The rhetoric of irony in academic writing. *Written Communication* 7: 419–455.

MYERS, G. (1990b) *Writing Biology: Texts in the Social Construction of Scientific Knowledge.* Madison: University of Wisconsin Press.

MYERS, G. (1990c) Every picture tells a story: illustrations in E. O. Wilson's sociobiology. In M. Lynch and S. Woolgar (eds.), *Representation in Scientific Practice.* Cambridge, MA: MIT Press.

MYERS, G. (1991a) Politeness and certainty: the language of collaboration in an AI project. *Social Studies of Science* 21: 37–73.

MYERS, G. (1991b) Scientific speculation and literary style in a molecular genetics article. *Science in Context* 4: 321–346.

MYERS, G. (1992) In this paper we report . . . speech acts and scientific facts. *Journal of Pragmatics* 17: 295–313.

MYERS, G. (1994) *Words in Ads.* London: Edward Arnold.

MYERS, G. (1995) Disciplines, departments and differences. In B.-L. Gunnarsson and I. Backlund (eds.), *Writing in Academic Contexts.* Uppsala University, pp. 3–11.

MYERS, G. (1997) Words and pictures in a biology textbook. In T. Miller (ed.), *Functional Approaches to Written Text: Classroom Applications.* Washington, DC: USIA, pp. 93–104.

MYERS, G. (1998) *Ad Worlds.* London: Edward Arnold.

NASH, W. (1986) *English Usage: A Guide to First Principles.* London: Routledge and Kegan Paul.

NATTINGER, J. R. and DeCARRICO, J. S. (1992) *Lexical Phrases and Language Teaching*. Oxford: Oxford University Press.

NEHAMAS, A. and WOODRUFF, P. (trans.) (1997) *Phaedrus*. Cambridge, MA: Hackett Publishing Co.

NICHOLS, P. C. (1996) Pidgins and creoles. In S. L. McKay and N. H. Hornberger (eds.), *Sociolinguistics and Language Teaching*. Cambridge: Cambridge University Press, pp. 195–217.

NORTH, S. M. (1986) Writing in a philosophy class: three case studies. *Research in the Teaching of English* 20 (3): 225–262.

NUNAN, D. (ed.) (1992) *Collaborative Language Learning and Teaching*. Cambridge, MA: Cambridge University Press.

NYSTRAND, M. (1986) *The Structure of Written Communication: Studies in Reciprocity Between Writers and Readers*. Orlando, FL: Academic Press.

NYSTRAND, M. (1989) A Social interactive model of writing. *Written Communication* 6: 66–85.

O'BARR, W. and ATKINS, B. K. (1980) Women's language or powerless language? In S. McConnell and R. Ginet (eds.), *Women and Language in Literature and Society*. London: Praeger.

O'BRIEN, T. (1995) Rhetorical structure analysis and the case of the inaccurate, incoherent source-hopper. *Applied Linguistics* 16 (4): 442–482.

OCHS, E. (1988) *Culture and Language Development: Language Acquisition and Language Socialisation in a Samoan Village*. Cambridge: Cambridge University Press.

ODELL, L. and GOSWAMI, D. (eds.) (1985) *Writing in Non-academic Settings*. New York: Guildford Press, pp. 281–307.

ODELL, L., GOSWAMI, D. and HERRINGTON, A. (1983) The discourse-based interview: a procedure for exploring the tacit knowledge of writers in non-academic settings. In P. Mosenthal, L. Tamor and S. A. Walmsley (eds.), *Research on Writing: Principles and Methods*. New York: Longman.

OGBU, J. U. (1987) Opportunity structure, cultural boundaries and literacy. In J. A. Langer (ed.), *Language, Literacy and Culture: Issues of Society and Schooling*. Norwood, NJ: Ablex, pp. 149–177.

OLSON, D. (1977) From utterance to text: the bias of language in speech and writing. *Harvard Educational Review* 47: 257–281.

OLSON, D. R. (1994) *The World on Paper: The Conceptual and Cognitive Implications of Reading and Writing*. Cambridge: Cambridge University Press.

OLSON, D. R. and ASTINGTON, J. W. (1990) Talking about text: how literacy contributes to thought. *Journal of Pragmatics* 14: 705–721.

ONG, W. J. (1982) *Orality and Literacy: The Technologizing of the Word*. London: Routledge.

O'SHEA, R. (1993) *Writing for Psychology: An Introductory Guide for Students*. Sydney. Harcourt Brace Jovanovich.

PALMER, F. (1990) *Modality and the English modals* (2nd edition). London: Longman.

PANDER MAAT, H. and KLAASSEN, R. (1994) Side effects of side effect information in drug information leaflets. *Journal of Technical Writing and Communication* 24: 389–404.

PANDER MAAT, H. and STEEHOUDER, M. (1992) Introduction. In M. H. Pander and M. Steehouder (eds.), *Studies of Functional Text Quality*. Amsterdam: Utrecht Studies in Language and Communication, Editions Rodopi, pp. 1–5.

PARADIS, J., DOBRIN, D. and MILLER, R. (1985) Writing at EXXON ITD: notes on the writing environment of an R and D organisation. In L. Odell and D. Goswami (eds.), *Writing in Non-academic Settings*. New York: Guildford Press, pp. 281–307.

PARK, D. (1982) The meanings of 'audience'. *College English* 44 (3): 247–257.

PARK, D. (1986) Analysing audiences. *College Composition and Communication* 37 (4): 478–488.

PATEMAN, T. (1983) How is understanding an advertisement possible? In H. Davies and P. Walton (eds.), *Language, Image, Media*. Oxford: Blackwell, pp. 187–204.

PENNYCOOK, A. (1996) Borrowing others' words: text, ownership, memory, and plagiarism. *TESOL Quarterly* 30: 201–230.

PERKINS, D. N. and SALOMON, G. (1989) Are cognitive skills context-bound? *Educational Research* 18 (1): 16–25.

PERKINS, M. (1983) *Modal Expressions in English*. London: Frances Pinter.

PETCH-TYSEN, S. (1998) Writer/Reader visibility in EFL written discourse. In S. Granger (ed.), *Learner English on Computer*. London: Longman.

PIENEMANN, M. (1989) Is language teachable? Psycholinguistic experiments and hypotheses. *Applied Linguistics* 10 (1): 52–79.

PILEGAARD, M. (1997) Politeness in written business discourse: a text-linguistic perspective on requests. *Journal of Pragmatics* 28: 232–244.

PLUM, G. (1998) Doing psychology, doing writing: student voices on academic writing in psychology. In C. N. Candlin and G. Plum (eds.), *Researching Academic Literacies: Framing Student Literacy: Cross-cultural Aspects of Communication Skills in Australian University Settings*. Sydney: NCELTR, Macquarie University.

POYNTON, C. (1985) *Language and Gender: Making the Difference*. Victoria: Deakin University Press.

PRELLI, L. (1989) *A Rhetoric of Science: Inventing Scientific Discourse*. Columbia: University of South Carolina Press.

PRINCE, E. (1992) The ZPG letter: subjects, definiteness and information status. In W. C. Mann and S. A. Thompson (eds.), *Discourse Description: Diverse Linguistic Analyses of a Fund-raising Text*. Amsterdam: John Benjamins, pp. 295–325.

PRIOR, P. (1994) Response, revision, disciplinarity: a micro-history of a dissertation prospectus in sociology. *Written Communication* 11: 483–533.

PURVES, A. (1988) *Writing Across Languages and Culture.* Newbury Park, CA: Sage.

QUIRK, R., GREENBAUM, S., LEECH, G. and SVARTVIK, J. (1985) *A Comprehensive Grammar of the English Language.* London: Longman.

QUIRK, R. and STEIN, G. (1996) Sipping a cocktail of corpora. In J. Thomas and M. H. Short (eds.), *Using Corpora for Language Research: Studies in Honour of Geoffrey Leech.* London: Longman, pp. 27–35.

RAFFEL, S. (1979) *Matters of Fact: A Sociological Inquiry.* London: Routledge and Kegan Paul.

RAFOTH, B. A. (1990) The concept of discourse community: descriptive and explanatory adequacy. In G. Kirsch and D. H. Roen (eds.), A sense of audience in written communication, *Written Communication Annual. Volume 5.* Newbury Park: Sage, pp. 145–152.

RANKINE, A. (1994) Review of G. Koch (ed.) *Kaytetye Country: An Aboriginal History of the Barrow Creek Area. Australian Aboriginal Studies* 2: 72–73.

RHYDWEN, M. (1993) The creation of a written language and a tool of colonisation. In M. Walsh and C. Yallop, (eds.), *Language and Culture in Aboriginal Australia.* Canberra: Aboriginal Studies Press, pp. 155–167.

RICHARDSON, P. (1991) Language as personal resource and as social construct: competing views of literacy pedagogy in Australia. *Educational Review* 43 (2): 171–189.

RICOEUR, P. (1976) *Interpretation Theory: Discourse and the Surplus of Meaning.* Fort Worth, TX: Christian University Press.

RICOEUR, P. (1979) The model of the text: meaningful action considered as a text. In P. Rabinow and W. M. Sullivan (eds.), *Interpretive Social Science: A Reader.* Berkeley: University of California Press, pp. 73–101.

RICOEUR, P. (1981) *Hermeneutics and the Human Sciences: Essays on Language, Action and Interpretation.* Cambridge: Cambridge University Press.

ROBERTS, C. and STREET, B. (1997) Spoken and written language. In F. Coulmas (ed.), *The Handbook of Sociolinguistics.* Oxford: Blackwell, pp. 168–186.

ROBBINS, S. P. (1994) *Management* (4th edition). Englewood Clifts, NJ: Prentice-Hall.

ROBBINS, S. P. (1996) *Management* (5th edition). Englewood Cliffs, NJ: Prentice-Hall.

RODMAN, L. (1991) Anticipatory 'it' in scientific discourse. *Journal of Technical Writing and Communication* 21: 17–27.

ROGERS, D., SHULMAN, A., SLESS, D. and BEACH, R. (1995) *Designing Better Medicine Labels.* Report published by the Communication Research Institute of Australia.

RORTY, R. (1979) *Philosophy and the Mirror of Nature.* Princeton, NJ: Princeton University Press.

ROTH, J. A. (1972) Some contingencies of the moral evaluation and control of clientele: the case of the hospital emergency service. *American Journal of Sociology* 77(5): 839–856.

RUNDELL, M. (1996) The corpus of the future, and the future of the corpus. Talk delivered at Exeter University at the conference on New Trends in Reference Science.

SACKS, H., SCHEGLOFF, E. and JEFFERSON, G. (1974) A simplest systematic for the organisation of turn-taking for conversation. *Language* 50: 696–735.

SALAGER-MEYER, F. (1997) I think that perhaps you should: a study of hedges in written scientific discourse. In T. Miller (ed.), *Functional Approaches to Written Text: Classroom Applications.* Washington, DC: USIA, pp. 105–118.

SANDS, R. G., STAFFORD, J. and MCCLELLAND, M. (1990) 'I beg to differ': conflict in the interdisciplinary team. *Social Work in Health Care* 14 (3): 55–72.

SAUER, B. (1994) The dynamics of disaster: a three-dimensional view of documentation in a tightly regulated industry. *Technical Communication Quarterly* 3: 393–419.

SAUER, B. (1995) Darkness visible: a rhetorical theory of representation in a dynamically changing material environment. MS. Department of English, Carnegie Mellon University.

SCHANK, R. and ABELSON, R. (1977) *Scripts, Plans, Goals and Understanding: An Inquiry into Human Knowledge Structures.* Hillsdale, NJ: Erlbaum.

SCHNEIDER, K. (1974) Primary and secondary symptoms in schizophrenia. In S. R. Hirsch, M. Shepherd and L. Kalinowsky (eds.), *Themes and Variations in European Psychiatry.* Charlottesville: University Press of Virginia, pp. 40–44.

SCHRIVER, K. A. (1989) Evaluating text quality: the continuum from text-focused to reader-focused methods. *IEEE Transactions on Professional Communication* 32: 238–255.

SCHRIVER, K. A. (1997) *Dynamics in Document Design.* Chichester, UK: John Wiley and Sons.

SCOLLON, R. (1998) *Mediated Discourse as Social Interaction.* London: Longman.

SCOTT, M. B. and LYMAN, S. M. (1968) Accounts. *American Sociological Review* 33 (1): 47–62.

SEYMOUR, E. (ed.) (1996) *Rethinking Labelling Regulation and Practice.* ACT, Australia: Communications Research Press.

SHATZMAN, L. and STRAUSS, A. (1973) *Field Research.* Englewood Cliffs, NJ: Prentice-Hall.

SHAW, B. (1984) How Aboriginal life histories can be written: a response to the review 'Language and dignity'. *Australian Aboriginal Studies* 1: 47–52.

SHIMAZUMI, M. and SARDINHA, B. A. (1996) *Approaching the Assessment of Performance in an Archive of Schoolchildren's Writing.* Paper presented at the TALC 96 Conference, Lancaster, UK.

SHORT, M. (1996) *Exploring the Language of Poems, Plays, and Prose.* London: Longman.

SHULMAN, A., SLESS, D. and ROGERS, D. (1996) Communication Research Institute of Australia. In E. Seymour (ed.), *Rethinking Labelling Regulation and Practice.* ACT, Australia: Communications Research Press.

SIEMENS, R. G. (1993) *Practical Content Analysis Techniques for Text-Retrieval in Large, Un-tagged Text-bases.* Conference Proceedings: SIGDOC '93. New York: Association for Computing Machinery, pp. 293–299.

SILVERMAN, D. (1993) *Interpreting Qualitative Data: Methods for Analysing Talk, Text and Interaction.* Englewood Cliffs, NJ: Prentice-Hall.

SINCLAIR, J. (1991) *Corpus, Concordance, Collocation.* Oxford: Oxford University Press.

SKELTON, J. (1997) The representation of truth in academic medical writing. *Applied Linguistics* 18 (2): 121–140.

SLESS, D. (1992) What is information design? In R. Penman and D. Sless (eds.), *Designing Information for People.* ACT, Australia: Communication Research Press, pp. 1–16.

SLESS, D. and WISEMAN, R. (1994) *Writing about Medicines for People: Usability Guidelines and Glossary for Consumer Product Information.* Department of Health and Human Services, Canberra.

SMAGORINSKY, P. (ed.) (1994) *Speaking about Writing: Reflections on Research Methodology.* Thousand Oaks, CA: Sage.

SMALLWOOD, I. (forthcoming) The vocabulary of Hong Kong secondary school texts.

SMITH, D. E. (1974) The social construction of documentary reality. *Sociological Inquiry* 44 (4): 257–268.

SMOLICZ, J. J. (1995) Language – a bridge or a barrier? Languages and education in Australia from an intercultural perspective. *Multilingua* 14 (2): 151–182.

SMOLICZ, J. J. and SECOMBE, M. J. (1985) Community languages, core values and cultural maintenance: the Australian experience with special reference to Greek, Latvian and Polish groups. In M. Clyne (ed.), *Australia, Meeting Place of Languages.* Canberra: Department of Linguistics, Research School of Pacific Studies, Australian National University, pp. 11–38.

SNYDER, I. (ed.) (1998) *Page to Screen: Taking Literacy into the Electronic Era.* London: Routledge.

SPERBER, D. and WILSON, D. (1986) *Relevance: Communication and Cognition.* Oxford: Blackwell.

SPINKS, S. (1996) *From Description to Analysis: An Inter-disciplinary Developmental Study of Student Writing*. Paper presented at the 11th World Congress of Applied Linguistics, Jyvaskyla, Finland (4–9 August).

SPINKS, S. (1998) Relating maker feedback to teaching and learning in psychology. In C. N. Candlin and G. Plum (eds.), *Researching Academic Literacies. Framing Student Literacy: Cross-cultural Aspects of Communication Skills in Australian University Settings*. Sydney: NCELTR, Macquarie University.

SPRADLEY, J. P. (1980) *Participant Observation*. New York: Holt, Rinehart and Winston.

STAKE, R. (1978) The case study method in social inquiry. *Educational Researcher* February: 5–8.

STANTON, A. H. and SCHWARTZ, M. S. (1954) *The Mental Hospital*. New York: Basic Books.

STAR, S. L. (1991) Power, technologies and the phenomenology of conventions: on being allergic to onions. In J. Law (ed.), *A Sociology of Monsters: Essays on Power, Technology and Domination*. London: Routledge, pp. 26–56.

STEIER, F. (1991) *Research and Reflexivity*. Newbury Park, CA: Sage.

STEVENS, V. (1995) Concordancing with language learners: Why? When? What? *CAELL Journal* 6 (2).

STICHT, T. (1985) Understanding readers and their uses of texts. In T. M. Duffy and R. Waller (eds.), *Designing Usable Texts*. London: Academic Press, pp. 315–340.

STOTSKY, S. (1991) On developing independent critical thinking: what we can learn from studies of the research process. *Written Communication* 8 (2): 193–212.

STRAUSS, A. L., SCHATZMAN, L., BUCHER, R., EHRLICH, D. and SABSHIN, M. (1964) *Psychiatric Ideologies and Institutions*. New York: The Free Press of Glencoe.

STRAUSS, J. S. (1969) Hallucinations and delusions as points on continua function. *Archives of General Psychiatry* 21: 581–586.

STREET, B. V. (1984) *Literacy in Theory and Practice*. Cambridge: Cambridge University Press.

STREET, B. V. (ed.) (1993) *Cross-cultural Approaches to Literacy*. Cambridge: Cambridge University Press.

STREET, B. V. (1995) *Social Literacies: Critical Approaches to Literacy in Development, Ethnography and Education*. London: Longman.

STREET, B. V. (1997) The implications of the new literacy studies for literacy education. *English in Education* 31(3): 26–39.

STUART-SMITH, V. (1998) Constructing an argument in psychology: rhetorical structure theory and the analysis of student writing. In C. N. Candlin and G. Plum (eds.), *Researching Academic Literacies: Framing Student Literacy: Cross-cultural Aspects of Communication Skills in Australian University Settings*. Sydney: NCELTR, Macquarie University.

STUBBS, M. (1980) *Language and Literacy: The Sociolinguistics of Reading and Writing.* London: Routledge and Kegan Paul.

STUBBS, M. (1996) *Text and Corpus Analysis.* Oxford: Blackwell.

SWALES, J. M. (1990) *Genre Analysis: English in Academic and Research Settings.* Cambridge: Cambridge University Press.

SWALES, J. M. (1993) Genre and engagement. *Revue Belge de Philologie et Histoire* 71 (3): 689–698.

SWALES, J. M. (1997) English as Tyrannosaurus rex. *World Englishes* 16: 373–383.

SWALES, J. M. (1998) Discourse communities, genres and English as an international language. *World Englishes.* 7: 211–220.

SWALES, J. M., AHMAD, U., CHANG, Y. Y., CHAVEZ, D., DRESSEN, D. and SEYMOUR, R. (1998) Consider this: The role of imperatives in scholarly writing. *Applied Linguistics* 19: 97–121.

SWALES, J. M. and FEAK, C. B. (1994) *Academic Writing for Graduate Students: A Course for Nonnative Speakers of English.* Ann Arbor: University of Michigan Press.

SWALES, J. M. and NAJJAR, H. (1987) The writing of research article introductions. *Written Communication* 4: 175–191.

TABOURET-KELLER, A., LE PAGE, R. B., GARDNER-CHLOROS, P. and VARRO, G. (eds.) (1997) *Vernacular Literacy: A Re-evaluation.* Oxford: Clarendon Press.

TALK WORKSHOP GROUP (1982) *Becoming Our Own Experts.* London: ILEA Teachers' Centre.

TANNEN, D. (1982) Oral and literate strategies in spoken and written narratives. *Language* 58 (1): 1–21.

TARONE, E., DWYER, S., GILLETTE, S. and ICKE, V. (1981) On the use of the passive in two astrophysics journals. *The ESP Journal* 1: 123–140.

THOMAS, J. (1985) The language of power: towards a dynamic pragmatics. *Journal of Pragmatics* 9: 765–783.

THOMAS, J. (1995) *Meaning in Interaction: An Introduction to Pragmatics.* London: Longman.

THOMPSON, G. and THETELA, P. (1995) The sound of one hand clapping: the management of interaction in written discourse, *Text* 15: 103–127.

THRALLS, N. and BYLER, C. (eds.) (1993) *Professional Communication: The Social Perspective.* Newbury Park, CA: Sage.

TOPPING, D. M. (1992) Literacy and cultural erosion in the Pacific Islands. In F. Dubin and N. A. Kuhlman (eds.), *Cross-cultural Literacy: Global Perspectives on Reading and Writing.* Englewood Cliffs, NJ: Regents / Prentice-Hall, pp. 19–33.

TRIBBLE, C. and JONES, G. (1990) *Concordances in the Classroom.* London: Longman.

TRIBBLE, C. (1997) Improvising corpora for ELT: quick-and-dirty ways of developing corpora for language teaching. Paper presented at the PALC Conference, University of Łodz, Poland, April.

TROSBORG, A. (1997) Contracts as social action. In B.-L. Gunnarsson, P. Linell and B. Nordberg (eds.), *The Construction of Professional Discourse.* London: Longman, pp. 54–75.

TURNER, R. (ed.) (1974) *Ethnomethodology: Selected Readings.* Harmondsworth: Penguin Books.

VALLE, E. (1997) A scientific community and its texts: a historical discourse study. In B.-L. Gunnarsson, P. Linell and B. Nordberg (eds.), *The Construction of Professional Discourse.* London: Longman, pp. 76–98.

VANDE KOPPLE, W. (1986) Given and new information and some aspects of the structures, semantics and pragmatics of written texts. In C. Cooper and S. Greenbaum (eds.), *Studying Writing: Linguistic Approaches.* Newbury Park, CA: Sage, pp. 72–11.

VAN DIJK, T. and KINTSCH, W. (1983) *Strategies of Discourse Comprehension.* London: Academic Press.

VAN EEMEREN, F. and GROOTENDORST, R. (1984) *Speech Acts in Argumentative Discussions.* Dordrecht, Netherlands: Foris.

VAN HARSKAMP-SMITH, S. and VAN HARSKAMP-SMITH, K. (1994) Torres Strait Islanders speak: building a model of critical literacy. *The Australian Journal of Language and Literacy* 17 (2): 101–108.

VAN LEEUWEN, T. (1995) Representing social action. *Discourse and Society* 6 (1): 81–106.

VAN LEEUWEN, T. (1996) The representation of social actors. In C. R. Caldas-Coulthard and M. Coulthard (eds.), *Texts and Practices: Readings in Critical Discourse Analysis.* London: Routledge, pp. 32–70.

VAN LEEUWEN, T. (1997) The Discursive Construction of Purpose. Paper presented at the Annual Meeting of the British Association for Applied Linguistics. Birmingham. September.

VAN LIER, L. (1997) Review of P. Bourdieu, J.-C. Passeron and M. de Saint Martin (1994), Academic discourse: linguistic misunderstanding and professorial power. *Applied Linguistics* 18 (4): 566–570.

VELOTTA, C. (ed.) (1995) *Practical Approaches to Usability Testing for Technical Documentation.* Arlington, VA: Society for Technical Communication.

VENTOLA, E. and MAURANEN, A. (eds.) (1996) *Academic Writing: Intercultural and Textual Issues.* Amsterdam: John Benjamins.

VYGOTSKY, L. S. (1978) *Mind in Society: The Development of Higher Psychological Processes.* Cambridge, MA: Harvard University Press.

VYGOTSKY, L. S. (1986) *Thought and Language* (revised edition). Cambridge, MA: MIT Press. (First published 1934.)

WALLER, R. H. (1975) Typographic access structures for educational texts. In P. A. Kolers, M. E. Wrolstad and H. Bouma (eds.), *Processing of Visible Language 1.* New York: Plenum Press, pp. 175–187.

WALLER, R. H. (1979) Functional information design: research and practice. *Information Design* 1: 43–50.

WALTON, C. (1990) The process vs. genre debate: an Aboriginal education perspective. *Australian Review of Applied Linguistics* 13 (1): 100–122.

WEBER, M. (1970) Bureaucracy. In H. H. Gerth and C. Wright Mills (eds.), *From Max Weber: Essays in Sociology.* London: Routledge and Kegan Paul, pp. 196–244.

WELDON, S. (1994) *From Patchwork Prose to Personal Style.* Unpublished MS, Lancaster University.

WHEELER, S. (ed.) (1969) *On Record: Files and Dossiers in American Life.* New York: Russel Sage Foundation.

WHITLEY, R. (1984) *The Intellectual and Social Organisation of the Sciences.* Oxford: Clarendon Press.

WIDDOWSON, H. G. (1994) The ownership of English. *TESOL Quarterly* 28 (2): 377–389.

WIERSMA, W. (1991) *Research Methods in Education: An Introduction* (5th edition). Boston: Allyn and Bacon.

WILKINS, D. H. (1974) *Notional Syllabuses.* London: Oxford University Press.

WILLINSKY, J. (1991) Popular literacy and the roots of the new writing. In C. Mitchell and K. Weiler (eds.), *Rewriting Literacy: Culture and the Discourse of the Other.* New York: Bergin and Garvey, pp. 255–269.

WILLIS, D. (1991) *The Lexical Syllabus.* London: Collins Cobuild ELT.

WINSOR, D. A. (1989) An engineer's writing and the corporate construction of knowledge. *Written Communication* 6 (3): 270–285.

WINSOR, D. A. (1994) Invention and Writing in Technical Work: Representing the Object. *Written Communication* 11: 227–250.

WINTER, E. (1977) A Clause – Relational Approach to English Texts: A Study of Some Predictive Lexical Items in Written Discourse. *Instructional Science* 6(1): 1–92.

WITTE, S. F. (1992) Context, text, intertext: toward a constructivist semiotic of writing. *Written Communication* 9 (2): 237–308.

WODAK, R. (1996) *Disorders of Discourse.* London: Longman.

WOODEN, S. L. and HURLEY, S. R. (1992) Bilingual (Spanish and English) adults: achieving literacy in the first language. Paper presented to the Annual Meeting of the Arizona Educational Research Organization, Phoenix, November.

WRIGHT, P. (1988a) Functional literacy: reading and writing at work. *Ergonomics* 31: 265–290.

WRIGHT, P. (1988b) The need for theories of NOT reading: some psychological aspects of the human–computer interface. In B. A. G Elsendoorn and H. Bouma (eds.), *Working Models of Human Perception.* London: Academic Press, pp. 319–340.

WRIGHT, P. (1988c) Issues of content and presentation in document design. In M. Helander (ed.), *Handbook of Human–Computer Interaction.* Amsterdam: Elsevier, pp. 629–652.

WRIGHT, P. (1996) Cognitive skills for reading functional texts: the multiple skills needed for reading in everyday life. In W. J. M. Levelt (ed.), *Advanced Psycholinguistics*. Nijmegen, Holland: Max Plank Institute, pp. 122–127.

WRIGHT, P. (1998) Designing healthcare advice for the public. In F. Durso (ed.), *The Handbook of Applied Cognition*. Sussex, UK: John Wiley and Sons.

WRIGHT, P., CREIGHTON, P. and THRELFALL, S. M. (1982) Some factors determining when instructions will be read. *Ergonomics* 25: 225–237.

YAHYA, Z. (1994) *Resisting Colonialist Discourse*. Bangi: Penerbit Universiti Kebangsaan Malaysia.

YOUNG, R. M. and BARNARD, P. J. (1987) The use of scenarios in human–computer interaction research: turbocharging the tortoise of cumulative science. In J. M. Carroll and P. P. Tanner (eds.), *Proceedings of CHI + GI '87: Human Factors in Computing Systems and Graphics Interface* (Toronto, 5–9 April), New York: ACM Press, pp. 291–296.

ZIMMER, A. and ZIMMER, F. (1978) *Visual Literacy in Communication: Designing for Development*. Bucks, UK: Hulton Educational Publications Ltd; and Teheran: International Institute for Adult Literacy Studies.

ZIMMERMAN, M. (1993) Free-text IR philosophy. In G. P. Landow and P. Delany (eds.), *The Digital Word: Text-based Computing in the Humanities*. Cambridge, MA: MIT Press.

Author index

Subject index